A Few Good Men from Univac

MIT Press Series in the History of Computing
I. Bernard Cohen, editor; William Aspray, associate editor

Editorial Board: Bernard Galler, University of Michigan, Ann Arbor, Michigan; J. A. N. Lee, Virginia Polytechnic Institute, Blacksburg, Virginia; Arthur Norberg, Charles Babbage Institute, Minneapolis, Minnesota; Brian Randell, University of Newcastle, Newcastle upon Tyne; Henry Tropp, Humboldt State College, Arcata, California; Heinz Zemanek, Vienna, Austria.

A Few Good Men from Univac

David E. Lundstrom

The MIT Press
Cambridge, Massachusetts
London, England

This book was printed and bound by Halliday Lithograph in the United States of America.

Library of Congress Cataloging-in-Publication Data

Lundstrom, David E.
  A few good men from Univac.

  (MIT Press series in the history of computing)
  1. Univac computer—History.   2. Computer industry—
History.   I. Title.   II. Series.
QA76.8.U6L86   1987   621.39'09   87-4193
ISBN 0-262-12120-4

This book is dedicated to George Cogar. He was my first instructor in the electronic computer, the first authentic genius I have worked with, and the first of the heroes of this narrative to pass from this life. May he rest in peace.

Contents

Series Foreword   ix
Preface   xi

1   In the Beginning   1
2   The Philadelphia Story   9
3   On Technology and Geography   19
4   Progress Is Our Only Product   26
5   To Each His Own   36
6   Anchors Aweigh!   47
7   If Anything Can Go Wrong, It Will!   55
8   The First Team   64
9   Tomorrow the World   72
10 To See or Not to See   81
11 Project Spin   92
12 Whatever Became of George Cogar?   101
13 The Large Computer Business   109
14 How Hard Is Software?   121
15 Visits to Chippewa Falls   131
16 Up, Up, and Away!   139
17 We Shall Never Surrender   151
18 Reprise   159
19 A Terminal Situation   168
20 Oops, I Lost the Computer!   177
21 Oink, Oink, Oink   188
22 Microspin and Spin and Spin   197
23 East Wind, Rain   211
24 E Unum Pluribus?   217

Epilogue   225
Chronology of Significant Events   229

Series Foreword

As much as is written about our technological society, few who have not worked in high technology industry understand the process by which ideas are turned into those products that drive our economy and enrich our lives. This book describes that process. It explains the differences between the work of the scientist and the engineer; how economic factors, personal idiosyncrasies, staff organization, plant location, and company priorities play as important a role as technical ideas in the structure and success of commercial products; and why the fate of our technological companies does or should rest on brilliant individual engineers like Seymour Cray.

These are the personal reminiscences of an engineer who spent thirty years, from 1955 to 1985, working on the design and development of computer technology. The book chronicles major projects of his two employers, the Engineering Research Division of Sperry Rand Corporation (now a part of Unisys Corporation) and the Control Data Corporation. Historians will find this work a welcome supplement to the abstract economic account of these companies by Franklin Fisher, James McKie, and Richard Mancke in *IBM and the U.S. Data Processing Industry,* or the top management portrait by Katherine Davis Fishman in *The Computer Establishment.* But David Lundstrom does not intend to write objective history here. His purpose, like that of Tracy Kidder in *Soul of a New Machine,* is to depict everyday life in an engineering organization. His heroes are the practicing engineers, his villains the corporate managers who underuse, misuse, and abuse the engineers. He uses this perspective to explain the past and present successes and failures of Control Data and Unisys, and to assess the Japanese challenge to the U.S. computer industry.

This book is part of a series devoted to the history of computers and data processing. Other volumes have dealt with, or will deal with, various aspects of the development of systems, hardware, and software, encompassing both general works and specialized monographs. Some of these are of a biographical or autobiographical nature, or concentrate on the history of an industrial company. This book does both. It is certainly to be hoped that other pioneers will make their experi-

ences available to us and that we will be able to publish additional
critical and biographical accounts of those who have made the modern
computer.

William Aspray, Associate Editor

Preface

The desire to write this book has been building over a number of years, fueled by what I perceive as three rather dramatic failures of understanding. First, the general public has almost no idea just what goes on in an engineering organization, the sort of people who work there and what they do. The subject has almost never been dealt with in books (exception: Tracy Kidder's excellent *The Soul of a New Machine*), and TV and movie representations are ridiculously distorted. A typical scriptwriter apparently has difficulty distinguishing the work of engineers from the work of scientists. Science and engineering are as unalike as coal mining and piano tuning. Judging from the media portrayals, one would think that an engineering group consists of a number of men and women in white lab coats who run about shouting, "The experiment is failing!" In thirty years in the electronic computer industry I have never known one single engineer who wore a lab coat and few who shouted. The alternative media presentation of the engineer is that of a dull fellow who spends his day bent over a drafting table. I have known a few of these, but they are comparatively rare and are mostly mechanism designers, a special breed.

Second, and more startling to me, the majority of people working in my own electronic computer industry do not understand how a computer gets designed, what really goes on in a development project, and why some developments are predictably losers from the very beginning and other projects almost sure to be winners. The dynamics of the interpersonal relationships in an engineering development group are so obvious to many old-timers that they can almost sort out the winning from the losing projects by walking through the development area, looking around, and taking a deep breath.

Third, and most important, it is not widely understood, by either the general public or by the people within the computer industry, just how important the single brilliant designer is to the outcome of a multimillion dollar project. The difference between success and failure, between completion of a project within the budget or a vast overrun of budget and schedule, between an outstanding product that sets the standard for its type and a mediocre "me, too" product, is almost always a single mind that conceives and holds in focus the entire project. Failure to utilize such a talent fully represents a management oversight comparable to leaving a multimillion dollar piece of capital equipment unused—and yet it happens all the time. The reader will meet a number of these brilliant and highly motivated designers in this narrative; almost all of them have been underused or misused for a large portion of their careers. It is these individuals who provide the cutting edge to the development of a computer, a product line, or even an entire industry. At a time when the United States is in a race to maintain our technological leadership and the fruit of that technology, our standard of living, failure to make the fullest use of our best people is unforgiveable.

This book is a personal reminiscence. It attempts to capture the feel of an industry at a time of great change and excitement. It is not history, although all names and dates used have been verified against documents written at that time. Remembrances of gossip over coffee and examples of cartoons pinned up over individual desks are included in this narrative to establish the atmosphere in which people lived and worked.

A Few Good Men from Univac

1

In The Beginning

The sprawling, nondescript complex of white frame and concrete block buildings was surrounded by a chain link fence. In the asphalt parking lot stood a steel tower topped by a rotating radar antenna, a sight familiar to me. The name on the wooden sign, Engineering Research Associates Division of Sperry Rand Corporation, did not sound promising. I was a young electrical engineer, just released from active service in the Navy the month before, and on this gray day in November 1955 I was looking for a job. Even at this early point in my career I knew that I was uninterested in the type of engineering that could be described as "research," which to me implied learning a great deal about a narrow specialty. I was always interested in the big picture—how the entire system fit together. But ERA was in St. Paul, next door to my hometown of Minneapolis, and they had advertised openings for electrical engineers. Little did I guess that the shabby buildings at 1902 West Minnehaha Avenue housed a creative center that would soon explode into the electronics computer industry and that ERA alumni would spread out to found dozens of companies that would influence the entire direction of computer technology.

After filling out the usual employment application forms in the personnel lobby on the street side of the plant, I met the personnel interviewer, Bob Patterson, a friendly gray-haired fellow with a fatherly manner. He offered to take me around the plant for interviews with the line engineering managers who had openings for electrical engineers. I later learned that Bob Patterson was highly regarded by the mostly young ERA engineers as a person with whom they could easily discuss their work-related problems.

The interior of the ERA plant, a former glider factory, was painted in two colors: battleship gray and that peculiarly depressing shade of pea green so often encountered in government buildings. This was not surprising, since the plant was government owned and leased to ERA. The floors were bare cement except for the personnel offices and certain offices of the higher management. These were graced with asphalt tile. As we walked along the corridors, I saw that the main building, an open hangarlike structure, had been partitioned into offices and labs. The partitions were only about eight feet high, and the upper part of the building was open to the roof. In the winter sparrows took up residence in the peak. Heating units and fluorescent lights hung on chains from the roof beams. The aisles were crammed with equipment—in boxes, on wooden fork-lift pallets, and on casters. Had I been familiar with Parkinson's law at the time ("It is now known that a perfection of planned layout is achieved only by institutions on the point of collapse," C. Northcote Parkinson, *Parkinson's Law and Other Studies in Administration*, 1957), I would have been greatly encouraged; here, obviously, was an organization that was growing far too fast to be concerned with physical plant.

My first interview was with Bob Buelow, head of Customer Engineering. A customer engineer, sometimes called a field engineer, a service engineer, or a field service engineer, maintains equipment that is installed at a customer's site. Customer engineers operate in one of two modes: P.M. (preventive maintenance), basically cleaning and adjusting of equipment with a good measure of boredom thrown in, or E.M. (emergency maintenance), characterized by periods of nonstop (that is, all night), frenzied activity usually triggered by the exclamation, "The machine is down!" I was extremely familiar with these two modes of operation from having just completed three years of duty as an electronics materiel officer aboard ship. The shipboard electronics materiel officer acts as sort of a seagoing customer engineering site manager, with a gang of Navy electronics technicians performing the P.M. and the E.M. I asked for another interview.

My next interviewer was genial, smiling Bill Keye, himself a brilliant engineer with several early patents in magnetic drum data storage. Keye was head of all commercial engineering activities at ERA. I should repeat here what Bob Patterson had explained to me: ERA had two parallel engineering organizations. Commercial engineering worked on company-funded developments for products that would be sold in the marketplace, and military engineering worked on government-funded projects that were security classified. Because I did not have security clearance at ERA yet (although I had been cleared for Top Secret by the Navy), I was not allowed into the areas where the military projects were being designed.

Bill Keye explained that he was forming an engineering group to set up the manufacturing procedures and to test the first production models of the Univac II, a new series of commercial electronic computers then under development. The work sounded interesting to me, so I was passed on to the manager of product development for Univac II, a tall, soft-spoken, good-looking man of obvious Swedish descent named Art Engstrom.

Art explained how the Univac II development effort was organized. The actual engineering design was being done by a separate development group headed by a manager named Ward Lund, who also reported to Bill Keye. The Univac II was to be a performance-upgraded version of the Univac I, a computer designed and manufactured by the Philadelphia branch of the company. Ward Lund's group had a model of the Univac I that they were modifying into a Univac II by replacing the mercury delay-line memory (an early and limited form of computer data and program storage) with a newly developed magnetic-core memory, by adding new magnetic tape units, and by adding some new computer instructions. The result was expected to be a doubling of the processing speed of the older machine. Engstrom's group would take the design from Lund's group and prepare it for production by making up the manufacturing drawings, parts lists, wire routing instructions, and test procedures. Because the manufacturing department in St. Paul had never built or tested a Univac I, let alone a Univac II, Engstrom's group would do the performance and acceptance testing on the first five production Univac II's while training the manufacturing technicians in the procedures. Actual assembly of the first five computers would be done by personnel supplied by the manufacturing department, but they would work under the supervision of Art Engstrom. Should I decide to work for Art, my first assignment would be to attend a four-month maintenance training course on Univac I in Philadelphia. This course was actually designed for customer engineers who would maintain the Univac I in the field, but it would give me a good working knowledge of the computer. I would then attend a four-week "differences" course taught by engineers from Lund's group. By that time the first five production Univac II computers would be completed and ready for testing.

Keep in mind that at that time—1955—I had no more understanding of computers than the average man on the street. There had been no courses on digital computers in the electrical engineering curriculum at the University of Minnesota. In the Navy I had encountered several devices that were labeled "computer," but these were special-purpose devices designed only to control the firing of guns or torpedoes. Some of the Navy "computers" were entirely mechanical, with gears and rotating shafts and dials. All that I knew for sure about electronic computers was that they were large, complex, expensive, and probably the wave of the future. My very first look at a digital electronic computer was a disappointment. The Univac I being redesigned into a Univac II in Ward Lund's lab was shut down and partially disassembled. Technicians and engineers were stringing wires on back panels and rewiring chassis at workbenches. The only impression that I got from the lab was complexity and confusion.

The Univac Scientific computer, designed and built by ERA, was much more impressive. It looked like the science fiction representations of a "giant brain." Two rows of gray metal cabinets, each about seven feet high and thirty feet long were lined up one behind the other. In the center of the front bay, a recessed nook contained a small flat work surface and hundreds of indicator lamps and switches that surrounded the operator, in front, on both sides, and overhead. The low rumble of the cooling blowers filled the room. Oddly, the only means to communicate with this behemoth seemed to be, except for the indicator lamps and switches, a small gray Flexowriter, a sort of combination typewriter and paper-tape reader/punch. Every now and then it clattered out a cryptic message to the operator, indicating that all was well with its thought processes.

The remainder of the plant, except for the classified areas that I could not visit yet, turned out to be a warren of small labs and office areas, all crammed with equipment and shabby gray metal desks and populated by engineers in a high state of enthusiasm. A few days later I received a written job offer from Bob Patterson. I quickly accepted and agreed to start work in Philadelphia in two weeks. The salary looked generous compared to my Navy pay, and I did not attempt to negotiate for more. I began packing my aging Olds convertible for the drive to Philadelphia.

The Philadelphia branch of the company, called the Eckert-Mauchly Division, was housed in facilities even less attractive than those of ERA. Nineteen hundred Allegheny Avenue proved to be a grimy brick warehouse in a semi-industrial district in north Philadelphia. I rode the freight elevator (there was no other) to the fourth floor and sought out the customer engineering offices. There I met Dave Keefer, the local head of customer engineering. Dave, a brash, bright engineer a little older than I, told me that the training course on Univac I had been postponed until after Christmas; hadn't I gotten the word? This proved to be only the first (and the least costly) of the many snafus that plagued the Univac II program, the result of poor communications (and worse working relationships) between the St. Paul and Philadelphia branches of the company. Somewhat upset, I called Bill Keye back in St. Paul and asked him what I should do. He told me that if there was nothing useful to be done in Philadelphia, I should come back to St. Paul for the month or so until the class started. While driving back to the Twin Cities, I consoled myself with the thought that at least I would be able to spend Christmas at home.

Back in the ERA plant in St. Paul, I was assigned one of the beat-up gray metal desks and was told to read all the documentation that I could find on the Univac I and Univac II. These manuals and books of engineering drawings, like nearly all computer documentation I have read since, proved to be badly written. The writer seemed to assume that the reader already understood the machine and needed only a little brushing up on the details of how the computer circuitry operated. I spent most of my time talking to the other engineers and learning the company lore.

Remington Rand, an old-line manufacturer of typewriters, file cabinets, punched card equipment, and, incongruously, electric shavers, had purchased two small, creative engineering firms that had entered the infant electronic computer business by completely different approaches. J. Presper Eckert and John W. Mauchly had developed the ENIAC (*Elec*tronic *Numeric Integrator and Computer*), which is generally recognized as the first electronic digital computer. (Portions of the ENIAC are now enshrined in the Smithsonian Institution.) ENIAC and a follow-up machine were developed under US Army contracts and were optimized to calculate artillery shell trajectories. After World War II Eckert and Mauchly incorporated as the Eckert-Mauchly Computer Corporation. Because businesses in the position to buy electronic computers had little interest in artillery shell trajectories, Eckert and Mauchly determined to design and sell Univacs (*Univer*sal *Automatic Computers*). The first Univac was delivered in March 1951 to the US Census Bureau. The development project proved to be so costly that Eckert and Mauchly were forced to put their company on the market in order to have funds to build more machines. By this time, December 1955, fifteen Univac computers had been delivered to such heavyweight companies as General Electric, US Steel, and Metropolitan Life Insurance.

Completely independently, a group of former US Navy officers and civilians who had worked together during World War II on secret (mostly cryptographic) projects had founded Engineering Research Associates. Their plant had been the home of the Northwestern Aeronautical Corporation, a wartime industry started by John Parker, an entrepreneur. ERA survived by working on classified government contracts, which led to their expertise in digital logic, a new technology at that time. Eventually, ERA contracted with the Navy for the development of a complete computer, which became the forerunner of the Univac Scientific Computer with which I was so impressed. The first ERA computer was developed under Task 13 of their continuing Navy contract. The engineers had therefore named the new computer the ERA 1101, 1101 being the representation of the number 13 in binary notation. (The binary system is a number system used in computers. It is based on powers of 2 rather than on powers of 10, as in the common decimal system.) The Univac 1100 Series computer numbering system has survived to this day.

ERA had been faced with the same problem as Eckert-Mauchly, insufficient capital to exploit their technical position by building and selling computers in the commercial marketplace. And they solved the problem the same way—by selling the company to Remington Rand. So in 1952 Remington Rand had acquired two of the leading pioneering firms in the electronic computer business: Eckert-Mauchly, which had chosen to attack the business computer marketplace, and ERA, which had specialized in scientific computing. Earlier, Remington Rand had built their own Norwalk, Connecticut, laboratory, where punched card and tabulating equipment was designed and where computer peripheral equipment would soon be designed.

A digression is in order to explain the distinction between "business" and "scientific" computing. In theory and indeed in practice, a general-purpose computer can solve any type of problem given enough time and the proper programming. The average home computer can, in theory, solve the space shuttle reentry equations, but the astronauts will have died of old age by the time the solution is complete. Business problems are typically quite simple mathematically—addition, subtraction, and multiplication carried out to two decimal places of accuracy but repeated thousands of times on successive payroll records, accounts receivable, etc. Thus computers used in business do simple things to a large number of records, so computer design stresses getting data into and out of the computer quickly. Scientific problems tend toward the opposite extreme. A typical problem might involve complex calculations carried out to twenty or thirty decimal places but with little input and output. I have seen a powerful scientific computer grind away for hours on a single problem, the output of which was a single printed line. Of course, modern computers are designed to be good at both business and scientific problems, but the early machines were usually optimized to solve one type of problem or the other. The differing design philosophies are important to my story.

To return to Remington Rand, senior management soon discovered that they had bitten off more than they could chew. The computer business became, and remained until recently, primarily an equipment leasing business, which requires enormous capital. The computer manufacturer would own the machines installed at the customer's site, gradually recovering its cost from the monthly rental being paid by the user. Remington Rand's three engineering groups were not integrated in any way, and they conducted a continuous political guerrilla warfare over who would get the largest share of corporate development funding. Most engineers suffer from the "Not Invented Here" (NIH) syndrome, which tells them that any product designed by a competitive group must be ill-conceived, sloppily designed, and certain to result in expensive failure. Exacerbating the normal NIH rivalry of ERA and Eckert-Mauchly was their difference in design philosophies—one scientific problem oriented and the other business problem oriented. Neither group could find much good to say about the design talents of the other.

Just six months before I joined the company, Remington Rand had merged with Sperry Corporation, to form the Sperry Rand Corporation. Sperry was a major defense contractor (the Sperry gyroscope was a familiar piece of equipment aboard Navy ships). Sperry had expanded into commercial businesses as well and could, they hoped, supply both the capital and the technical management skills needed to exploit the Remington Rand computer business. As a first essential step, the Sperry Rand management had combined the three engineering operations, keeping the prestigious Univac name, into the Univac Division of Sperry Rand.

The first general manager of the combined division was William C. Norris, who was the senior surviving member of the small group of ERA founders. One of the other founders had died. John Parker had taken his profit and left the company. The founders of ERA had profited enormously on the sale of their stock to Remington Rand, so Norris was already quite a wealthy man. The original shareholders of ERA received eighty-five times their investment when the company was sold. Bill Norris was pointed out in the hall to me—a thin, medium-sized man in his mid-forties with gray hair and an austere manner. Raised on a farm in Nebraska, he had an electrical engineering degree from the University of Nebraska and had served as a lieutenant commander in the Navy during World War II.

I had been at ERA for a month, time enough to be thoroughly brainwashed by my fellow engineers about the superiority of ERA designs. But I still had to attend the course given by those kludgemachers at Eckert-Mauchly Division. (For the uninitiated, a kludge, pronounced klooj, is a common engineering term, always used contemptuously, to describe the other fellow's equipment. It implies a clumsy and inelegant design that just possibly may operate, but barely!) I set out for Philadelphia once again, this time in style. I had traded in my old convertible for a brand new 1956 Buick hardtop.

2

The Philadelphia Story

Once again back at 1900 Allegheny Avenue, I checked in with Dave Keefer, rented a room within walking distance of the plant, and at Dave's recommendation, rented a garage for my Buick. The neighborhood around the plant was the sort where you counted your hubcaps on arriving at work and again on leaving! There was a small company parking lot provided for the instructors, but none for the students, and on-street parking was hazardous to the car's health.

The other twenty or so students arrived. All but one other engineer had been hired by customer engineering. They would eventually be going to customer sites to maintain their assigned computers. The class was about equally divided between graduate electrical engineers and electronics technicians. The technicians were all recently discharged from the armed forces, where they had received their electronics training and had performed maintenance for the Navy or Air Force. All students were in their twenties, and all were eager to learn. The classroom at Allegheny Avenue was a large room with two walls of blackboards and rows of long tables for the students. Each of us was issued a book of "B" size (11 inches by 17 inches) logic diagrams of the Univac, but before we were allowed to look at it, we had to be initiated into the mysteries of the binary number system. I am afraid that the reader will have to submit briefly to the same discipline.

The binary number system is based on the number 2 raised to various powers: 2 squared equals 4, 2 cubed equals 8, and so forth, just as the decimal system is based on the number 10 (10 squared equals 100, 10 cubed equals 1000, etc.). Mathematicians invented number systems based on every conceivable number hundreds of years ago; the binary system was not invented by computer engineers. The use of binary numbers in computers came about because of the limitations of electronic circuits. It is easy to design circuits that have two reliably stable states (think of them as "on" and "off") but difficult and expensive to design circuits with more than two stable states. Some years ago research was done on tristable devices (three stable states), and Burroughs Corporation tried at one time to popularize a vacuum tube having ten stable states (which would have allowed computer arithmetic to work directly in decimal). But nothing came of these efforts. Computer designers today, as in 1956, must work with a large number of electronic circuit devices that have only two stable states. The basic unit for design of computer arithmetic is therefore a digit that can have only two values, a *bi*nary digi*t*, or bit. The bit is represented as 0 or 1 and is sometimes referred to as being "true" or "false," "on" or "off," "high" or "low," or any other pair of opposites the designer chooses.

As part of our education, our class had to learn to do simple arithmetic (add, subtract, multiply, and divide) in binary notation, with each number represented by a long string of 1's and 0's. This takes a lot of patience and more scratch paper! Imagine trying to do long division using roman numerals and you will get the general idea. I have never used this ability to calculate in binary. I think it is something of a tradition, like teaching English schoolboys Greek and Latin. As it is impossible to imagine an educated English gentleman unfamiliar with Greek and Latin, so it is impossible to imagine a computer engineer unable to perform binary arithmetic.

Representing something useful in binary notation, such as a single decimal digit, requires four bits. (There are 2^4, or sixteen, possible combinations of four bits.) Representing a character that can be alphabetic or numeric requires a minimum of six bits (sixty-four possible combinations, figuring twenty-six letters of the alphabet plus ten numerals plus some minimal punctuation marks). If you want to get more elegant and distinguish upper- from lowercase letters and add a wide selection of punctuation marks and some control characters for the printers, you need seven or eight bits. A group of bits forms a character called a byte. If you see the term "byte" in computer literature without any modifying explanation, it means eight bits, because that is what IBM uses; it has become the de facto standard. Control Data got by for years using a 6-bit byte, foregoing lowercase letter representation. This was perfectly acceptable to scientific users, who were mostly interested in numbers anyhow, and a 6-bit byte made more efficient use of the computer storage.

Many engineers dislike inefficient use of circuitry. The fact that four bits are required to represent the ten possible combinations of decimal digits, zero through nine, leaving four possible bit combinations unused, offended some engineers so much that they worked in a system of eight symbols, known as octal. A single octal digit represents three bits; therefore, eight symbols are needed to represent all the possible combinations of three bits. Octal digits are written just like decimal digits except that there are no 8's or

9's. Counting in octal goes 0, 1, 2, 3, 4, 5, 6, 7, 10, 11, and so forth. The representation 10 in octal indicates 1 times 8 plus 0 times 1, or 8, and 11 in octal represents 1 times 8 plus 1 times 1, or 9, and so forth. The beauty of this system is that three bits define each octal digit, with no bit combinations unused. Because octal numbers look like decimal numbers, they must be identified as octal in computer literature. Such numbers as the memory requirements for computer programs are sometimes stated in octal. Two 3-bit octal digits can be crammed into a 6-bit byte, making efficient use of the computer circuitry. Use of octal was widespread at ERA but not at Eckert-Mauchly. Similarly, for efficiency of data storage, an 8-bit byte can be treated as two 4-bit halves, known as nibbles. Because each 4-bit nibble can represent a decimal digit, two decimal digits can be stored in each 8-bit computer byte if numeric-only information is to be represented. To represent the four bits of a nibble, computer engineers came up with another numbering system—hexadecimal, meaning "sixteen." A hex character is represented by the numerals 0 through 9 plus the six letters A through F, sixteen characters in all.

Only one more term remains to be defined: the computer word. A word is the number of bits that are processed by the computer simultaneously, as a single entity. Most current IBM computers use a 32-bit word. Control Data, with its strong emphasis on scientific computation requiring high precision (a large number of decimal places), has traditionally used a 60-bit word and now uses a 64-bit word in their newest computers. Most low-cost home computers use an 8-bit word; that is, the word is equal to the byte. The size and cost of a computer increase roughly in proportion to increases in word length. Also, the speed increases, especially for complex arithmetic operations. The Univac I used the longest word I have ever heard of, eighty-four bits organized as twelve characters (the term "byte" had not been invented yet) of seven bits each. This extremely long word was a characteristic of the memory technology used in the Univac I and was not typical of computers, then or now.

Once we students had mastered binary arithmetic, we were allowed to open our books of logic diagrams and, with the instructor's help, trace through the logic circuitry of the Univac, learning exactly how it performed each instruction. One of our first instructors was George Cogar. Tall, raw-boned, with big protruding ears, George looked somewhat like pictures of the young Abe Lincoln before Abe grew his beard. George was from the mountains of West Virginia, with an appropriate drawl, and he was the first genius I encountered in the computer business. George had never finished high school; he had gotten a USAFI (United States Armed Forces Institute) equivalent degree in the Air Force, where he had learned electronics with extraordinary ease. I first suspected that George was more than just bright when I watched him writing at the blackboard. Instructing us in the circuitry of the adder, he wrote from one end of the blackboard to the other, filling in circuit details complete with component values and never looking at the book of diagrams that lay open on his desk. "George, how can you draw all that circuitry and never look at the prints?" I finally asked him. He explained that he could see it all in his head. Just circuits and logic diagrams—he could not do the same thing with printed text. Although George was a comparative newcomer to the technical staff at Eckert-Mauchly and had not been one of the Univac designers, he was already recognized as the expert of last resort in troubleshooting certain sections of the machine. He was later called to help us with the problems that plagued Univac II in St. Paul. We became friends and drank a good deal of beer together.

We students were disappointed to learn that the first month of the course would consist of classroom instruction; only later would we be allowed to go to the other plant farther west on Allegheny Avenue where the Univacs were being assembled and tested. There were no computers at 1900 Allegheny Avenue.

As we students threaded our way through the logic diagrams of the Univac I, trying to understand exactly what each computer instruction, or "op code," did, I was astonished at how simple the computer really was. In my hazy thinking about electronic computers or "giant brains," as the press still called them, I had assumed that a computer could, of course, perform differential and integral calculus and perhaps do Fourier transforms and other higher mathematical functions. Wrong! Besides the "housekeeping" functions of moving data in and out and between various storage devices, the only things the computer could actually *do* were add, subtract, multiply, divide, shift characters to the right or to the left, and make decisions based on whether two computer words were equal or on whether one word was greater than another. By "one word being greater than another," I mean, of course, that the binary bit pattern represents a greater numerical value, there being no other way to compare the "value" of an A with that of a semicolon, for example. The only "reasoning" ability the computer has is in those last two instructions. By "make decisions" I mean that, if the test condition is met, that is, if the two words are equal, the computer takes its next instruction from a specified memory location; if the two words are not equal, the computer takes its next instruction from a different specified memory location. The whole power of a stored-program computer, as opposed to a fast calculator, rests on the computer's ability to test and "branch" in its program (that is, to take its next instruction from one memory location or from a different memory location) and on its ability to treat its programmed instructions exactly the same as data. This ability enables the computer to modify its own sequence of instructions as it performs them. It took me some time to understand fully the power of these two seemingly simple abilities.

Of course a digital computer can perform higher mathematical functions, but it does them by means of lengthy, repetitious series of calculations, such as series expansions. Much of the theory for these calculations was developed by mathematicians hundreds of years before the invention of the computer, but the calculations, which require only the four basic mathematical functions, are so lengthy and time consuming that they are seldom done with pencil and paper. I finally realized that computer development represented no breakthroughs in mathematical theory whatsoever, but it was a great triumph of practical down-to-earth engineering.

The machine instruction set of the Univac I was mnemonic, meaning "memory aiding." That is, an A instruction was an add, a B instruction was a bring, etc. This was just as well because development of higher-level computer programming languages was in its infancy and programs had to be written directly in machine instruction codes. We students were required to write some simple programs, which we later tested on the computers. As we worked our way through the logic of each instruction, the mystery of the computer began to dissipate. The operation of the adder, the multiplier, and the shift registers gradually became clear.

What was not clear to me at all was how all the data got into the computer in the first place. We had seen the console typewriter, but this could handle only a trickle of information. The functions that the computer could perform were so elementary; its usefulness presumably lay in its ability to process vast amounts of data rapidly. Where did this data come from and how did it get into the machine? We were to study the input/output system last of all, so I had to wait for an answer to my questions.

Finally came the great day when we were allowed to work on an actual computer! We met our instructor a mile west on Allegheny Avenue, at the other old warehouse where Univacs were being assembled and checked out. At this time fifteen Univac I's had been installed at customer sites and another six machines were on the test floor.

Each Univac I was a little larger than a single car garage with a flat roof. Two big cooling blowers in the base of each machine and the line of magnetic tape transports attached to each computer provided continous background noise. The outer skin of each computer was entirely composed of hinged gray metal doors, which gave access to rows of removable chassis, aglow with the filaments of vacuum tubes. Wherever a door was open—and there were many open—a large fan hung from brackets on the ceiling was turned on to blow air on the exposed chassis. The test floor was therefore both noisy and breezy! In the center of one of the long sides of the computer was a special door with a clear Plexiglas panel in the center. This access door allowed an engineer to walk inside the computer, to check out the wiring interconnecting the chassis or to service the memory banks. The Plexiglas panel in the door allowed the service engineers to see if anyone was working inside the machine, or, heaven forbid, if smoke was arising from the circuitry within. The memory of the Univac I consisted of mercury acoustic delay lines, large horizontal cylinders studded with vacuum tubes, which occupied the center third of the space inside the computer. Their capacity: 1000 84-bit words or 12,000 bytes, less than most home computers today! I found it quite a thrill to stand inside the computer surrounded by a million dollars' worth of electronics. Wires covered all four sides and the ceiling. The powerful suction from the two cooling blowers beneath coarse metal grill covers in the floor tugged at my pants legs.

Cooling the Univac was accomplished by circulating chilled water from an external cooling compressor through cooling coils located around the periphery of the machine under the banks of the vacuum tube chassis. The blowers under the false floor of the computer drew air from inside the computer, forced it through the cooling coils and up the sides, cooling the chassis (if the doors were closed). The now warm air was exhausted into the interior of the computer near the ceiling, and the blowers pulled it down again. When some of the outside doors were opened to give access to the chassis, the cool air escaped into the room without cooling the chassis, hence the need for the external fans. The Univac test technicians, and later we students, discovered that the cooling coils under the false floor of the computer made excellent refrigerators for soft drinks or beer. We often discovered a stray beverage can nestled against the cooling coils when we lifted the floorboards to retrieve a dropped tool. The Univac I, with its 5000 vacuum tubes, needed a lot of cooling. It consumed about 100 kilowatts of power. For comparison, an electric range with all the burners set at the highest temperature consumes about 10 kilowatts.

Because vacuum tube circuitry requires high voltages, the interior of the computer was actually quite a hazardous place to work. A cord called the trolley wire was strung along the ceiling inside the computer in such a way that it could be reached from any place in the interior. A quick jerk on the trolley wire shut off all electrical power. Standing orders on the test floor dictated that no one was ever to work alone inside the machine; a buddy was always to be standing by. I never heard of any worker being injured on either the Univac I or later on the Univac II, but the high voltages gave rise to a lot of gallows humor. A cardboard skeleton of the kind sold at Halloween was once found hanging from the trolley wire by one bony hand!

The power supply for the Univac, housed in a separate gray metal cabinet about the size and shape of a garden tool shed, was the setting for a more elaborate practical joke. In the center of the power supply cabinet was a long wire ribbon, a "bleeder resistor," which zigzagged back and forth across the six-foot height of the interior. Studded with movable taps for the various voltages, it presented a wicked and cruel appearance. The members of one test crew managed somehow to obtain a department store mannequin. They dressed it in khacki pants and sport shirt, the apparel worn by most of the test technicians. The mannequin was hung on the bleeder resistor after the test crew carefully moved a voltage tap so that voltage monitors would indicate a problem with the power supply. The mannequin was left for the next shift to discover!

Once we students became familiar with the general workings of the computer, we were encouraged to gain experience in writing and running simple programs. Inevitably, most of these programs turned out to be humorous, as we discovered what a great toy a computer can be. The operator's console of the Univac was a separate desk, with a sloping panel of indicator lights and switches, not as impressive as the Univac Scientific Computer in St. Paul but still impressive. In the center of the console was a typewriter keyboard, and a typewriter printer alongside allowed dialogue with the computer. Although some of the students attempted serious programs, such as income tax preparation, far more typical was a program called Psychiatrist. It began with the message: "I am your friendly Univac Psychiatrist. Please answer the following questions to the best of your ability." The program then asked a series of questions starting with name, sex, age, sexual habits, etc., allowing the respondent to type in answers. Finally the program came to the critical question: "What is your annual income?" If the victim typed in a number larger than $15,000 (remember, this was 1956,) the program would reply: "You indeed have serious problems which will require years of analysis to resolve. Please see the receptionist for your next appointment." If the response indicated less than $15,000, the program would reply: "You have a few minor problems that I am sure you can work out. Please show (fills in the name) out. Show the next patient in."

Despite the lighthearted approach to our jobs, we students learned rapidly, and we were soon finding and correcting with commendable speed the malfunctions that had been inserted into the machine by our instructors. At the same time we began to appreciate just how complex the relationship between individual circuit elements and logic can be in a big computer and why it was said that when a machine reaches a certain level of complexity, it develops a personality of its own, usually malevolent. The most maddening problems for a test engineer to find are those errors that occur intermittently and that cannot be made to recur. We heard the story of one such intermittent error that took the *instructors* weeks to find. It seemed that if a certain number of records were read from the magnetic tape to the computer with the tape moving in a forward direction and then a record was read from magnetic tape moving in a backward direction, a read error would occur—sometimes! Every portion of the read circuitry had been checked over and over, and the problem could not be duplicated. Finally, one of the instructors picked an arbitrary number: 500. He wrote a short program to read 500 tape records forward and then one record backward. The read failed every time.

The trouble was quickly isolated to a sluggish mercury relay in the read circuitry. Just out of curiosity, the instructor tried the same program using 510 records. No failure. He tried again using 490 records. No failure. Some of these things border on witchcraft!

About this time I met "Pres" Eckert and some of the senior engineers who had designed the Univac. The already famous inventor turned out to be medium size, balding, with bright eyes and rapid-fire speech. Pres no longer had any interest in Univac I or in Univac II. He was already at work designing his first transistorized computer, called the LARC, for Livermore Atomic Research Computer. The LARC was an early example of what came to be called a supercomputer, a machine designed to operate at the maximum speed that the state of the art allowed. The Livermore Laboratory had, and still has, an insatiable appetite for more and more computer speed. The director of the computer center there, Sidney Fernbach, became famous for the number and diversity of supercomputers that he had installed.

The LARC program was in trouble and seemed certain to overrun its budget and schedule. A story told by rival engineering groups gives the flavor. The LARC was a huge machine physically, and its designers were having problems with electrical noise, unwanted random electrical signals. To ameliorate the noise problem, the designers had to minimize the electrical contact resistance between the metal framework of the computer and the plug-in chassis that slid into the frame. The entire LARC frame and the contact areas on the chassis that touched the frame were gold plated! Gold is a wonderful contact material because in addition to its low electrical resistance, it resists surface corrosion, which can be a problem with copper or silver (Univac chassis contacts were silver plated). It was said of the gold-plated LARC that if you were short of lunch money, you could always run your fingernails over the chassis and scrape off a few dollars' worth of gold on your way to lunch!

Our class continued to spend half-days in classroom instruction. Gradually I began to understand how data got into and out of the computer. An integral part of the Univac system design was a row of magnetic tape recording devices, dubbed Uniservos. The technology for recording digital data, as opposed to voice and music, on magnetic tape was new at the time, and the Eckert-Mauchly engineers had pioneered a whole new technology to make it practical and reliable. For example, magnetic tape of quality good enough to record digital data, where the loss of a single bit can be disastrous, was not commercially available, so Eckert-Mauchly made their own. The tape was a half-inch-wide strip of thin nickel-plated bronze. A reel of this tape held 1500 feet, and it was, of course, terribly heavy. A reel made a wonderful paperweight. Crinkled lengths of the silvery tape, damaged by faulty Uniservos, also made good Christmas tree decorations. We never lacked for an adequate supply!

Each Uniservo stood about six feet high and three feet wide. A typical Univac I system had ten Uniservos. The data was recorded on the tape at 128 characters per running inch of tape, and the tape moved at 100 inches per second. Thus a Uniservo could move 128 times 100, or 12,800 characters per second into or out of the computer. This was a phenomenal data rate for the time. To give a tape speed comparison: The ordinary cassette tape recorder moves eighth-inch-wide plastic tape at 1⅞ inches per second, fifty-three times slower than the Uniservo.

On the front of each Uniservo were two tape reels, one for supply and one for take-up; the magnetic heads for erasing, recording, and reading the tape; the capstan (drive wheel) that moved the tape; and two long loops of tape, one on the supply reel side and one on the take-up reel side. These loops were held in position by Rube Goldberg-like assemblies of pulleys, springs, and ordinary fishing line. Such "buffer loops" are a feature of high-performance magnetic tape transports even today. They are necessary because the tape is accelerated so rapidly (in a few thousandths of a second) from a stop to a speed of 100 inches per second that the supply and take-up reels are unable to respond quickly enough. The tape would break if buffer loops were not provided. As the tape accelerates, it is pulled from the loop on the supply reel side and dumped into the loop on the take-up reel side. Photocells sense the changing length of the loops and command the supply reel to spin off more tape and the take-up reel to wind up the excess. Adjustment of the buffer loops and replacement of worn fishing line were constant problems for the customer engineers. A new magnetic tape transport, called the Uniservo II, substituted vacuum columns for the pulleys and the fishing line. The Uniservo II was under development in St. Paul and would be used on the Univac II.

I could now understand how a large amount of data could get into and out of the computer, but how did all this data get onto magnetic tape in the first place? I was told that the Uniservo tapes were prepared "off-line," that is, on devices not wired to the computer. The devices that put data onto the magnetic tape were the card-to-tape converter and the Unityper. The device that took the output tapes prepared by the computer and produced printed reports was the tape-to-print station. These three devices would be studied in the last few weeks of the course.

One day I received a message from Art Engstrom saying that I was needed in St. Paul. With regret I realized that I would have to postpone learning about the off-line data preparation devices. I packed up my Buick for the return drive, comforting myself with the thought that I would be seeing most of my classmates again in St. Paul. They would be helping to test the Univac II.

I left Philadelphia with a thorough respect for the engineering capabilities of the Eckert-Mauchly Division. They had taken the poorly suited vacuum tubes and other electronic components available at the time and through painstaking, conservative engineering design built a practical and usable computer *system*. I looked forward to what I could learn from the ERA engineering staff.

3

On Technology And Geography

Back at the old glider factory I found that development of the Univac II was not going well. Ward Lund's lab looked as chaotic as ever, and a never-ending stream of wiring changes were being made. I now understood enough about Univac I to understand the modifications that would convert the design to a Univac II. These fell into three catagories.

1. The mercury acoustic delay line memory of the Univac I was being replaced with a newly designed magnetic-core memory of 2000 words—doubling the memory capacity! The magnetic-core memory, in which each bit is stored as the magnetic polarity of a tiny doughnut-shaped magnet made of iron oxide, was just coming into use in the computer industry. Each tiny doughnut, or toroid, was threaded by fine wires through the center hole. Electrical pulses sent through these wires served to change the magnetic state of each core to store a 0 or a 1 as desired and to read out the previous state stored in the core. As the technology improved, the size of magnetic cores got smaller and smaller, but the basic technology of core memories remained a standard in computer memories for an amazingly long time, fifteen to twenty years, before it was replaced by semiconductor memories. Even today you may hear some old-timers in the industry ask: "How much core does the computer have?"

2. The Uniservo I magnetic tape transports were being replaced by the new Uniservo II's. Besides getting rid of the troublesome fishing line and pulley arrangement for the tape buffer loops, the new Uniservos could record up to 215 characters per running inch of tape instead of 128 characters, nearly doubling the capacity. In addition, up to sixteen Uniservo II's could be used on a system, up from ten Uniservo I's.

3. A number of small changes were being made to the processor itself to add some new or improved instructions.

None of these changes seemed to be particularly difficult. What was going wrong?

While pondering the cause of the problem, I had a number of administrative duties: planning the test procedures to be used on Univac II, ordering engineering drawings and tools, establishing working relationships with the manufacturing people, etc. I had made friends with a couple of other young engineers with whom I usually ate lunch. We were soon joined by Dick Karpen, a tall, good-looking senior engineer who had worked on maintenance of the Univac I at the Livermore Laboratory.

Dick Karpen told a story of negotiating across the table from Pres Eckert on the LARC contract. Eckert was making a detailed technical presentation on LARC to the Livermore staff, which included Karpen. In a creative frenzy Eckert paced back and forth, describing how the multiply unit worked. His right-hand man, Frazer Welsh, interrupted: "Pres, that's not the way it works!" "Yes, it is," replied Eckert, "I just changed it." The LARC was eventually delivered to Livermore and performed as promised, but it was a financial disaster for Univac, having cost several times the contract amount to develop. We at Univac took consolation from the fact that archrival IBM had had a worse disaster with *their* early supercomputer, optimistically named STRETCH, because it was intended to stretch the technology. Cynics—and there are many in the computer business—nick-named the IBM computer SHRINK, because it never met its performance criteria, which had to be revised downward continually. The history of supercomputers is littered with costly failures. These were only two early examples.

Dick was well acquainted with most of the senior engineers in Philadelphia who had designed Univac I and with their design methods. He explained exactly why the Univac II design group was having so much trouble. The truth is, *technology does not travel well.* Moving a technical project from one location to another is much like transplanting a living tree: The difficulty is proportional to the length of time that the tree has been growing in its original location; the difficulty is proportional to the physical distance the tree is to be moved; if the tree is to survive, a lot of dirt has to be moved along with it; the best result to be hoped for is that the growth will be set back by three to six months, and, at worst, the tree will not survive.

This problem in transferring technology, which I have seen demon-strated time and time again, arises from the nature of engineers and engineering. Most engineers hate to write. When absolutely forced to, they will keep their descriptions as cryptic as possible and will plagiarize existing documents wherever they can. A complete engineering design consists of a great stack of engineering drawings, supplemented by a stack of specifi-cations and test procedures. If the developing engineering group has strong discipline and if the engineers are conscientious, this great pile of paper will represent perhaps 90 to 95 percent of what the receiving group needs to know about the design. Missing will be the subtle tricks of timing, methods of compensating for known weaknesses in components, etc. These are not in writing because no one ever thought of a need to write them down. "Everybody knows about that." And, indeed, in the developing organization this may be true: Everybody does know about the tricky timing in the read circuit; it was the topic of hallway conversation for weeks.

If the developing engineering group dislikes the receiving group or feels that they are rivals for scarce development funds, the amount of information supplied may be more like 70 to 75 percent. "Let those smart guys figure it out for themselves like we had to!" is not an uncommon attitude. The top engineering designers especially are often disdainful of lesser intellects. But even assuming that the receiving group gets the 90 to 95 percent of the design information that they need, they will still be lacking two essential things: the overall design philosophy of the development, a sort of mind's-eye overview of what the machine is supposed to do and how the design is going to accomplish the tasks, and the many design approaches that were tried but failed. Although the overall design philosophy influences every design decision, most engineers are incapable of verbalizing their inner thoughts on this philosophical level. The failed design approaches are never written down because no one likes to publicize his failures, and it is easy to rationalize that the failed approaches are not a part of the completed design. They are "nobody's business."

The group receiving the completed design, then, has to ferret out the missing 5 to 10 percent of the design for themselves, despite their not knowing the overall design philosophy that guided, perhaps subconsciously, every decision of the original designers. Any change that the receivers make with an eye to reducing costs or improving performance runs the risk of repeating one of the unsuccessful (and undocumented) experiments of the original developers. In a nutshell, this was the position in which the development group for Univac II found themselves. Starting with an operating Univac I, they had anticipated only minor changes to accommodate the new memory. They found themselves in a mine field. Each seemingly innocuous change caused unexpected problems elsewhere in the computer that, on being corrected, caused still other unexpected problems. Change followed change, and the schedule for our five production computers continued to slip.

ERA Division now compounded the problem of communications by opening a brand new headquarters plant on West 7th Street in St. Paul on the east bank of the Mississippi River. Our Univac II production group was to move to the new plant and assemble the first five production computers there; Ward Lund's development group was to remain in the old glider factory. This five-mile gap appeared trivial when compared to the thousand-mile Philadelphia–St. Paul abyss, but it contributed its share to the future problems.

Facilities in the new plant were almost as spartan as those in the old plant. True, I could now look out a window (when they were washed, which occurred infrequently) at a view of the parking lot, but the floors were still bare cement except for the executive offices in the front of the plant. One definite improvement was the presence of a small bar and steak house next door. My friends and I soon ate lunch there nearly every day. Gannon's steak house became known jokingly as the Univac Executive Cafeteria, a designation it retains to this day.

My former classmates arrived from Philadelphia. They were put to work helping to complete the five Univac II's that were being assembled in a large room just across the aisle from my office. Two other friends also appeared: Dave Keefer and George Cogar. Management had become seriously concerned about the delays in the Univac II development and had recruited both men to help. George Cogar would work half-days with Ward Lund's development group and then teach us test engineers a "differences" course on the changes made to convert the Univac I to Univac II the other half-days, a dual assignment that seemed to bother him not at all. George eventually returned to Philadelphia, but Dave Keefer stayed on in St. Paul to work with Dick Karpen on a preliminary design for the Univac IIR, a version of the Univac II that would use magnetic amplifiers instead of vacuum tubes. (Magnetic amplifier circuits were thought for a brief time to be the most suitable replacement for vacuum tubes in computers. They were superseded by transistors before much design was done with them.) Dave Keefer and George Cogar often joined our lunch group. Some of the most pleasant times of my long career were spent around a lunch table or at the bar drinking beer after work with this talented group. Dave Keefer in particular had a vast store of anecdotes about the early days in the computer business. He had worked briefly at IBM and told a story of being admonished by his supervisor for wearing an "inappropriate" tie!

The attitude of the typical ERA engineer toward IBM is worth an aside at this point. IBM was universally regarded as the enemy, the only competitor in the infant computer industry that counted. IBM was respected and feared for its management acumen and for its superb marketing force but disliked for its presumed arrogance, stuffiness, and concern with image.

Engineers, it was believed, were second-class employees at IBM while all status was enjoyed by marketing. For this reason it was believed that IBM computers were and would continue to be technically inferior because no really first-class creative engineer would want to work there. Nevertheless, the IBM sales force was so well trained and highly motivated that "they could sell manure in a brown paper sack!" The Univac products, therefore, had to be twice as good as the IBM products to have a chance in the marketplace. Mixed in with this attitude was a usually unspoken resentment of IBM's East Coast, Ivy League image. Nearly all the engineers at ERA were graduates of midwestern state universities. A statement often heard in one form or another was: "They [IBM] think that we are a bunch of dumb farmers out here; we'll show them!" This attitude certainly extended upstairs to Bill Norris, as a later chapter will show. A better, more unifying factor for Univac would be hard to find. Even the long-standing Philadelphia–St. Paul feud would be forgotten in our eagerness to beat IBM to the market with a new product.

The Eckert-Mauchly people told the story, believed at the time, that IBM had pretty much ignored the electronic computer, considering it to be a toy for government-funded laboratories. That is, they considered it so until Metropolitan Life Insurance in New York bought one of the early Univac I's. Met Life was a company known for its tightness with a buck, never spending one dollar unless they could see a two-dollar return. When they bought a $1½ million Univac system, so the story went, there was panic in Poughkeepsie! IBM launched a crash effort to develop their 70X series, which proved to be no great shakes technically but which filled the marketplace gap until IBM could develop something better. Nearly every engineer at Univac understood that *we* were the world leaders in electronic computers at that time. The topic of many a lunchtime conversation was how we at Univac could maintain and exploit our lead.

My security clearance had been processed, so I was now allowed to tour the classified military section of the old glider plant. A number of fascinating projects were revealed to me. I found out what was connected to the radar antenna that I had noticed my first day at the plant. A prototype device called a video processor analyzed the radar return signal and generated its digital coordinates so that a computer could analyze and track the radar return. A senior engineer named Malcolm Macaulay was working on a large cathode-ray-tube display on which radar "blips" and computer-generated alphanumeric messages could be displayed simultaneously. My years in the Navy staring at radarscopes gave me an instant appreciation of its value. Down the hall two small working prototype computers named Transtech and Magstech had been built to evaluate the relative effectiveness of transistors and magnetic amplifiers as components to replace vacuum tubes in full-scale computers. This was exciting stuff!

The military engineering side of ERA was headed by Frank Mullaney, Bill Keye's counterpart. Mullaney is a tall, thin, mournful-looking Irishman who enjoys a unique distinction: In all the years I have known him, I have never heard anyone speak a critical word about Frank Mullaney; he is universally liked and respected. Working under Mullaney were two up-and-coming engineers, Seymour Cray and Bob Kisch. Cray and Kisch had just written a paper describing their pioneering work in using a computer, in this case the Univac Scientific, to design the next model computer. The program optimized the placement of plug-in circuit cards and calculated the backplane wiring lengths and routing—elementary stuff by today's standards but an innovation that was widely admired at the time. Although a relative newcomer to ERA, Seymour Cray was already regarded as one of the top, if not the top computer designer in St. Paul. Coming to ERA with a bachelor's degree in electrical engineering and a master of science degree in applied mathematics from the University of Minnesota, he had taken to computer design like one born to it. He was similar to George Cogar in that respect. Of medium height and absolutely average appearance, Seymour Cray was normally soft spoken but capable of biting sarcasm when confronted with foolishness. Oddly enough, he is a very distant relative of mine.

Back in the workaday world of the Univac II, I was formally appointed project engineer in charge of the test floor. I was assigned another engineer as assistant. The equipment and drawings ordered earlier were flooding in: oscilloscopes on rolling carts, meters, hand tools, and engineering drawings by the thousands. The engineering drawings we had mounted on tilting-top, rolling stands, two for each computer. These were soon known as Unidollies. My assistant and I designed portable workbenches for holding tools, fuses, and small parts. These were made up in the model shop and dubbed Unibenches. I assigned men from customer engineering to the test crews for the first five production computers, with an engineer-in-charge responsible for each one. The five computer mainframes were now erected on the test floor of the new plant, without, however, all the plug-in chassis containing the vacuum tube circuitry and without a full complement of Uniservos. These five machines had already been sold, so a sign was hung above each one with the name of the customer.

In the early days of computers, each company buying one wanted to be sure that the general public, and especially their shareholders, knew about the new acquisition. After all, computers were extremely expensive and the newest thing in technology. Possession of a computer demonstrated that the company was financially solid and that the management was progressive. Virtually all computer rooms were built with a glass wall, or at least with a number of viewing windows so that passersby could see but not touch the new marvel. The test floor at the new plant on West 7th Street followed this trend. Viewing windows were cut in the walls along the main aisles of the plant. Members of our test crews often looked up to see curious faces with noses pressed against the glass. Some of the technicians became mildly irritated at this unwanted attention and responded in typical fashion. Signs were made up identifying those with their faces to the glass as improbable or obscene animal species: "Blue-balled Baboon" is one I recall. These signs were hung above the viewing windows, invisible to the viewers outside the test room but obvious to the weary technicians glancing up at the windows. After a few management visits to the test floor, we were ordered to take the signs down.

Finally, the great day came when we were ready to turn on the power of a Univac II computer for the first time. The plug-in chassis were removed to protect them from any miswired power. My assistant stood by the circuit breaker while I checked to see that there was no one inside or even standing near the computer. He threw the switch.

4

Progress Is Our Only Product

There was a flash and a "pop," and the power was off. We had blown dozens of "grasshopper" fuses. A "grasshopper" fuse, used by the hundreds in Univacs I and II, is a brightly colored phenolic plastic strip about an inch and a half long. The color of the phenolic strip indicates the current rating of the fuse. A fuse wire is kept in tension between two spring-loaded clips, one on the front side of the phenolic strip and one on the back side. If the fuse blows, the spring clip on the back side snaps down, closing a contact to an alarm circuit that drops all power on the computer and also lights an indicator that shows the section of the Univac having the blown fuse. These grasshopper fuses had been designed for telephone switchboards and were rated for about 40 volts. Univac used them on all voltages up to 410 volts! The high voltages did not interfere with the ability of the fuses to protect the circuitry but did make for some spectacular pyrotechnics. When one of the higher voltages blew, there would be a flash, a pop, and a puff of smoke, and a blackened spot the size of a silver dollar would appear on the connection board behind the fuse. Transparent plastic covers were provided for the fuse boards, but in test, of course, we had removed all the covers. The number of flashes and pops as we first put power on the empty computer frame convinced us that we were in deep trouble. There was nothing we could do but trace through the wiring of the entire machine, checking for the proper voltage on every chassis pin.

The sheer number of errors found, dozens on each work shift, became a flood that threatened to drown our group in paperwork. The system for correcting errors worked like this: Each error found was reported on a "trouble report," a 7-by-9-inch card that described the problem, the serial number of the computer, the person reporting, etc. Filled-out trouble reports were left in a red wooden box provided on each computer's Unibench. Each problem was classified by the person reporting as either a "wiring error" or a "design error." A wiring error meant that the machine was wired wrong but that the engineering drawings or wiring tabulations (printed lists of wire connections) were correct. Wiring errors were corrected on the spot. The trouble report was required so that the test crews on the other machines could check for the same error and so that the manufacturing assemblers could be shown what a lousy job they were doing. A design error, indicating that the engineering drawings or wire tabs were wrong, was much more troublesome to correct. For example, the drawings of the computer backplane might call for +300 volts on pin 72 of a certain chassis; a study of the circuitry might indicate that this voltage should be on pin 73. Our test group was not authorized to make this sort of correction without approval of the group having design responsibility, Ward Lund's group, which was five miles away. It should have been simple to phone the responsible engineer and ask if this was the wrong pin, but these problems accumulated by the dozens and soon by the hundreds as we went into three-shift, around-the-clock testing. I soon had two men assigned full-time collecting trouble reports from the red boxes and correcting the documentation. The deadly five-mile communication gap began to cost us dearly in time and money. The trouble reports would be collected and logged, and formal questions would be written up for the design group and sent to them by interplant mail. This took a day. Ward Lund would guarantee us an answer within three working days. Sending replies back and distributing the answers to the person originating the trouble report would take another day. We were losing a week between problem finding and correction, and in the meantime testing of a particular computer section might be held up. I authorized one man to drive his car back and forth every day between plants to save the time taken by the interplant mail system.

The problem that we worried about most was undocumented wiring in the machine. This can occur in the following manner: A wire is specified to connect from pin 6 of one chassis to pin 73 of another chassis. The assembler by mistake connects the wire to pin 71 instead of to pin 73. Soon afterward, before the original error is found, an ECO (engineering change order) comes through to delete this wire. The assembler, working from a tabulated list of changes, looks at pin 73, sees no wire there, and assumes that the wire has already been removed. She goes on to the next change on her list, leaving in the machine a wire that now appears nowhere in the documentation. In something as complex as a computer, a random undocumented connection can cause strange and unpredictable symptoms and can be almost impossible to find. Eventually things got so bad that we had to strip out all the wiring on three machines and start over.

With these constant changes and little progress in getting the computers operational, morale in the test group dropped. One of the technicians adopted as our slogan the phrase that is the title of this chapter: "Progress Is

Our *Only* Product," a takeoff on the General Electric slogan, "Progress Is Our Most Important Product." The reader may well ask—and I did ask—why didn't we just shut down the testing until the development computer documentation had stabilized. The answer is that there was so much marketing pressure for the delivery of these already late computers that management did not want to lose even a week on the schedule despite the cost. Testing continued ten hours a day, three shifts, and a half-day on Saturday.

Apart from the frustration of the never-ending change orders, I was having a great time. I made more acquaintances among the other engineers, and I learned more about Univac products every day. Next door to our Univac II group was an engineering group called General Development that was designing peripheral equipment. Peripheral equipment refers to those electromechanical devices that are used with but are not a part of the computer mainframe or Central Processing Unit (CPU). The Uniservos are peripheral equipment, as are a number of the other fascinating devices with which I was about to become acquainted.

Perhaps the most interesting peripheral to watch in action is the high-speed printer. When the first electronic computers were invented, the only printing devices available for typing out the data from the computer were the Teletype machine, invented for typing out telegrams, and the electric typewriter, which could easily be modified to type out computer messages. These devices were limited in speed to about fifteen characters per second. Computer system designers soon realized that even a whole row of these character-at-a-time printing devices could not keep up with the rate at which a computer could generate data, so the high-speed printer had to be developed. The one designed by Eckert-Mauchly Division was of the type known as a "drum" printer. The first version operated at 600 lines per minute, or 10 printed lines per second. Such printers are used to print financial data more often than correspondence, so they are set up to use ledger-width paper rather than standard 8½-inch-wide paper. Widths of pages printed vary from 120 columns to 160 columns at a normal spacing of 10 columns per horizontal inch (Pica typewriter spacing). The first high-speed printer that I ever saw was an Eckert-Mauchly design, another gray metal box about four feet high, three feet wide, and two feet deep. A loud machine-gun-like "rat-tat-tat" came from the printer as it spewed out continuous-form paper in a steady flow, punctuated by sudden bursts of blank paper between forms.

To understand how a drum printer works, you must visualize a steel cylinder about five inches in diameter and sixteen inches long. Holding the cylinder with the long axis horizontal, you will see engraved on the surface a horizontal row of A's in all 132 column positions. Rotating the cylinder slightly, you will see a row of B's (actually mirror-image characters like the type slugs on a typewriter), next a row of C's, etc. all around the circumference of the cylinder. The alphabet (uppercase letters only) is followed by the numerals 0 through 9, and the common punctuation marks, for a total of forty-eight characters.

In operation the print drum (or cylinder) rotates at a constant ten revolutions per second. Opposite each column position on the drum is a print hammer, actually a small electromagnet. When each electromagnet is "fired," or pulsed with current, the hammer pushes the paper against an inked ribbon that is between the rotating drum and the paper, and the character that is at that instant opposite the hammer on the drum is printed in that column. Because the drum never stops rotating, the maximum time available to print this one character is 1/48 (because there are forty-eight characters around the drum) multiplied by 1/10 of a second (because the drum rotates ten times in one second) or about 1/480 of a second. The printer gains its speed by printing all the A's in a line simultaneously, then all the B's, and so on, until by the time the drum has completed one revolution, all the characters in the line have been printed. The paper steps up one line and the process is repeated. The printing takes place so fast that the eye cannot follow and, except for the noise generated, the machine would almost appear to be pulling preprinted paper through the mechanism.

The timing of the print hammers has to be extremely precise or the printed characters will be cut off at the top or the bottom and the line of print will appear wavy. To answer the frequent customer complaints about wavy lines, printer engineers developed the "band" or "train" printer. These printers work on exactly the same principle as the drum printer except that the typeface characters are contained in a horizontal oval or racetrack form, and the characters move horizontally across the paper rather than rotating vertically. The band or train printer requires timing of the print hammers just as precise as does the drum printer, but small errors in timing show up as characters squished together or spread apart rather than displaced vertically. The human eye is more tolerant of this type of print error, and so the manufacturer gets fewer complaints. Look closely at the next computer-printed document that you get in the mail and you can probably tell if it was printed on a drum- or a band-type high-speed printer.

In the General Development lab I could see the answer to the question I had raised in Philadelphia about how all the data got onto magnetic tape in the first place. A card-to-tape converter read ordinary punched cards ("IBM cards") into a small memory, then recorded the contents of its memory onto a Uniservo magnetic tape. The tape was then removed by an operator and mounted on one of the Uniservos attached to the Univac computer. Such a device, which is not wired directly to the computer but supplies information by means of a recorded media, is known as an off-line device. The first high-speed printer that I saw was also operated off-line from its own Uniservo tape transport. As computer programs became more sophisticated, devices such as the punched card reader and the high-speed printer were moved on-line, or directly wired to the computer. The duties of the computer operator became simplified, being reduced to adding more cards to the card reader and removing the printed output from the high-speed printer.

Punched cards, of course, had been around for many years before the computer was invented. IBM had built a profitable business from leasing equipment for punching cards, sorting cards, and tabulating (printing out the information on) cards. We at Univac disliked the universal term "IBM cards" because Remington Rand had its own competitive line of punched card equipment. These used round holes and stored ninety characters on a punched card, as opposed to IBM's rectangular holes and eighty-character cards. The Remington Rand cards never caught on in the marketplace although they were superior from a strictly technical standpoint. Besides having a greater capacity per card, round holes are easier to punch than rectangular holes, and punch dies stay sharp longer. In a concession to the marketplace, early Univac card readers were usually designed so that they could read either eighty-column or ninety-column punched cards.

Another interesting peripheral invented by Eckert-Mauchly was the Unityper. This was a typewriter keyboard that recorded the data keyed in directly on magnetic tape, bypassing the use of punched cards. A small six-inch-diameter reel of the Uniservo metal tape was mounted above the keyboard. It was recorded incrementally; that is, one character at a time entered from the keyboard was magnetically recorded on the tape and then the tape was stepped forward a fraction of an inch to the position for the next character. When one of these small reels was full, it could be mounted on a Uniservo and read into the computer or copied to a standard large reel of Uniservo tape. This device was years ahead of its time. It never caught on in the marketplace, which continued to use the punched card as the primary computer input media. It was left to my friend George Cogar and some other former Univac people to exploit the keyboard-to-magnetic-tape concept some years later.

ERA had pioneered the development of magnetic drums, and there were drums of several types in the General Development lab. A magnetic drum has computer data recorded on the surface of a rapidly rotating cylinder. If you think of an aluminum cylinder with magnetic tape wrapped around it, you will be close to the idea. As a matter of fact, some of the earliest magnetic drums were made in just this way; they were wrapped with magnetic tape material. The great advantage of a drum over a magnetic tape in storing and retrieving computer data is that all the data on the drum are accessible within the same short length of time. A tape has to be read from one end to the other, and if the record that you want happens to be in the middle or at the other end of the tape, it can take more than a minute to get to it. Data are recorded on a magnetic drum in tracks around the circumference, which appear as rings or hoops, spaced only a few hundredths of an inch apart. To record or to read the data on these tracks, the drum may have either fixed heads or moving heads. Fixed-head drums have a large number of magnetic heads positioned all around the surface of the drum so that one head is located above every track. Getting the record wanted, therefore, requires only selecting the correct head and waiting until the desired record appears under the head as the drum rotates. Drums typically rotate at 2000 to 5000 revolutions per minute, so this time interval, known as the rotational latency time, is a few thousandths of a second. Moving-head drums have only one or a small number of heads that must be moved parallel to the axis of rotation until they are over the desired track. The time for the head to move, called the positioner latency time, must be added to the rotational latency time to determine the total time required to access a given record. Moving-head drums are thus slower in accessing a data record but lower in cost because of the reduced number of magnetic heads.

Eckert-Mauchly had developed a large moving-head drum for use with the LARC. The FASTRAND drum actually was made up of two huge nickel-plated cylinders, each about six feet long and eighteen inches in diameter. These were mounted with the long axes horizontal, one above the other in a glass-fronted cabinet. A single moving-head mechanism mounted between the two drums would whip back and forth horizontally, dragging behind it a long flexible cable like a tail. The FASTRAND was the subject of much obscene joking by the General Development engineers.

An enormous early prototype of a magnetic disk file had been built by the ERA engineers. A magnetic disk file serves exactly the same function as a magnetic drum. Instead of the surface of a cylinder, the magnetic material coats both sides of a number of disks or platters. These disks are stacked on a common shaft with spacers between them, and all rotate together. One magnetic head is required for each surface of each disk, but they are normally all ganged together, so that all the heads move in and out like the teeth of a comb between the rotating platters. The advantage of a magnetic disk file over a magnetic drum is simply that more magnetic surface area, and hence greater data storage capacity, is available in a given volume of space. Removable disks had not been invented at this time. The prototype disk file in the lab was huge, with an eight-foot-long horizontal main shaft containing thirty-inch-diameter disks. In operation it was rather menacing. The open disks generated quite a breeze when rotating at full speed. Referred to as the "sausage slicer" by the engineers, it was never made into a product by Univac. Large disk files of this type were developed by other companies in later years, however.

The peripheral equipment that interested me most was the Uniservo II. The principal challenge facing the engineers was design of the vacuum-column buffer loop boxes, which were to replace the pulley-and-fishing line buffer loops of the Uniservo I. The vacuum loop boxes were tall, narrow, glass-fronted chambers just a fraction of an inch deeper than the half-inch width of the tape. The bottom of each loop box was connected to a vacuum pump. If the depth of the box was just right and the vacuum was adjusted properly, the tape would be held in smooth loops under slight tension but with almost zero frictional resistance to movement. The General Development engineers were working on some concepts of their own for future magnetic tape transports, but in the meantime they were adapting the Uniservo II design to the Univac Scientific, the ERA-designed line of computers.

Across the aisle from the General Development lab was another ERA computer development, the Univac File Computer. A vacuum tube machine, it was smaller than Univac II, and it was oriented around the ERA-developed magnetic drums. As its name implies, the File Computer was intended for electronic inventory management. Early passenger reservation systems were configured for Northwest, Eastern, and Capitol airlines using the File Computer. These were only seat inventory systems, not full Passenger Name Record (PNR) systems.

Down the aisle in the opposite direction from the General Development lab was a small research lab that was working on advanced techniques for making "thin film" memories. A thin film memory utilizes tiny spots of magnetic material that have been vacuum-deposited on a glass substrate instead of cores that have been compression-formed from magnetic oxide. Thin film memories operate somewhat like core memories. One of the funniest stories going around the plant, told by the engineers to illustrate the difference between engineers and scientists, concerned a Ph.D. researcher in this lab. The man, who I will call the Professor, looked like every casting agent's idea of the absentminded professor. Slight, with thinning gray hair and thick glasses, he had an intense peering expression and a shuffling gait. Like the absentminded professor of legend, he would often get so absorbed in what he was doing that he had to be reminded when it was time to eat. He *did* wear a white lab coat.

The research in thin film memories was being funded by the US Air Force. It was hoped that the new technology would be applicable to airborne computers because of the small size and mechanical ruggedness of the memories. One day a group of Air Force officers was visiting Univac for a technical briefing on the progress being made under their research contract. The Professor was holding forth when someone interrupted him, reminding him that it was lunchtime and that the visitors were hungry. Reluctantly the Professor broke off his presentation and accompanied one of the Air Force majors to the men's room. The Professor and the major were standing at adjacent urinals doing their business when the Professor remembered an important point that he had forgotten to make. In his excitement he swung around to face the major and urinated all down the major's pant leg!

As a result of my visiting around the plants and my lunchtime conversations, I found out where in the pecking order of engineering prestige the Univac II program stood: near the bottom. Besides being primarily Philadelphia designed and hence subject to Not Invented Here prejudice, Univac II was a vacuum tube computer. Even the most junior engineer understood that the future development of computers had to be done with one of the solid state technologies: transistors or magnetic amplifiers. Vacuum tube machines were too large, too unreliable, too power consuming, and too difficult to ship and install in customer offices. The Univac I and II, for example, were made to come apart into sections for shipping, but the individual sections were still too large to fit into freight elevators in many existing buildings. Dave Keefer told a story about delivering the first Univac to Metropolitan Life in New York City. Sections of the computer were hoisted by crane up the outside of the building, then swung in through an opening where the windows had been removed. Not many customers would be willing to put up with the expense and trouble of such an installation. Virtually all the solid state computer design work was being done under Univac's various government contracts—LARC in Philadelphia for the Livermore Laboratory and several Navy developments in St. Paul. The engineers working on these projects were enjoying positions of the highest prestige among their peers. Where were the efforts to develop commercial solid state computers?

I discussed my concerns with Art Engstrom and later with Bill Keye. As a young engineer, somewhat naive and not at all worried about getting another job should my efforts be interpreted wrongly, I composed a carefully worded letter to Harry Vickers, president of the entire Sperry Rand Corporation, asking, in effect: "Where are we going with commercial computers?" In my first flush of enthusiasm for the computer business I had bought a hundred shares of Sperry Rand stock, so I took the position of a stockholder with an inside knowledge of the business from my experience on the Univac II project. Vickers's reply was so full of resounding generalities and so lacking in specifics that I strongly suspect that it was cut and pasted together from old press releases by the public relations department as a general response to stockholder questions. The letter accomplished nothing. Vickers's reply did elicit a mild curiosity among the St. Paul management. Vickers had sent them a copy of his reply but not a copy of my inquiry.

After hundreds of change orders, the Univac II's were beginning to function as computers. The test crews could now resume using them as versatile toys, just as we had done as students in Philadelphia. Each computer console had a small amplifier and loudspeaker connected into a data path within the computer. This served as a troubleshooting aid for the customer engineer. When certain test programs were run to check the operation of the computer circuits, the loudspeaker would put out a distinctive series of tones. An experienced troubleshooter could tell from a distance just which test was runnning. If the machine "hung up" or stopped with an error, the tones would cease and the customer engineer was alerted. Budding programmers in our test crew soon worked out a program to produce a desired tone. Dubbed "Music Maker," the program allowed the console operator to type in a musical note and the interval of time it was to be held. He could then transcribe sheet music for the computer. These tunes, tinny but recognizable, absolutely fascinated the assembly workers in our area. They would drift in from all over the assembly floor whenever the music started. We finally had to ban all music playing during working hours. The programmers, working after hours, then improved on the original routines with a program that made the tape loops on the Uniservos jump up and down in time to the music! This caused a sensation among the assembly workers.

An open house in the new plant was scheduled one weekend for family and friends of employees. We determined to show the visitors our musical Univac. The exhibit fell flat. The visitors were more interested in the console typewriter clattering out its occasional cryptic messages. It took me a while to figure out what was going on. Apparently the visitors, knowing nothing at all about computers, saw nothing unusual in a million and a half dollar Univac system playing a crude "Beer Barrel Polka" while the tapes jumped up and down in time to the music. What was unusual to see was an electric typewriter typing by itself. The assemblers it seemed knew just enough about computers to understand that they are not designed to play music and that some clever programming had been done. To the assemblers the console typewriters were old hat, having been around since the first prototype computers.

Both plants of the Univac St. Paul operation were in 1957 in a frenzy of creativity. Each little project area held some new and exciting development, and the talk over coffee in the lunchrooms was always of what this or that group was up to. Despite my growing disillusionment with the senior management, I was tremendously excited to be an engineer in the computer business. I firmly believe that engineering creativity feeds on itself and that the physical proximity of engineering groups doing innovative work stimulates innovation in other project areas of the same plant. As the nuclear scientist says of an atomic reaction, Univac St. Paul had "gone critical." It was now generating new product ideas much faster than they could be absorbed or exploited. I did not suspect that this creativity was about to explode, spinning off dozens of new companies, some of which would grow to be major factors in the computer industry.

5

To Each His Own

One summer morning in 1957 an almost incredible rumor swept the West 7th Street plant: Bill Norris, head of the entire Univac Division (including Philadelphia and the Norwalk lab) had resigned, and with him Frank Mullaney! The rumor was soon confirmed by a cryptic notice on the company bulletin boards. The whole St. Paul operation was astir with speculation over what would happen next. Then events struck closer to home. My own boss's boss, Bill Keye, together with another senior engineer, Howard Shekels, resigned. They were reported to be joining Norris and Mullaney in starting a new company in Minneapolis, just across the Mississippi River from St. Paul. As was and still is the custom at Univac, a farewell luncheon was organized for Keye and Shekels. It was held in a banquet room at a large restaurant nearby. Because Keye and Shekels were old-timers and popular, a large crowd had signed up for the luncheon. Keye would say of his plans only that, yes, he was joining Norris and Mullaney and that he wanted to try a small company again. We all knew that Keye had been one of the pioneers at ERA and that he had made a good deal of money on his ERA stock when the company was sold to Remington Rand.

The more knowledgeable among the Univac engineers now cast a watchful eye on Seymour Cray and Bob Kisch to see if they would be the next to leave. They were known to be close to Mullaney, and their departure would represent a loss of what was often considered to be the top design team at St. Paul. Other hallway rumors concerned the financing of the new company, to be called Control Data Corporation. The organizers were reported to be offering stock at a dollar a share to friends and co-workers from Univac. One evening I got a call from a friend from Univac saying that if I wanted to subscribe for Control Data stock, there would be a meeting at the home of Willis Drake in the nearby suburb of Edina that evening. When I arrived, I had to park way down the street from Drake's house because of the cars lining both sides of the residential street. Some forty or fifty Univac people crowded into Drake's living room, standing along the walls. Drake, whom I did not know, spoke briefly about the new company, warning us that it was a speculative investment. He said that they would working in digital technology but that they would not be directly competing in computers with Univac or IBM. Norris and Keye were not present, nor was anyone else that I recognized. No mention was made of Cray or Kisch. I decided that the company would probably fail, but I wanted to own a little of their stock so that I could follow their activities. I signed one of the subscription forms passed out, requesting two hundred shares at a dollar a share. Little did I realize that I had just missed my first chance to become a millionaire! Twelve hundred and seventy-five shares of that initial stock, which I could easily have afforded, if held through the two stock splits, was worth one million dollars in 1968!

Shortly after the stock subscription activity died out, Seymour Cray and Bob Kisch resigned to join Control Data. The new company's headquarters was established in a warehouse building at 501 Park Avenue in downtown Minneapolis. From that time on, senior Univac engineers would leave in ones and twos to join Control Data. Because the two companies were separated by the Mississippi River, the defectors to Control Data were known around Univac as wetbacks. "Have you heard who is joining the wetbacks?" became a frequent question in the hallways at Univac.

The relationship between the two companies was peculiar. Univac engineers had so many friends and acquaintances at Control Data and so many Univac engineers owned Control Data stock that the relationships at the working level were almost fraternal. Control Data was never really looked on as a competitor, even when they became a serious one, and they certainly were never thought of as The Enemy. That designation was reserved for IBM alone. On a management level it was quite a different story. Sperry Rand soon filed a lawsuit against Control Data, charging theft of trade secrets. Bill Norris never concealed his low opinion of the abilities of the senior Sperry Rand management based in New York City. In my opinion, one reason there has been little opportunity for nepotism at Control Data is the contempt that Bill Norris had for the abilities of Marcel Rand, the son of Remington Rand founder Jim Rand. Marcel Rand was at one time executive vice-president of the entire Remington Rand operation and Norris's boss. The management feuding continued for many years. It could perhaps be finally considered settled in 1983, the year that Sperry bought into Magnetic Peripherals Incorporated, a joint-venture company dominated by Control Data.

Through all this management upheaval the Univac II project continued to make slow progress, getting the latest set of wiring changes, shutting down the computers to make the changes, and then retesting the machines.

With the departure of Bill Norris, a new general manager was appointed for the St. Paul Univac operation only, an engineer from Northwest Airlines named Bob McDonald. As a result of the departure for Control Data of much of the senior management of ERA, Pres Eckert and his group from Philadelphia came to have a much larger say in the operation of the Univac Division, although executive management remained based in New York. The Philadelphians decided that St. Paul had fouled up the Univac II long enough and offered to come to St. Paul to help straighten us out. Two senior engineers and a group of test technicians from the Univac I test floor arrived in St. Paul. The chief test technician was a man who was competent technically but crude in personal appearance and speech. His last name was Loss, and he had the nickname, even in Philadelphia, of "Total." The engineers were fortunately more diplomatic and also competent. The Philadelphia invasion caused about as much resentment as you would expect. I believe that if the Philadelphians had come a year earlier, they would have been welcomed and their help would have improved the delivery schedule dramatically. By this time we in St. Paul had learned the hard way nearly all that they had to teach us.

Under the assault from the combined Philadelphia and St. Paul test groups, the last remaining problems in the Univac II were tracked down and corrected. An evaluation report, a sort of giant checklist of the computer's condition and performance, was completed for each computer, and the power was shut off for disassembly and shipment. Our test crew was broken up, with each man leaving for his assigned customer site in the United States or Canada. The men were to help reassemble and retest the arriving machines and would then stay on as on-site customer engineers. At least they were well trained, intimately familiar with every single wire in the computer! George Cogar returned to Philadelphia. Dave Keefer resigned from Univac and moved to Arizona. I paid a largely ceremonial visit to each Univac II customer site, verified that the machine was operating properly, and said good-bye to my former co-workers. It was getting lonely!

The Philadelphians had taken over responsibility for the follow-up Univac II production. I was now in that embarrassing condition known as "between assignments," a condition common to working engineers, especially in poorly managed companies, and Univac at this time certainly was a poorly managed company. Someone noticed in my personnel file that I had spent three years in the Navy in charge of electronics maintenance aboard ship, so I was offered a job on one of the Navy-funded projects working on system studies. It involved moving back to the original plant at 1902 West

Minnehaha, where the government classified work was done. I thought that it would be interesting to see more of the other half of the company. I accepted the offer.

"System studies" for what eventually became the Naval Tactical Data System (NTDS) proved to consist of a number of short studies of the feasibility of connecting the various pieces of shipboard electronic equipment into a general-purpose digital computer. I certainly agreed with the objective. The ships on which I had served had had completely separate electronic systems, interconnected manually if at all. For example, there was a "surface search" radar to detect other ships, an "air search" radar to detect aircraft, and a "fire control" radar to direct the aiming of the guns. It was possible to manually switch a cathode-ray-tube (CRT) display from "surface" echoes to "air" echoes, but this was seldom done because the identification of each radar blip and the past tracking information were handwritten on the face of the CRT with a grease pencil. If the tube was switched from surface to air echoes, all the surface tracking information would have to be erased and new information for air contacts written. A computer-controlled CRT, such as the one I had seen earlier demonstrated by Malcolm Macaulay, used the computer to calculate and display the echo identification and tracking history *electronically* on the face of the tube. Thus the presentation could be switched at will, or both surface and air information presented simultaneously on the same CRT, using different computer-generated symbols to identify surface and air echoes.

Another potentially great improvement was in ship-to-ship communications. Reporting of radar contacts between ships of a fleet had been done by using voice radio. For example, one ship might report: "I have an unidentified air contact bearing 315 degrees range 100 miles." Note that the bearing and distance are given from the ship making the report. The ship receiving the report might be some miles distant. The receiving ship must calculate by trigonometry the bearing and distance of the air contact from *its* ship and then plot the resulting position with a grease pencil. This could take several minutes, and a fast-moving aircraft would have changed position by the time the plot was completed. The Navy had funded Univac to study the feasibility of communication between the computer on one ship and the computer on the other ship with no operator intervention at all. The sending computer would send the contact information in digital form by radio to the receiving computer, which would then perform the trigonometry and display the reported contact on a computer-controlled CRT within seconds. Our study group concluded that this was all perfectly feasible with existing technology but that a lot of special equipment and a major programming effort would be required.

Much progress had been made in designing a transistorized computer small enough and rugged enough for use aboard ship. Univac's first full-scale operating prototype was known as the M-460. It looked like a chest-style home freezer except that it was painted battleship gray. The hinged, counterbalanced lid could be raised to gain access to the chassis, aluminum frames about three feet square that slid up and down in grooves in the inside of the chest. Each of the printed circuit cards, containing the transistors and other components, was about the size of a graham cracker. The cards plugged into the chassis. The M-460 was cooled by air drawn in at the base and blown upward through the printed circuit cards. A novel feature was a "dipstick" for testing the computer. Because the chassis were inaccessible when they were seated in their connectors at the bottom of the chest, a fiberglass rod with a spring-tip probe was made up. This rod could be slid down a premeasured distance along a test strip on the edge of each chassis to pick up the signal from a desired circuit. The dipstick was clever but difficult to use, and the packaging was soon changed. Comparing this computer with the only other one with which I was familiar, the Univac II, I was excited. The M-460 had 32,000 words of 30-bit core memory compared to only 2000 words of 84-bit memory for the Univac II. It was, except for rather primitive input/output channels, much faster; it took only one-tenth the electrical power, and it was so incredibly small!

A newer computer package looked more like a side-by-side refrigerator-freezer. The chassis were slid in horizontal channels in this model, which acquired the official military designation AN/USQ-17. Another improvement was in the cooling system, which used chilled water and air recirculated in a closed-loop system like the Univac II. One advantage of the closed recirculating cooling over the open air flow of the M-460 was discovered by accident. Smoke was seen pouring from the M-460 one day. After the power was shut off, the lid opened, and the fire extinguished, it was found that one of the resistors on a printed circuit card had overheated. It had set fire to the printed circuit card material. The flame, fed by the vertical draft airflow, fanned out in a perfect V above the burning card, setting fire to six or eight more cards above it. The engineers had assumed that the fiberglass-based epoxy cards were fireproof. They were wrong! In the lab the card material burned with a hot, smoky flame. With the closed-loop cooling of the AN/USQ-17, such a fire would quickly exhaust the oxygen in the cabinet and extinguish itself.

These studies for the Navy were interesting but frustrating. Like all engineers, I wanted to build something, not just write reports. A constant problem for Univac during this period was the resignation of key engineers. The engineers who are technically the sharpest are invariably the most restless and the first to leave if they are not kept busy on challenging assignments. Control Data was continuously draining our engineering talent. It was widely believed at the time that the founders of Control Data had taken a Univac telephone directory with them, and when they needed, say, a designer of memory circuitry, they would simply flip through the directory until they found a name they remembered as a good memory designer. In addition to the Control Data "brain drain," a number of other companies, General Electric and RCA that I recall, were just getting into the computer business. They found Univac St. Paul a fruitful recruiting ground for experienced computer engineers, who were in short supply nationally. No one that I knew well ever left Univac for IBM, but Univac alumni soon were to be found in almost all the other computer companies.

In 1959 Malcolm Macaulay, who had first demonstrated his large, computer-driven CRT display for me, left Univac with half a dozen other designers. They founded a small company in St. Paul that they named Data Display Incorporated. They continued to do just what they had done at Univac—design and build large computer-driven CRT displays, mostly for classified government applications. Macaulay was later ousted as president by a group of local investors in favor of Ed Orenstein, formerly a vice-president. Macaulay emigrated to Australia, where he founded a CRT terminals company in Melbourne. Orenstein and the rest of the founding group from Univac continued as an independent company until 1965, when they sold out to Control Data and became the Data Display Division. In 1969 Orenstein and virtually the entire senior engineering staff left Control Data to found another new company, Data 100. Data 100 continued to design and build CRT displays and remote job entry terminals. In 1979 Data 100 was sold to Northern Telecom, a Canadian telephone company. (Northern Telecom, which had also acquired Sycor, a Michigan CRT display company, the next year took a $300 million write-off!) Within months Orenstein and most of the senior technical staff left Northern Telecom. With Orenstein as a major investor, a number of the same original staff from Univac founded Lee Data, another CRT display firm. Lee Data became a high flyer on the stock market and was written up in the *Wall Street Journal*. Lee Data can be considered as the fifth generation spin-off from Univac; it included some of the same people who were on the original

NTDS display project. This pattern of spin-offs and mergers is common in the computer industry. Some of the causes are examined in a later chapter.

To return to the story of the NTDS development, a great rumor soon spread through the hallways: Univac had been awarded a $50 million contract to develop a "service test" system based on a new shipboard digital computer! This meant that the computers and related peripheral equipment would move out of the laboratory, be manufactured in small quantities, installed aboard Navy ships, and evaluated under actual operating conditions. If the evaluations were successful, the equipment would presumably be supplied to the entire fleet! The rumors were soon confirmed by a notice on the bulletin board. Joy swept the plant!

Univac St. Paul was now in a position like that of the avid fisherman who, after years of trying, has finally hooked a giant muskie. Now that he has it on the line, how is he going to land it? The original designs for the M-460 and the AN/USQ-17 computers had been done by Seymour Cray and some of the other senior engineers who had since left for Control Data. No engineer remaining had the gut-level understanding of the computer logic that was needed for successful service test implementation. In addition, the prototype computers had some reliability problems, and the mechanical design of the cabinets and the accessibility for servicing were not satisfactory. The St. Paul management of Univac decided on a bold step: a complete redesign of the computer, saving only the machine instruction set (repertoire) so that programs written to run on the prototypes would run on the new computer. A team of computer designers was pulled together primarily from the Athena project, a special-purpose, ultrahigh reliability computer designed by Univac to check out Athena rockets for the Air Force. I was offered and I accepted a position as a supervisor in the peripheral equipment design department of the NTDS project.

At this point, Bob McDonald, the new general manager of the entire Univac St. Paul operation, made one of the shrewdest management moves that I have ever seen in all my years in the computer business: He called a three-day, out-of-plant kickoff meeting for all personnel assigned to the NTDS project down to the supervisor level. All departments were represented: engineering, manufacturing, quality assurance, purchasing, contracts. We were to meet for a long weekend at the George A. Hormel mansion in Austin, Minnesota, about seventy-five miles south of St. Paul. The French Provincial mansion belonging to the meat packing family was set in acres of dense pine woods just off the main highway. I had a special reason for approving of the choice of the meeting site. George A. Hormel II, son of the family, had been a classmate of mine at prep school. I always remembered him sitting at the piano in the senior class room, a cigarette dangling from the corner of his mouth, entertaining his classmates with a good impersonation of songwriter Hoagy Carmichael. George was an excellent musician, and he had married Leslie Caron, the dancer and screen star. Unfortunately they were divorced before this trip to Austin. I did see George while there, and he played a snatch of the old school song for me, but, alas, I did not get to meet Leslie!

The senior Univac management, including Bob McDonald, had rooms in the mansion itself; lower-ranking members of the team such as me roomed in a motel nearby, but we had all our meals as a group. At the first session McDonald explained the importance of the contract. It was probably the most significant that Univac had ever received. If it was successfully executed, the follow-up business could be many times as large as the original contract value. Univac had the contract to design the overall system and to design and build the computers and some peripheral equipment and adapters. The CRT display system was to be designed and built by Hughes Aircraft Company, and the digital radio communications system was to be designed and built by Collins Radio Company. This was a disappointment to some of the engineers who had been working on displays and communications equipment. Univac would develop a higher-level language for programming the computers and would write some of the test and evaluation programs, but the operational programs that would run in the computers when the ships were at sea in a training or combat situation would be written by Navy personnel at the new Fleet Programming Center under construction in San Diego.

The total meeting, consisting of forty to fifty men, then broke up into groups of six or seven, deliberately chosen to mix up the different backgrounds. For example, an engineering manager might be teamed with a manufacturing supervisor, a contracts administrator, a purchasing agent, and a member of Bob McDonald's staff. The teams were reshuffled periodically and were given various assignments to work on together. Emphasis was on thinking ahead to various problems that might interfere with meeting the schedule and performance commitments and on brainstorming various solutions to these anticipated problems. Of course the small group meetings also served to get everyone acquainted with each other and with the ways of thinking of the other departments. The meals together and the large group meetings built a team spirit. The personal acquaintances made all through the NTDS organization did much to ease the inevitable conflicts as the project moved from design to manufacturing to delivery. The active involvement of Bob McDonald and top management made the importance of the project obvious to everyone. We left Austin all charged up and raring to go! In my opinion, this kickoff meeting anticipated by twenty years the "involvement team" concept being touted as one answer to the Japanese challenge to US industry. I have *never* participated in another such meeting in the twenty-five years since.

The newly formed and emotionally charged-up NTDS project team was moved into a "new" plant, a rented warehouse adjacent to the old glider factory on Minnehaha Avenue. The two-story warehouse had very high ceilings and bare wooden floors. The ground floor became the manufacturing area, shipping and receiving, and parts storage crib. The upper floor was made into offices for engineers and programmers. Except for a few managers' offices built along the outside walls, the entire upper floor was divided by shoulder-high partitions, open at the bottom, in a "bullpen" arrangement. These spartan accommodations, with all groups in close contact with one another, certainly proved effective in encouraging close communications. The entire project was headed by a short, bald-headed manager with piercing blue eyes named Arnie Hendrickson. He proved ideal for the assignment, combining shrewd management guidance with technical savvy. The design effort was divided among three departments: computer design, peripherals design, and systems and programming. These groups were supported by a mechanical design group responsible for the cabinetry, a reliability and failure analysis group, and a drafting and technical publications group, perhaps 150 people all told.

The strong team spirit continued to grow as we started on the design tasks, but it was tempered by a continuing good-natured cynicism about the bungling of Sperry Rand senior management. One engineer coined the phrase, which was widely quoted in the computer industry: "Once again Univac has snatched defeat from the jaws of success!" All the Univac engineers had the bone-deep feeling that if only Univac management could get its act together and exploit the excellent engineering being done, even IBM could be beaten in the marketplace. We looked on most other computer companies as something of a joke and not to be taken seriously as competitors.

The Sperry Rand corporate management, located in Rockefeller Center, was then operating on what we dubbed the "messiah" theory of management. Usually we would first read about the new messiah, our next Univac vice-president, in *Electronic News*, the leading trade paper. About two weeks later the corporate public relations department would make an official announcement full of praise for the new appointee, who always had a brilliant record at his previous company. None of these new vice-presidents had any real computer experience, of course. We would often get an early look at the new messiah as he made his ritual tour of the Univac plants, accompanied by swarms of staff people. For some months the corporate publications would be full of news of how the new savior was going to "coordinate" this and "consolidate" that, but things never seemed to change much on the working level. Official pronouncements would grow less and less frequent as time went by until there was finally no word at all of how the messiah was doing. Then *Electronic News* would have a photo and a short news article on the next messiah. The former messiah, proven false, would fade away with no announcement of his destination, and the new man, hailed by all as the true savior, would make his ritual tour of the plants.

To be fair, it must have been difficult for a vice-president, new to the corporation and new to the computer business, to sort out the conflicting claims and priorities. Pres Eckert, while never directly in charge of the St. Paul operation, had a lot of influence with management, which he often used to shoot down St. Paul development proposals. Another story told by Dick Karpen illustrates what a formidable opponent Eckert could be. In the early days of Eckert-Mauchly a customer was scheduled to visit the factory to see a demonstration of the Univac I serial number 5. Came the day of the visit and the computer was still not working properly. It would stop and hang up for no apparent reason. Eckert was standing beside the computer demonstrating it to the customer when it stopped. Without missing a breath, Eckert explained: "...and if it detects an error it stops like this," while he pushed the stop button. Anyone who can think that fast on his feet is obviously a formidable opponent.

Another rival for development funds for digital computers was our sister division, Sperry Gyroscope (contemptuously called "Sperry Gyrokludge" by St. Paul engineers). Sperry had for a long time built special-purpose analogue computers for the Navy, and they were beginning to realize that digital computers, about which they knew nothing, might be the way of the future. Of course they wanted to develop their own design, duplicating in many cases work being done in St. Paul. Sperry Gyroscope was ingenious in thinking up reasons why they could not use an existing Univac-designed computer but would have to develop a new one for their unique purpose. "Gyro" had an enormous plant on Long Island, so large that bicycles were provided for riding from department to department within the plant. Long

Island was much closer both physically and emotionally to corporate management in Rockefeller Center than St. Paul was. I often felt sorry for Bob McDonald, who had to defend St. Paul's interests in this highly political environment. Sperry Gyroscope eventually did develop their own shipboard digital computer. Their first attempt was a disaster. St. Paul engineers were called in as consultants to aid them in getting it running. They brought back stories of obvious design errors that kept the NTDS engineers in stitches. Kind of reminded me of Univac II.

Figure 1
Univac Scientific Computer System. Photograph courtesy of the Charles
Babbage Institute and Unisys Corporation.

Figure 2
William C. Norris. Photograph courtesy of
Control Data Corporation.

Figure 3
George R. Cogar.

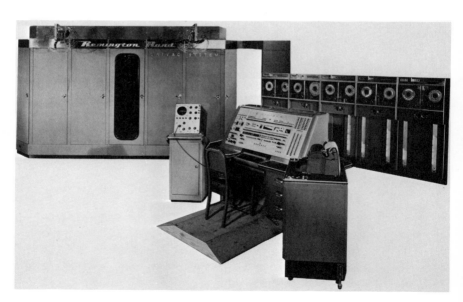

Figure 4
Univac II Computer System. Photograph courtesy of Unisys Corporation.

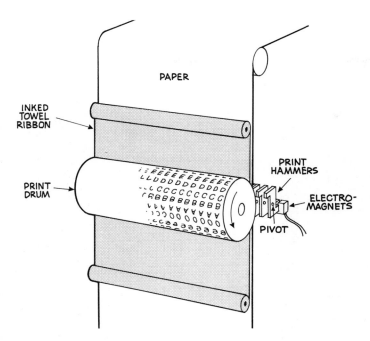

Figure 5
A drum printer mechanism.

Figure 6
The development wedge. *1,* Design team; *2,* product engineering; *3,* drafting and technical publications; *4,* manufacturing engineering; *5,* assembly department.

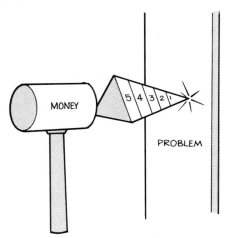

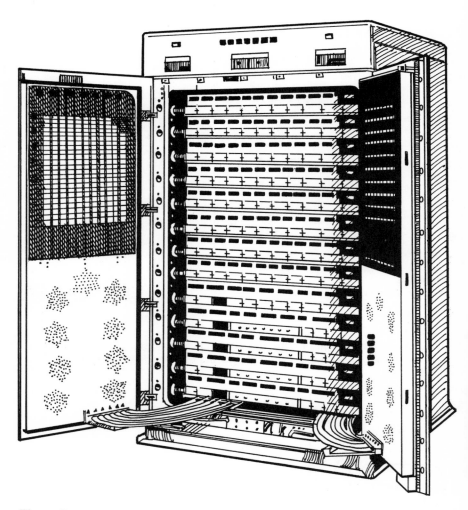

Figure 7
The Univac NTDS Computer.

6

Anchors Aweigh!

The NTDS project had a peripheral equipment department, but a minimum amount of peripheral equipment was to be designed. Magnetic tape transports and controllers were to be designed and packaged for shipboard service. Keyboard data entry devices, special adapters, and a manual computer input/output channel-switch panel were to be developed for shipboard installation. No magnetic drums or disk files were planned for the service test implementation because it was believed that the rolling and pitching of a ship at sea would wreak havoc with the bearings of a rapidly spinning device, which attempts to act like a gyroscope. My major duty as supervisor in the peripheral equipment department turned out to be the writing and interpretation of the official NTDS Input/Output Specification for the other Navy contractors. This document, only fourteen pages long, described in excruciating detail the data and control signals exchanged between the computer and the peripheral devices connected to it. Because this specification was critical to the operation of the entire NTDS system, each draft and each proposed change, no matter how minor, had to be reviewed and approved by the Navy NTDS Project Office. The principal concern of the Project Office was that the other NTDS contractors, particularly Hughes Aircraft, not be given the opportunity to use a change in the input/output specification as an excuse to claim a "change of scope" of their contracts, thus leading to requests for increases in funding and schedule. I spent a great deal of time talking long distance on the telephone and flying to the Los Angeles area, where both Hughes Aircraft and Collins Radio had facilities.

In order to gain the detailed knowledge of the computer that I needed to perform my job, I worked closely with the computer design group located just a few cubicles away. The "logic design team" consisted of four men. Herman "Hi" Osofsky was a tall, curly-haired, quiet mathemetician. He was the chief logic designer and personally designed the "control" section of the computer, the heart of the design that controls the transfers of instructions and data between the other sections. He was respected for his ability to do both logic design and circuit design. Some people, myself included, thought of Hi Osofsky as a younger Seymour Cray. Bob Burkholder was from the Boston area, a recent Massachusetts Institute of Technology graduate. Bob was the youngest and brashest of the group. In contrast to the other engineers who drove mostly conservative Fords and Oldsmobiles, Bob Burkholder drove a Morgan sports car, a British two-seater of classic lines and such exclusivity that I had never even heard of one until I saw his. He and his wife had picked up the Morgan from Peter Morgan himself at the factory in England where it was hand-built on a wooden chassis. As the designer of the "input/output" section, most of my liaison was done with Bob Burkholder. Finley McLeod was responsible for the "memory" section, and Glen Kregness was responsible for the "arithmetic" section of the computer. These four sections: control, input/output, memory, and arithmetic, make up the traditional central processing unit (CPU) of a computer system. (In the newest computers, the functions of the control and arithmetic sections are sometimes combined into what is called the ALU (Arithmetic and Logic Unit). The memory and input/output sections, however, have retained their separate identities.) These four designers, backed up by the chief circuit designer, Lee Granberg, formed the creative cutting edge of the computer design group, which may have totaled twenty-five people in all.

The memory section of a computer accounts for the largest part of its volume but consists of the same circuit combinations repeated over and over. Once the interface of the memory section to the control section is completely defined, the design of the memory section can proceed semi-independently of the rest of the logic design. The control, input/output, and arithmetic sections, however, are so interdependent that the design of any one section requires continuous consultation with the designers of the other sections. For this reason, Hi Osofsky, Bob Burkholder, and Glen Kregness had their desks in the same cubicle.

I spent many an hour in this cubicle waiting for a break in Bob Burkholder's train of thought so that I could question him on a fine point of interpretation. This was my first opportunity to watch a computer being designed from conception to operating hardware. Osofsky, Burkholder, and Kregness each worked with a pencil and a clear plastic template on large, tear-off desk pads. The design appeared as a pattern of circles, each neatly labeled and each representing a logical gate function. The circles were connected by a dense network of lines and arrowheads, also labeled at each entry to and exit from each circle. Each designer would be absorbed in his own intellectual problem until a need to communicate would arise, perhaps every minute or so. "Hey, Glen, can you give me another overflow signal from the D register?" "Just a minute. Yes, I can give you a positive output; label it from Z103." "Thanks. Label it to H607." "OK." This might be the extent of the conversation. With the signal's origin and destination duly noted on each designer's desk pad, both returned to their solitary contemplation.

Less frequently the need for a short conference would arise. This might take place in their cubicle, or the designers might move to an adjacent conference room where a large blackboard was available. The creative concentration in the little cubicle was intense, awe inspiring. Watching it I felt a little like I imagine a surgeon feels when he first opens a living person's chest and exposes the heart, moistly beating.

A serious design problem that affected the machine instruction set or the external characteristics of the computer would have to be resolved with the systems and programming group in the next set of offices. Here the great advantage of having all the NTDS project people in the same area really became evident. Questions that might have taken two or three weeks to resolve with an exchange of memos could be solved in fifteen or twenty minutes with the principal hardware and software designers standing in front of a blackboard. Most of these problems had to do with handling of limit or unusual conditions. The design of the computer had started, as is common, with a definition of the computer instruction set, or repertoire. This defines in general terms just what the computer logic will do on recognizing each computer instruction, or op code, written by the programmer. But what will the computer do if the programmer attempts to divide by zero? This is an invalid instruction, but it might be done by mistake. In what state would each computer register be left if this instruction is attempted? How would the programmer be notified that he has attempted an illegal instruction? Is it possible for him to try to use the result of this instruction, which, in general, is meaningless? What will happen if input data from the magnetic tape transport is broken off in mid-record? Will the computer wait for it to resume? For how long? How will the control program know that the input transfer was never completed? How can the transfer be restarted without destroying existing data? These and hundreds of similar questions must be answered down to the last bit before a systems design can be completed. The answers to these questions were kept in a masterfully organized document known as the Blue Book. Contained in a four-inch thick loose-leaf notebook, this document defined all the NTDS system interrelationships in successive levels of detail from a broad overview down to the exact bit patterns found in each computer register following each type of data transfer. Each change or added bit of detail agreed on in a design conference had to be immediately reflected in the Blue Book, and changed pages had to be sent to all programmers working on the system. This documentation system proved to be both simpler and more effective than the elaborate hierarchical documentation control systems with which I worked in later years.

As the logic design team finished with each section of the logic, their hand-drawn diagrams were taken over by a second echelon of engineers and engineering assistants. Engineering assistants stand in somewhat the same relationship to engineers as warrant officers to commissioned officers. They are without an engineering degree but are promoted from technicians on the basis of their experience and demonstrated ability. The job of this second echelon is to transform the rough sketches representing the designers' intentions into the detailed formal drawings, wiring tabulations, specifications, etc. required for manufacturing to build the computers in large numbers. Considerable engineering judgment is required because these second echelon product design engineers are making decisions involving wire lengths and routing, power distribution, maintenance features, etc. that will affect the performance, manufacturing cost, and maintainability of the computer. Continual interaction with the designers is required, and trade-offs are always necessary between the theoretically best way to wire the computer and a design that is practical to assemble and maintain. An old story concerns the desirability of hiring only Swiss watchmakers to assemble computers! (The theoretical speed of a computer increases as its physical size decreases.)

A third echelon of the computer development process consists of the drafters, the technical writers, and the technical illustrators who actually produce the final printed documentation under the direction of the product design engineers. A fourth echelon is made up of the manufacturing engineers who lay out the assembly areas, break down the manufacturing process into steps, order tools and fixtures, and define each step of the manufacturing processes to the assemblers. The assembly workers who actually build the computers might be considered a fifth echelon.

Development of a new technical product is much like driving a wedge into a hard material. The point of the wedge, the cutting edge, is the creative design team. In my experience this is most often a single individual. It is *never* more than four or five. If the "point" of the wedge is a team, they must be compatible, friends as well as co-workers, one brain with several bodies.

The speed and efficiency with which the design is completed is directly dependent on the sharpness of the point. The only condition worse than having no sharp point on a technical development project is having two such points. Two highly creative leaders on the same project will inevitably disagree on some approach to the task. A large proportion of their time and creative energies will then be wasted in arguing and politicking over the approach to be taken, and the loser will often quit rather than implement an approach that he has argued against. The single, clear, unified design philosophy will get the job done quickly. The wider portions of the wedge, farther from the point, represent the successive echelons just described. The width of the wedge at its blunt end represents the size of the final manufacturing program; obviously a much larger organization is necessary if a thousand jet aircraft are to be built than if seventeen computer systems are to be built. The hammer is money. Just as a dull wedge can be driven into granite if it is hit often enough with a large enough hammer, so even a second-rate development organization can eventually accomplish its task given enough time and money. This "brute force" approach, besides being prodigiously wasteful, also leaves a lot of rubble lying around the area to be cleaned up later. We will see some examples of the brute force design approach in a later chapter.

To complete the analogy, the development wedge must be a cohesive whole or it will shatter under the stress imposed by an unyielding problem and a heavy hammer blow. Team spirit is greatly encouraged by physical proximity. It is much easier to pass the blame for poor design decisions to someone who is in another plant and easier still to blame someone in another city than it is to blame someone you drink coffee with every morning.

Concurrent with the design of the logic of the computer under the direction of Hi Osofsky was the design of the various printed circuit cards directed by Lee Granberg. Granberg was the archetype of the "white socks engineer." This term requires some explanation. Soon after graduation from engineering colleges, young engineers tend to sort themselves into two broad categories. Some see engineering as a stepping stone to management, marketing, or some other less technical and higher-paid job function. These engineers tend to pattern their dress and grooming after those who they see as successful in such fields. The "real" or "white socks" engineers disdain such ambitions and get their satisfaction in the laboratory. This type of engineer usually makes some concession to his professional status by wearing a suit coat or at least a sport jacket to work (technicians never wear suit coats), but his tie is usually half-masted or removed, and, almost as a badge of his calling, he wears white cotton sweat socks summer and winter.

Lee Granberg represented the extremes of technical competence and indifference to personal appearance. He was a brilliant circuit designer. It was said that he "thought like a transistor." The circuits that he designed for the NTDS computer input/output drivers were so much better than anything that the other NTDS contractors could design that I ended up giving copies of his circuit designs to the other contractors. (The Navy owned the rights to all designs because they had paid for all the development.) Granberg could usually be found in his laboratory testing the performance of his circuits or pouring over the latest technical specifications from semiconductor manufacturers. His loosened tie was invariably gravy stained, his suit baggy, his shoes run over at the heels, and his socks white.

Another story illustrates the close working relationships required in a good wedge. The logic of the controllers for the Univac-supplied peripheral equipment was designed by George Osborne, an engineer. The logic design for a peripheral equipment controller is a much smaller task than the logic design for a computer, but it requires an equal level of competence. George was good at this job but he had one fault. After completing the logic design, he would go over the design again in an attempt to reduce the number of circuits required to perform the functions. This, of course, reduced the size and cost of the controller and so was desirable. Unfortunately George would repeat this "optimization" process over and over, reducing the circuit card count by making each circuit serve several different purposes at different times in the controller's master timing cycle. The logic thereby got so convoluted that no one but George was able to understand it and troubleshoot it. George's professional pride in design made him strive to eliminate every logic element not absolutely essential, and he would continue the process almost indefinitely, trying to get rid of one more circuit.

Recognizing the problem, George's manager assigned an engineering assistant to "help" George. The key duty of this man, an experienced and practical type, was to follow closely the progress of the design and then, at just the critical point, snatch the logic drawing off George's desk with some remark like: "This one done, George? I'll get it into drafting and you can get started on the next one." His timing was critical. If he took the drawing too soon, either the controller would not work at all or George would get angry and demand his drawing back. If he waited too long, George would improve the design until it was impossible to troubleshoot. This critical trick of timing, which is a common problem in engineering organizations, has given rise to an often-heard axiom: "The real secret in engineering management is knowing when to shoot the engineers and build the machine!"

Another factor affecting life on the second floor of the warehouse was the behavior of the local stock market. Many on the NTDS project had invested in Control Data stock, some quite heavily, and its steady rise in price was a cause for glee. One engineer had a graph posted over his desk. On one axis the legend read "Price of Control Data Stock," and on the other axis the legend read "Number of People I Have To Be Nice To." As the price of the stock climbed, the number of obsequious contacts required diminished toward zero. Almost every engineer knew someone who was starting a small electronics-related company, usually with "tronics" in the name. Besides the computer spin-offs from Univac (and later from Control Data,) the medical electronics industry was just starting to grow in the St. Paul–Minneapolis area. Initial-issue stock was usually offered first to friends and acquaintances at one dollar a share. A typical engineer at Univac might own one hundred shares or so of half a dozen small companies. Of course many soon folded or were merged into larger companies, but the winners tended to more than offset the losers, especially if Control Data was among the holdings. Many engineers had their broker's telephone number prominently posted above their desks, together with graphs showing the prices of their stock holdings. Other engineers organized investment clubs that met monthly and purchased mostly local stocks.

With so many of the engineering staff both cynical about the Sperry Rand Corporation messiah management technique and deeply involved in making profitable stock investments, it might be thought that productivity would be low and work sloppy. Quite the opposite was the case. Because the NTDS project was tied down by Navy contract as to deliverable product, schedule, and funding, it was largely protected from meddling by corporate staff. As another old engineering axiom says: "The best product planning is that done by the customer!" The Navy program office responsible for NTDS did seem to provide good direction. They seemed to learn quickly who among the various manufacturers' personnel they could trust, and they were always willing to consider suggested changes if backed up by good engineering reasons. The security classification of the work prevented casual executive visits to some areas. Thus we were largely isolated from company politics. The relative financial independence felt by at least the shrewder investors among the engineering staff did not detract one whit from their eagerness to do a good job on a challenging project. One factor in this attitude may have been a desire to show their friends who had taken the riskier course of starting a small company that those who stayed at Univac could do good engineering work, too.

Gradually the desk-pad sketches of the logic designers became formal engineering drawings and lists of computer-printed wiring instructions. Lee Granberg's circuit drawings and laboratory breadboard circuits became formal parts lists for purchasing agents to order components and large-scale blowups of printed circuit board wiring to be sent out for printed circuit card fabrication. Mechanical parts of the computer began to appear in the assembly area on the first floor. The cabinet was to be similar to the AN/USQ-17, a battleship-gray box the size and shape of a side-by-side refrigerator-freezer. The inside surfaces of the doors were covered with switches and indicator lamps. The entire top of the computer was filled with connector panels for cabling to peripheral equipments. (In Navy ships most cabling runs in open racks along the "overhead," or ceiling.) The scattered design activity was beginning to come together into a working computer. In the meantime I was having a ball with my liaison work with the other NTDS contractors.

7

If Anything Can Go Wrong, It Will!

Everyone has heard of Murphy's law: If anything can go wrong, it will. It has a certain reality for computer engineers. Complex electrical and mechanical devices have been known to behave as if they had a spark of malevolent intelligence. In an earlier chapter I gave an example of the downright spookiness of intermittent computer errors. An entire body of engineering humor has been built up around Murphy's law and its corollaries: Equipment that is going to fail will always do so during a demonstration to your best customer! Experienced engineers have learned to design cautiously, taking nothing for granted, as if Murphy's law were a serious physical principle.

The input/output specification that defined the data interchange between the NTDS computer and all its peripheral equipment had been written with extreme care. Every condition that the NTDS project designers could think of had been defined in that specification based on conservative engineering principles. One reason why the designers were so cautious was the unknown level of electrical "noise," or unwanted electromagnetic interference, to be encountered aboard ship. A Navy ship is a welded steel box with a great deal of electrical power running all through it to drive gun turrets and raise aircraft elevators. The areas where the computers were to be installed were full of high-power radar and radio sets, mostly designed and installed piecemeal over a period of years and having unknown levels of radio-frequency power leaking from their cabinets and cabling. The Navy was unable to supply us with quantitative data on just what level of electrical noise we could expect. Equipment and techniques for measuring these unwanted signals were not well developed at that time (1960), and field measurement would have required the availablity of at least two types of ship with all their electronic and electrical equipment operating. If the cables from the computer to the cabinets of the peripheral equipment, some of which were several hundreds of feet away, were to pick up a false bit occasionally, the operation of the system would be crippled. We Univac designers therefore assumed the worst conditions that we could imagine and designed for those conditions. Besides worrying about electrical noise, the designers considered the effects of wiring errors on the circuitry. For example, the input/output driver circuits in the NTDS computer were so conservatively designed that any wire in the cables could be accidently shorted to ground without damage to the driver circuits. Once all the conditions relating to the computer input/output had been defined and all problems that we could think of had been anticipated and incorporated into the specification, the input/output specification was given to the Navy NTDS Project Office to approve and distribute to the other contractors. Then the fun began.

Nearly every line in the input/output specification and its companion specification defining cabling between equipment cabinets was misinterpreted by one contractor or another. For example, in computer terminology the bits making up a computer word are *always* numbered from the least significant bit (the right-hand bit) to the most significant bit. The NTDS computer used a 30-bit word, so its bits were numbered from bit 0 to bit 29 in the specification. One contractor reversed this nomenclature, numbering the bits in his equipment from the most significant to the least. Another contractor reinterpreted all references to "input" and "output" as being input or output from *his* equipment, thus reversing all the names of control signals. "Input" to the computer, of course, is "output" from a peripheral, and vice versa. Another contractor claimed that the specifications on rise times and voltage tolerances on the output circuits could not be met. His engineers were persuasive and would have convinced me except that I had seen Lee Granberg's design of the output driver circuits, which met all the specifications perfectly. I gave them a copy of Granberg's circuit schematics, and that ended the argument. Another contractor claimed that, in order to meet the timing requirements, his device would *always* have to have at least seventy-five feet of cable attached! Day after day, the conversations continued, mostly by long-distance telephone but occasionally in face-to-face visits. I came to appreciate more and more the difficulties of communicating over a 2000-mile distance and the great differences in corporate cultures. The engineers at Collins Radio had been exclusively concerned with radio communication equipment. The engineers at Hughes Aircraft had worked almost entirely with radar and with CRT displays for radar. Neither group had worked closely with computers. Almost without realizing it, my colleagues and I at Univac had been transformed from graduate electrical engineers, sharing a common base of theory and practice with all other graduate electrical engineers, into specifically *computer* engineers. Easy nonambiguous communication with other electrical engineers could no longer be taken for granted.

Finally we were ready to turn the power on the first prototype computer. Most of the project team was gathered around for the big event, which proved to be not nearly as exciting as the first Univac II power-up. No fuses blew and no smoke arose. Of course there were no printed circuit cards in the machine for the first power-up. Voltages were checked on all the chassis, and the cards were then inserted and tested one chassis at a time. A newly developed computer, no matter how carefully designed, never works when first powered-up with all its circuit cards in place. Errors are made by the assembly workers, errors are made in transcribing the original logic sketches to formal drawings, and errors are made by the logic designers themselves. All these errors interact, and the source of the problem has to be determined before a formal correction can be made. The computer design team of Osofsky, McLeod, Kregness, and Burkholder actively participated in the checkout process, along with members of the second echelon of product design engineers. Each error, except simple assembly mistakes, caused a ripple through the entire documentation system, as each piece of paper had to be corrected to represent the current condition of the computer on a day-to-day basis. The checkout process proceeded smoothly, thanks to the close working relationships of the team and the presence of the designers, who could make on-the-spot changes to the logic design if necessary. The first prototype was running simple programs six weeks after the power was first turned on—quite a contrast to the months taken by Univac II. Soon the other sixteen service test computers began to appear in phased assembly behind the first prototype.

There is no topic in engineering about which more nonsense has been written than reliability. The theoreticians have gotten hold of the subject and well-nigh obscured it with page after page of nearly unintelligible equations purporting to predict reliability. These predictions are better than nothing, but not much. The basic principles are simple. Reliability of electronic equipment is expressed as Mean Time between Failures (MTBF), which is the number of hours that a piece of equipment can be expected to operate before failing. Keep in mind that a year contains about 8800 hours. Suppose that you intend to design a computer using a certain transistor. The manufacturer says that its MTBF is a million hours. This works out to about 114 years, so it sounds pretty good. But wait, your design will use ten thousand of these or similar transistors. Now the predicted reliability of your computer, based on just this one component, is one million hours divided by ten thousand individual components, or one-hundred hours—only four days! The transistors do not have the good sense to all operate for one million hours and then fail all together like the wonderful one-horse chaise. All the manufacturer promised you is that on the average they would last one million hours. In the real world, one transistor will fail after one hour and the next will last two million hours; the one million hour average is still met. Besides, how are you going to verify that the manufacturer was not overly optimistic when it promised a million-hour MTBF? You cannot learn anything meaningful by testing one transistor. You must test a large sample, which is both time-consuming and costly. Even if you do test, say, a thousand transistors, how can you be sure the manufacturer did not send you its best components for your test, the "pick of the litter"? In my observation, successful design of reliable equipment depends on obtaining the most thorough, painstaking understanding of each component, the process by which it is manufactured, and the manner in which it is likely to fail.

The NTDS reliability and failure analysis group consisted of three experienced engineers and one technician. This group had a theory, which no one was able to disprove, that there is no such thing as a purely "electrical" failure; all failures can be traced to some visible mechanical defect if the analytical tools are fine enough. Their laboratory included dental x-ray equipment, microscopes, a jeweler's lathe, and precision micromanipulators. The technician was a genius at taking photographs through a microscope and producing enlargements of the interior of a transistor.

The first project that this reliability group tackled was a study of the connectors with which the printed circuit cards were plugged into the aluminum chassis. There were hundreds of these in the computer. Because vibration and shock were to be expected aboard ship, especially in a situation where the ship was maneuvering in rough weather and firing her guns, the contact between the male connector on the cards and the female connector on the chassis had to be reliable. Samples of a premium-priced, purportedly reliable connector were obtained and analyzed. The sample connectors, plugged together, were x-rayed from several angles. The x-rays penetrated the molded plastic connector shells and showed the metal contacts clearly. In some samples the x-ray photos showed that, although the male and female pins at one end of the connector mated perfectly, tolerance buildup in the molded plastic shell allowed the pins at the far end to make contact at only two points or in one case, at only one point. The connectors would still have tested good on any electrical check, but the margin of safety was much reduced. The connector manufacturer was visited and shown the x-ray photos. He then improved his plastic-molding process so that Univac got the four-point contacts that the Navy was paying for. The connectors, which had gold-plated contacts to resist surface corrosion, proved to be reliable in service.

The 8-by-10-inch glossy photographs taken through a microscope of the inside of a failed transistor were especially dramatic. A watchmaker's touch was needed to dissect a transistor without disturbing the positions of the delicate internal elements whose failures were to be analyzed. A technique to "freeze" the transistor interior was developed. A pinhole was cut in the case, and a hypodermic needle containing a clear plastic resin was inserted. After injection the resin would set and stabilize the internal elements. Then the entire case was cut away on a jeweler's lathe. The failure analysis group loved to startle the other engineers on the project with their dramatic photographs of the miscellaneous junk found inside the case of a failed transistor. Small particles of metal, dirt, human hair, and nasal mucus were the most common. The story was told of the desiccated remains of a fly found inside a large power transistor, but I never actually saw that. The most common cause of failure involved misaligned or incomplete welding of the microscopically fine wires that connected the external leads of the transistor to the semiconductor surface itself.

The failure analysis group would collect evidence of failures of a particular transistor or other component and then schedule a visit to the manufacturer's plant. The manufacturer, forewarned, would have its quality control manager and perhaps its production engineer in charge of that particular component line ready to refute any claims of poor quality. The Univac failure analysis engineer would begin with a statement such as "Your lead-welding process on the XXXX transistor line is out of control." The manufacturer's quality control manager would reply that this was impossible, the lead-welding machines were checked and calibrated every shift, he had just spot-checked production from that line, etc. The Univac engineer would then throw on the table three or four of those damningly clear 8-by-10 glossy enlargements of the interior of the failed transistor. Typically the quality control manager would turn white and mutter something to the effect that he would see to the problem right away. In the reliability field, one picture is certainly worth a thousand words!

Probably the most embarrassing failure found by the NTDS failure analysis group showed up in x-ray photos of a large power transistor made by a company that has always taken great pride in manufacturing reliable equipment. The design of the top, or cap, of the transistor had been changed to a lower-profile style. Someone had forgotten to pull the old-style headers from the production stock bins. The headers are leads coming up through the bottom of the case to which the extremely fine wires making connection to the semiconductor chip itself are welded. The old-style headers were too high for the new cap; they shorted out against the inside of the new, lower-profile cap. The x-rays showed this perfectly. The old headers just barely touched the inside of the cap, making marginal contact, so that any slight pressure on the cap or a slight temperature change would cause the transistor to short out. This sort of unpredictable intermittent failure drives computer test engineers absolutely crazy!

Because intermittent computer errors can be so difficult to locate, the NTDS computer design provided for full "margin" testing. The theory is that, if an electronic circuit is right on the ragged edge of failing, changing the voltage applied to it or increasing the speed at which it must pass an electrical pulse will push it over the edge and cause it to fail continuously. Both the voltage change and pulse speedup techniques were implemented on the NTDS computer. A switch located on the power supply of each chassis allowed the maintenance technician to raise or lower the voltages to all circuits on that chassis. Another switch speeded up the "clock" pulses, the continual stream of signals that synchronized all data transfers in the computer, by 25 percent. The margins (the range of conditions over which the computer will operate) of the NTDS computer were so wide that the voltages could be lowered and the clock pulses speeded up and the computer would still continue to operate for days. One computer installed aboard ship got a margin test that the designers never intended. In operation the computers were sealed up with both doors closed, cooling being accomplished by recirculating the air inside the computer through a chilled-water heat exchanger in the base of the machines. One day the water-chilling system was shut down for some maintenance work, and an oily rag was found in the chilled water line to one computer. It was discovered that the computer had been operating for weeks with the chilled water supply nearly cut off by this rag, running at a much higher temperature than designed for. The computer had operated perfectly all the while.

Arnie Hendrickson, the engineering project manager for the whole NTDS project, once told of being asked by the Navy NTDS Project Office what MTBF goal had been established for the computer. This machine was built so early in the shipboard use of computers that the contract had not specified a required MTBF, unthinkable in a Navy contract today. Arnie told us that he made up the answer on the spur of the moment: two hundred hours. The last MTBF that I heard actually measured for the first seventeen computers in service was twenty-five hundred hours, and it was increasing. This means that the computers, if used twenty-four hours a day, seven days a week, were failing once every three or four months. The reliability of the computers actually caused a problem for the shipboard electronic technicians responsible for maintaining it. The computer failed so seldom that the opportunity for an individual technician to troubleshoot and fix a problem was limited. With no practical experience, the technician would soon forget his classroom instruction on computer maintenance. Computers were the newest thing, with great sex appeal for the technicians, so everyone wanted to work on computers rather than on radar or some other old familiar equipment. The shipboard electronics officers had to insert some artificial problems into the computers to give their technicians troubleshooting experience.

My personal satisfaction with the computer design reached a climax one day when I was visiting a destroyer in which one of the first NTDS computers was installed. A member of the Navy NTDS Project Office, a lieutenant commander, was complaining to the ship's chief electronics technician that he was not receiving any formal reports of failure of the computer system, reports from the ship that he needed to complete an analysis. He was getting reports on the display system, he said, but none on the computer. "Hell, it don't hardly ever fail, sir," said the chief. I had to turn my head to hide my laughter.

Testing of my own particular area of responsibility, the NTDS input/output specification, had been done some months earlier. The Navy has a number of electronic facilities on Point Loma in San Diego, a beautiful high peninsula with the Pacific Ocean on one side and San Diego Bay on the other. A new Fleet Antiaircraft Warfare Training Center was being built just across the road from the older Naval Electronics Laboratory. Our first integration test of the entire NTDS system was to be conducted there. A prototype computer had been sent, together with a complete display system from Hughes Aircraft and a communications system from Collins Radio. This was the first time that the three newly designed pieces of equipment were to be connected and operated. There was an undercurrent of nervousness on the part of the three manufacturers and, most of all, on the part of the Navy NTDS Project Office, which had retained overall responsibility for the total system.

Several of the senior engineers from each company were present along with the Navy Project Office people. I knew them all, of course, from my frequent liaison visits. I had two assistants in conducting the tests: a junior engineer from the NTDS peripheral equipment department who would take oscilloscope pictures of the waveforms of the input/output signals, and a programmer from the NTDS systems and programming group who had written some simple input/output test routines to pass data back and forth to the other equipment. We connected the cables and found some miswired pins. Within three hours the computer was running the input/output test routines, communicating with the Hughes and Collins equipment. The sighs of relief in the room were audible. We had overcome the obstacles caused by physical separation and misunderstandings among three different contractors and made the system hardware work together. The engineering development portion of the NTDS project was all downhill from this point, although the programming portion of the project was just beginning. The programming difficulties in "tracking" the radar contacts, or determining their expected position by computer calculation so that each radar blip could be associated with an already identified ship or plane, proved to be much more difficult than anticipated. More hardware problems were found and corrected, but there was no longer any doubt that a good reliable system would emerge. The installations aboard the first three service test ships, two destroyers and an aircraft carrier, went smoothly. I had a chance to visit all three ships. I did not expect any input/output problems, and I did not find any.

One source of controversy is worth mentioning. Because we were unsure just how good an electrical ground would be provided by the steel hull of the ships, I had specified that all NTDS equipment connected to the computer must be grounded to a large copper bus bar to be run through all electronics compartments. Allowing for the worst possible conditions, I specified this bus bar as one million circular mils. This is equivalent to a solid copper rod one inch in diameter! Fortunately the Navy had a standard cable that size, so availability and installation technique were not problems. The ground bus did add thousands of pounds of weight and several thousand dollars to the cost of each installation. It was constantly being criticized by engineers who suggested that such a bus was unnecessary. Years later at a reunion I met the man who had been the civilian head of the Navy NTDS Project Office. He told me, laughing, that he still gets cost reduction suggestions to remove that oversized ground bus. He keeps rejecting these suggestions, he said, until someone can *prove* that the shipboard systems will work just as well without it. He *knows* that the systems work well with the bus and figures that a few thousand dollars worth of copper is a good investment. In such ways are things positively *prevented* from going wrong!

Univac established a reputation for quality shipboard computers that has kept them a favorite supplier of the Navy to this day. Univac has won follow-up contracts for shipboard computer equipment totaling hundreds of millions of dollars. Such can be the payoff for designing with a skeptical attitude, taking nothing for granted and overkilling the problem where system performance is critical to the customer.

8

The First Team

As the seventeen NTDS service test computers were completed and shipped, work for engineers on the project kept decreasing. A follow-up Navy contract was obtained for Hi Osofsky and the computer design team to work on a more advanced version of the computer. The systems and programming people had plenty of work to do; their group was split in two, with one half assigned to San Diego to help the Navy develop its own programming capability. As a reward for a job well done, the NTDS managers and supervisors were offered the chance to go on a one-day cruise on the aircraft carrier that had received the first NTDS computers. The NTDS equipment was working well. No one down in the computer spaces had any problems to report or needed my advice. I felt superfluous.

After the VIP cruise I was again between assignments. Working on a military project like the NTDS can be satisfying for an engineer because of the opportunity to use the most advanced technology available and because budgets are usually generous—generous, that is, for items that are readily reimbursed by the government, such as experimental components and test equipment. Overhead items, such as office space and furniture, are inevitably spartan. The great disadvantage of working on these projects is the on-again, off-again nature of contract funding. The shuffling of engineers as contracts are won or lost is less traumatic in companies like Univac and Control Data, which have large commercial development programs to move engineers to and from. Large aerospace companies are infamous for their mass hirings and firings of engineers as contracts are won or lost. The system is terribly wasteful of engineering talent because organizing and honing a good development team takes a long time.

My next assignment was back at the headquarters plant on West 7th Street, in a job that combined marketing support with product planning. The marketing support aspect of the job was kind of fun. I would travel to government installations, for example, Rome Air Development Center (in Rome, New York, unfortunately, not Rome, Italy) to try to sell them on using NTDS-type computer equipment for their applications. The product planning part of the job should have been a prestigious assignment; it was not. To understand why the reader has to learn another one of the only half-humorous "laws" that computer professionals have learned to take seriously: All the good computer designs are bootlegged (that is, done without formal management approvals and budgets); the formally planned products, if they are built at all, are dogs!

With the possible exception of IBM, I believe that this law holds throughout the computer industry and perhaps throughout all high technology development organizations. The products that are really outstanding are those whose development has been driven by individuals who believe devotedly in them and who push them over, under, around, but never through the formal product planning system. Certainly my experiences at Univac and later at Control Data have verified this law.

One group of engineers from the commercial side of Univac saw the potential of the NTDS computer for use in commercial "real-time" processing. After prolonged pleading with upper management, they finally got grudging permission to repackage the NTDS computer with less expensive commercial-grade cabinetry and with some improvements to the input/output system that were already planned by Hi Osofsky and his design team. The resulting direct takeoff from the military development was sold as the Univac 490 Real Time Computer. With its follow-up derivatives, the Univac 491, 492, etc., it was a staple of the product line for many years. Another example: A design team that had included my friend Dick Karpen worked for two years on the specification for a new scientific computer to replace the aging Univac Scientific 1103/1105 product line. Suddenly, the manager of the NTDS systems and programming group presented a design that he and some of his colleagues had been working on in their "spare time" (that is, bootlegged). This design, an extension of the NTDS computer in the general direction of the Univac 1103, was built instead of the formally planned computer. It became the Univac model 1107 computer.

Fiasco after fiasco have been perpetrated by committees of individually talented, knowledgeable computer designers. Consider what happens when a group of six or eight senior engineers is given a charter to define a new computer product line. Probably the majority of the committee members will be competent designers who just happen to be between assignments. Each will have two or three favored design concepts that he has thought up over the years and never had a chance to implement in a previous design. A typical committee is certain to include one or two individuals who have reached a senior position through a talent for company politics rather than through design accomplishment. These people, who are seldom stupid, are especially dangerous to the group because they have had a lot of free time on their hands, which they have spent reading trade journals and computer society publications. Computer publications are filled with articles, mostly written by academic theoreticians, on the latest esoteric concepts in computer architecture. The authors, who have never been responsible for building anything that *works*, are convincing. The committee meets, each member convinced that any new design that fails to incorporate his favorite concepts ("floating floogeldorp," "relocatable razzmatazz") will be hopelessly behind the state of the art. The concepts may be individually quite good, but they are *never* compatible with one another or with the architecture of the existing product line that the committee is chartered to replace.

Returning to my "wedge" analogy, the committee's wedge has multiple points. The resulting committee design can be implemented if enough time and money are spent, but the design is never "clean," and it is unlikely to be cost effective. The worst horror stories about committee design concern attempts by two companies or, worst of all, two countries to design a computer jointly. The differences in company culture and in experience with previous machines makes it almost impossible for the various designers to communicate a clear concept of just what exactly they want the new computer to be. A later chapter will contrast the committee design approach with that taken by Seymour Cray, undoubtedly the most accomplished computer designer in the world.

My responsibilities in my new marketing support/planning job did not include any new computer design committees. I was used as a consultant on the input/output specifications for two new computers, and I spent much of my time planning for new peripherals to be added to the product set. This required writing proposals and study papers, but no decisions were being made or design projects started as the result of my recommendations. I got a call one Sunday afternoon in early 1963 from Dick Clarke, a mechanical engineer and an acquaintance from the General Development lab next door to the old Univac II area. Clarke had become a wetback and had joined Control Data several years previously. He was now director of product management for Control Data's Peripheral Equipment Division. He invited me to visit the Peripheral Equipment Division to see what they were doing. Because of my frustration with the lack of new developments at Univac, I accepted Clarke's invitation.

Control Data had prospered greatly since Bill Norris and Frank Mullaney had left Univac. The number of employees had grown from ten at the time of incorporation to about three thousand. A combination of government and commercial business brought revenues of over $40 million in 1962. Business was increasing rapidly. Contrary to what had been said in the initial prospectus, Control Data had almost immediately developed and marketed a major computer, the model 1604. The derivation of the product number of the Control Data 1604 is another example of inside humor that computer designers seem unable to resist. The last commercial computer on which Seymour Cray and Bob Kisch worked at Univac was the model 1103. The address of Control Data's first building was 501 Park Avenue. Adding 501 to 1103 gives 1604!

The model 1604 used a medium-long word, 48 bits, good for engineering and scientific calculation. It was evidently built by engineers for engineers. The cabinet was battleship gray and opened like a book, with chassis that were hinged to swing out. Formed largely of machined aluminum, it was massive and satisfying to that sort of engineer or scientist who is really interested in the internal construction. The door latches closed with a solid "thunk." Complementing the workmanlike unadorned gray of the computer cabinet was an elegant curved desk console containing enough switches and indicator lights to satisfy the most devoted button-pushing buyer. Almost as an afterthought, Seymour Cray had designed one of the first minicomputers (legend had it, over a long weekend), the Control Data model 160. A 12-bit machine, the 160 was intended as an input/output station or a remote satellite to the 1604. It was packaged in an ordinary office desk, an unusual and clever cabinet that seemed to fascinate customers. These computers represented good performance for the price. They had sold well on the small scale that an infant company could afford to exploit. The thing about Control Data's success that so infuriated us at Univac was that they had greatly prospered by exploiting the straight-forward strategy that we had discussed so often over lunch: using the transistor technology developed on military programs to produce commercial scientific computers for the engineering market where Univac St. Paul already had a good reputation.

By the time of Dick Clarke's call Control Data had designed the Control Data model 3600, a much enlarged and upgraded version of the 1604. It was dramatically different in appearance—one of the most beautiful computers ever built. An industrial design consultant had styled the cabinetry. The outer surface of the computer was made up of hinged door panels with narrow aluminum frames enclosing panels of blue glass. The printed circuit cards could be seen dimly through the glass, and the whole effect was dramatic and space age. The 3600 had been designed under the direction of Bob Kisch.

Seymour Cray decided that he needed more of a challenge than the upgrading of the 1604. According to stories told at the time, he also grew impatient with the interruptions and visitors at corporate headquarters. He bought eighty acres of land on the Chippewa River near his boyhood hometown, Chippewa Falls, Wisconsin, ninety miles east of Minneapolis–St. Paul. Folklore says that he announced to Bill Norris one day that he was going to have a computer laboratory on half of this site, later famous throughout the computer industry as the Chippewa Lab. Seymour built his house on the other half of the site. He started on the design of what was to be the fastest computer in the world at that time, the Control Data model 6600. The machine was not yet announced, but enthusiasm for the 6600 was widespread throughout Control Data.

While driving ahead in the large scientific computer business, Control Data had also started on a never-ceasing series of acquisitions of small companies working in complementary areas. Bill Norris's announced intention was to reach a critical size so that CDC could not be driven out of business by IBM. Acquisitions ranged from one-man companies to those of several hundred employees. The first acquisition, made in the year Control Data was founded, 1957, was Cedar Engineering. Cedar was a Minneapolis company that built small electromechanical devices for industrial control systems. With 165 employees, it was larger than Control Data at that time. Cedar was needed to give Control Data an instant manufacturing capability.

The 1604 computers were built entirely by Control Data, but all the associated peripheral equipment—the paper tape and magnetic tape transports, printers, and punched card equipment—was purchased from other manufacturers and integrated into the computer system. These were known as OEM buyouts, for Original Equipment Manufacturers. Control Data correctly foresaw that an increasing portion of the computer system value would be represented by the peripheral equipment. To keep this money in-house and to keep control over the product performance and quality, it was decided that Control Data would design and manufacture a complete line of computer peripherals. This was an audacious decision. Even today only a handful of the major computer manufacturers build all their own peripherals. Design of peripheral mechanisms is time consuming and expensive, and engineers capable of good mechanism design are rare.

Cedar Engineering was chosen as the nucleus for the peripheral design effort. Although the former Cedar business was continued, Tom Kamp, the plant manager of Cedar, and some of the other people were reassigned, establishing Control Data's Peripheral Equipment Division. A new plant, a single-story concrete-block building, was constructed in the Minneapolis suburb of Bloomington.

Neither the original Control Data founders nor the Cedar Engineering employees had the necessary expertise to design computer peripherals. Fortunately, a pool of suitable engineering talent was available: Univac's General Development group. As described earlier, this group in the West 7th Street plant had developed capabilities for designing nearly any computer peripheral except punched card equipment. The level of frustration among these engineers was high. Most of their proposals to develop new peripherals for Univac were being rejected by upper management in favor of competing development efforts by the Philadelphia branch of the company. The old Philadelphia–St. Paul rivalry was as strong as ever, with the Philadelphians having the upper hand in company politics.

Control Data was thus in an ideal position to recruit peripheral equipment designers. No advertising or personnel recruiters were needed. No travel or relocation allowances need be paid. All recruiting could be done on the basis of personal acquaintance with occasional memory jogging (if the rumors were true) from the purloined Univac telephone directory. For those engineers who were not attracted by the glamour of the most aggressive, fastest-growing company in the computer industry, there was the ultimate lure of the stock option. Everyone at Univac was keenly aware of the dramatic rise in the price of Control Data stock and the possibilities for wealth that a stock option might provide. Senior engineers were normally offered stock options to "swim the river"; few refused job offers. Univac had no such incentive as stock options for working engineers, and the sluggish behavior of the Sperry Rand stock would not have made options attractive in any case.

Of course, Control Data was not the only company raiding Univac for computer design talent during this heady period. Honeywell's computer division located in the Boston area was particularly active in recruiting whole departments of the Eckert-Mauchly branch of Univac, now located in the suburb of Blue Bell, north of the Pennsylvania Turnpike. ERA engineers usually resisted relocation to the east coast but would consider jobs offered on the west coast. General Electric and RCA were other major companies scrambling to get into the computer business by drawing on the pool of engineering talent developed and inadequately used at Univac. Univac was, and sometimes still is, referred to as "the world's finest postgraduate school of computer science."

On that gray winter Sunday afternoon, I drove to the new Peripheral Equipment Division plant, and Dick Clarke met me at the door. We toured through the not-quite-deserted plant. A few engineers were in even on Sunday working on their projects. I was astonished at the number of peripheral developments going on. The bread and butter product manufactured at the new plant was a magnetic tape transport. The single model developed first was soon broadened into a complete family of magnetic tape transports in different performance ranges, and variations were being sold to other computer manufacturers on an OEM basis. Also in production were a paper tape reader, wanted by all scientific computer customers at that time, and a family of factory shop floor data-collection devices. (The data collectors were shortly thereafter transferred to another division because they did not belong in the mainstream of computer peripherals.) The thing that surprised me was the range of other peripherals in various stages of development. We saw a punched card reader, a high-speed drum printer, several magnetic drums, and two separate magnetic disk file developments—one removable disk pack and one gigantic fixed-disk file for eventual use on the 6600 computer. We sat and talked in Clarke's office in the executive row in the front of the plant. The windows had blue glass, impossible to see through but nice looking from the outside. I later learned that Tom Kamp, the general manager of the plant, was particularly fond of blue. He owned a blue car and a blue house, and he generally wore blue suits!

There in Clarke's office I filled out an employment application form and I promised to think over what I had seen. I did not think very long. When a few days later I got a formal job offer, I promptly accepted. The salary was a little more than I was making at Univac (a 10 to 15 percent increase was the norm), and I had a promise that my name would be submitted for a stock option. I felt like a baseball player being called up from the farm club to the major leagues. I wrote a letter of resignation from Univac the same day and planned a vacation in Acapulco between jobs. The customary farewell luncheon was scheduled, and I said good-bye (for now) to my friends at Univac. I expected to see, and did see, a great many of them again when they crossed the river.

My perception at the time was this: Control Data was succeeding brilliantly by doing just exactly what Univac should have done given an aggressive management. They were using their senior design talent, the most experienced computer engineers in the world at that time, to drive as far and as fast as possible to preeminence in the large scientific computer market. This was the prestige portion of the market, comparatively small in number of customers but high in dollar value per account. This made the market particularly suitable for coverage by the relatively small marketing force that a young company could field. The large computers were supported by a complete line of in-house designed peripherals and by smaller down-sized computers (such as the 160). It is usually easier to design a smaller, low-cost version of a high-performance computer than it is to design a higher-performance version of a small machine. This is because all the technical problems of the entire product line must be solved in designing the high-performance computer. The smaller, lower-cost versions can then be produced as subsets of the large machine hardware by substituting lower-cost and slower components or by replacing special-purpose circuitry with programmed sequences of instructions that perform the same functions but more slowly than in the large machine.

The fact that Control Data was carrying out this successful strategy while staffed primarily by Univac "graduates" was the final indictment of the inept and confused Univac management of that day. My luncheon companions and I used to say of Univac: "Where the management is weak, the accountants run the company." We believed this to be true because the accountants were the only ones who had a clear vision of what they wanted to accomplish—they wanted an organization where every figure fit into a neat catagory and all the figures added up horizontally and vertically. At Control Data it was clear the *engineers* were running the company, with spectacular results. I could hardly wait to join the first team.

9

Tomorrow the World

With my fresh Acapulco suntan, I reported for work at Control Data on income tax day, April 15, 1963. After the necessary employment forms were filled out, I was assigned to a partitioned cubicle in the front office area of the Peripheral Equipment Division (PED) plant. The quarters were not much more luxurious than those at Univac, but at least the floor was tiled and the furniture was new. Dick Clarke introduced me to Tom Kamp, a tall, thin, intense man of Dutch descent who reported directly to Bill Norris. Tom Kamp was one of the few executives of Control Data who was not a Univac alumnus. Within two years he became the first vice-president of Control Data who was not a member of the founding group of wetbacks.

Control Data had outgrown the original rented headquarters building at 501 Park Avenue and had bought a large tract of land near the Minneapolis–St. Paul International Airport. A complex of buildings, which eventually housed headquarters staff, marketing, a data services center, the Government Systems Division, and the Research Division, was built on this site over a period of several years. The new headquarters building, although only three stories high, was rather dramatic. The walls of the two upper stories were all glass and were shaded by a system of floor-to-ceiling vertical louvers on the outside of the building. The louvers were on pivots and were connected by a system of bars to an elaborate gear-and-clockwork mechanism that was intended to rotate the louvers throughout the day so as to keep the sun from shining directly into the offices. The clockwork mechanism never worked properly, and the louvers were soon left in fixed positions. The center of the headquarters building was a large open atrium extending up to a skylight above the third floor. The mostly midwestern engineers of Control Data liked to tell the story of the young, newly hired graduate from "Moo U" (variously identified as one of the agricultural colleges in the Midwest), who, on entering headquarters for the first time looked up in awe to the ceiling of the atrium and remarked, "Sure would hold a lot of hay!"

On my first trip to headquarters with Tom Kamp I was introduced to Bill Norris, who, of course, I knew by sight from the hallways at Univac. The same was true with most of the managers of Control Data. I knew nearly all the senior managers by sight even if I had not met them personally at Univac. This certainly made for a strong family feeling in meetings, and, combined with the intense dedication that everyone felt to make the company succeed, made Control Data at that time a pleasant place to work.

Tom Kamp, as general manager of the Peripheral Equipment Division, had reporting to him not only my boss, Dick Clarke, but also the directors of engineering, manufacturing, and quality assurance, and a controller, a traditional manufacturing organization. I soon found that, although I knew a good deal about the functions of peripheral equipment, I had a lot to learn about the business aspects of manufacturing and selling peripherals. The only product that was being produced and sold in quantity, bringing money into the division, was the magnetic tape transport. In the back of the PED plant was the nearest thing that Control Data had to a real production line: a row of tape transport frames on casters. These were rolled along as various subassemblies were bolted on to each frame. At the end of the line the completed tape transports were rolled into a test area where they were operated for several hours by a Control Data 160 minicomputer. The transports were put through their paces by magnetically writing and then reading back various data patterns, rewinding the tapes and then trying other sequences until the quality assurance technicians were convinced that all was well. Plastic dust covers were slipped over the tested tape transports, and they were rolled back into the finished inventory area ready for shipment.

The first Control Data tape transport model was designed with an engineering budget of $250,000, a remarkably low figure for a major peripheral development and one that Tom Kamp is fond of quoting. The reason why the development could be done so inexpensively was that the engineers assigned were extremely competent and hard working and all had had previous design experience on tape transports at Univac. The director of engineering was Paul Bulver, a genial mechanical engineer who I had first met in the Univac General Development Lab. Bulver had done pioneering work on the vacuum capstan, which was the heart of the Control Data design. In appearance the Control Data tape transports were not much different from the Uniservo II's. Tall, narrow vacuum loop boxes held the buffer loops of tape on either side of the magnetic read/write heads. The major difference was in the rotating drums, or capstans, that actually pulled the tape past the heads in one direction or the other. (Tape transports can read tape while moving it either forward or backward.) The older Uniservo design moved the tape by wrapping it around a capstan coated with cork or some other high-friction material. The capstan did not rotate until tape motion was called for. When the tape was to be moved, an electric clutch was engaged. This clutch had three positions: neutral, in contact with a friction plate that was always rotating clockwise, and in contact with a friction plate that was always rotating counterclockwise. Thus the capstan could rotate either clockwise or counterclockwise, depending on the tape motion wanted. To ensure accurate reading of the recorded information, magnetic tape must be brought up to full speed within a few thousandths of a second. Adjustment of the electric clutches to do this was a continuing problem with the Uniservos.

The vacuum capstan was a clever innovation. Two capstans were provided on the Control Data tape transports, one rotating constantly clockwise and the other rotating constantly counterclockwise. Instead of a high-friction surface, the circumferences of the capstans, in contact with the tape, were pierced with hundreds of tiny holes through the rims into the center axes. To keep the tape wrapped around the capstans from moving, compressed air was blown into the center of the capstans. The compressed air escaped through the holes in the rims and held the tape away from the capstans. When tape motion was desired, an electric valve in the center of one capstan flipped the air supply from pressure to vacuum. The tape was instantly sucked down to the surface of the capstan and moved in the direction in which that capstan was rotating. This vacuum capstan system proved to be fast and reliable in starting the tape. It did, however, require an air compressor and vacuum system in each transport, which made the units comparatively large and expensive.

Working for Paul Bulver and in many ways the technical spirit of PED was Lloyd Thorndyke. Lloyd had worked for a short time on the magnetic tape system for NTDS and had indeed shared an office with me briefly, so I knew him well. Of medium height with a crew cut, Lloyd had a positive manner of speaking and a rasping voice. He was raised in the small town of Pipestone in southwestern Minnesota. He had a degree in physics, not in engineering. Lloyd tends to polarize his peers into those who admire him (the majority) and those who make fun of him. Like most of the Univac and Control Data engineers I have known, Lloyd is a skier. In his positive manner, he liked to tell others how to adjust the automatic-release safety bindings that hold the skis to the ski boots: "Every time you fall and the ski comes off, tighten up the bindings one notch. When you break a leg, back off one notch!" He demonstrated the success of this technique when he came back from a ski trip to the Rocky Mountains with Tom Kamp. Lloyd had tightened his bindings one notch too tight; he was in a wheelchair! Lloyd took a lot of ribbing as he rapidly wheeled around the hallways at PED.

Lloyd has a unique ability to discuss the most complex mechanism in terms of the basic laws of physics governing motion, acceleration, force, and energy. He is at his best in talking to a technically oriented customer or prospective customer for Control Data peripherals. In a few sentences and using only a blackboard, he can trace the route through the various design alternatives and explain the choices made and the logic behind them in a totally understandable, totally convincing presentation. When excited, Lloyd tends to talk faster and in a higher pitch than normal, and his detractors compared him to Donald Duck in a tirade, but in general he enjoyed the sort of technical status at PED that Hi Osofsky had on NTDS. His mind was the cutting edge of the peripheral development wedge. He was called on (or intervened without request) to solve occasional design problems with the tape transports, but his time was largely devoted to development of the new disk files.

To my surprise, a subject for continuing debate within PED and between PED and the Control Data Computer Division was the cost of the magnetic tape transports. At that time a high-performance magnetic tape transport such as our top-of-the-line model 606 sold for about $40,000. The PED manufacturing cost, the parts and labor needed to assemble and test a transport, was about a third of that amount initially and was soon reduced as volume production increased. It seemed to me, naive even after seven years in the computer business, that the product had a good markup and that everyone should be delighted. Tom Kamp did not see it that way. He bought and had shipped into our lab an IBM tape transport that was equivalent to ours, although it used a different technical approach. The manufacturing cost of the IBM transport, according to intelligence received, was half of our cost! The two transports, ours and IBM's, were set up side by side in the lab and critiqued by our engineers. To me the differences in physical construction were striking. The Control Data transport was much more solid, with massive welded frames and a lot of machined surfaces; it was fastened together with bolts and nuts. By comparison the IBM unit was flimsy, with a lot of sheet metal and little machining; it was fastened together with rivets or quick fasteners of various types. If the end customer was an engineer and if the retail prices were the same (actually the CDC unit was slightly cheaper), the customer would certainly buy the CDC unit;

it was much more satisfying and workmanlike in appearance. However, the IBM unit performed as well as ours, and reports from the field indicated that it was at least as reliable in service as the CDC unit. Gradually I began to understand that the IBM tape transport represented another level of sophistication in engineering, "value engineering." This topic would grow more and more important as time went by and the technology to design and build good reliable peripheral products became spread around the industry. At the time that Control Data's first tape transports were designed, high-quality, high-performance tape transports were not available to the OEM market. IBM would sell tape transports to Control Data—at full retail price! If Control Data wanted tape transports of a quality to complement our excellent computer mainframes, we had to build them ourselves or buy IBM tranports and forego *any* profit. Price competition in OEM tape transports became a factor only after many more competent manufacturers entered the market.

The continuing negotiations with the Computer Division centered not on the base manufacturing cost of the PED tape transports, but on the "interdivisional price" at which the units were sold by the manufacturing division (PED) to the using computer division. If I had thought about the matter at all, I probably would have assumed that the transports were transferred at cost. But that would have left PED without any internally generated "profit" with which to fund new development projects. In cases where this is done, the manufacturing division is reduced to a servile "resource center" status, dependent on corporate-allocated funds to finance future product developments. Tom Kamp, a strong leader, was not about to assume such a dependent role, and he insisted that a portion of the markup between manufacturing cost and selling price be kept by PED. The formulas for determining this distribution of markup occupied a good deal of Dick Clarke's time. An early proposal was to divide the profit equally between the manufacturing and selling divisions. To use round numbers, suppose that a tape transport that costs $10,000 to manufacture can be sold at retail for $40,000. The total markup is thus $30,000. If this is divided equally, PED would "sell" its transports at $10,000 cost plus half of the $30,000 ($15,000), or $25,000. Computer Division would not accept this proposal, arguing that they were getting a lower percentage markup based on their cost of acquisition ($25,000). As I recall, a compromise was reached that allowed each division an equal percentage of markup on *their* cost basis. In the example just given, if PED took a 100 percent markup on its cost ($10,000 mark-up on a $10,000 cost), the interdivisional price would be $20,000. Computer Division now takes a 100 percent markup on its cost ($20,000 on a $20,000 cost), giving a retail price of $40,000. Computer Division gets twice as much dollar profit per unit as PED but the same percentage on its cost.

A formula to provide this distribution of markup was a starting point for negotiation, but the issue remained a subject for countless meetings. How to account for manufacturing start-up costs, for cost reductions achieved as a result of redesign or increased production volume, and a host of related topics became subjects of additional meetings with Computer Division. Another issue causing almost as much acrimony between divisions as the cost issue was the responsibility for long-range production scheduling. Computer Division had, in those early days, a crude system for forecasting their tape transport requirements: They would estimate how many computer systems they were going to deliver per month, multiply by the average number of tape transports sold per computer system, add a few more tape transports for adding-on to computer systems already delivered, and submit the result to PED as a monthly requirement. Every few months Computer Division would count the tape transports in their warehouse and would find several hundred on hand! They would then send a panicked message to PED to cancel their deliveries for the next few months until they had used up their inventory. This cancellation would wreak havoc with the production schedules at PED, potentially causing layoff of production workers and penalties for cancellation of parts orders. These panics were invariably caused by a combination of overly optimistic sales projections and computer systems shipment delays caused by software not working as promised. Eventually, after many angry meetings, a scheme was worked out to put much greater responsibility on the using divisions for taking what they had forecast, at least for the immediate three- to six-month period. Beyond six months, they could amend the forecast, but only by certain percentages. Otherwise the using division had to take what was ordered, regardless of their inventory. This forced a much more conservative and realistic forecasting approach and reduced, but never completely solved, the scheduling problem.

Another controversy pitted Tom Kamp and the Peripheral Equipment Division against most of the rest of Control Data. Kamp, whose background was production engineering, was keenly aware of the cost savings resulting from higher production volume. He used to tell us that each doubling of the monthly production rate would cut at least 10 percent off the unit manufacturing cost. Because the internal sales to Computer Division were limited by the number of computers sold, the most logical way to increase volume and decrease cost was to sell our tape transports to other computer manufacturers (the OEM market). However, nearly everyone in Control Data believed that our tape transports were technically far superior to any others being offered on the OEM market. The Computer Division executives believed, with some justification, that to sell our tape transports to other computer companies would enable them to offer a better overall system and thus aid competitor's sales. The dispute was resolved by Bill Norris, who sided with Kamp. By the time I arrived, tape transports painted National Cash Register tan were already moving down the production line, interspersed with those painted Control Data gray. Of course, another reason that Kamp fought for the right to develop the OEM market was to give him a business not dependent on the Computer Division and hence to increase his political independence.

The effort to promote sales of tape transports to other manufacturers was spearheaded by Bob Beese, product manager for tape transports. Bob was a pure sales type with thinning blond hair, a florid complexion, a gregarious manner, and an endless supply of new jokes, quite a contrast to the pure engineer types who made up most of my acquaintances. Bob was aided by Dick Clarke and occasionally by Tom Kamp. Kamp liked to get personally involved in high-level customer negotiations. Bob Beese became one of my regular luncheon companions, and I began to learn about marketing from him.

Because tape transports are too big to fit in a sample case, sales efforts were directed toward getting prospective customers to visit our plant, where they were given a tour of the engineering and production areas as well as a sales pitch on our tape transports. We were selling our technical capabilities and our future product plans as much as we were selling our current products. Once OEM customers make the investment to engineer a peripheral into their product lines, make up brochures, train their sales force and customer engineers on the product, they do not want to have to switch vendors every time a better model comes along. An ongoing development effort by the supplier is important. Because of the large number of prospects coming to tour the PED plant, I was soon drafted as a tour guide to handle the overflow visitors when Bob Beese was tied up. This was enjoyable, an almost daily contact with knowledgeable customers (they do not send the dummies to evaluate OEM peripherals) who had been surveying what our competitors had to offer and who were up to date on all the latest computer industry gossip.

When showing visitors around the PED plant and demonstrating CDC peripheral equipment, my favorite stop was the newly announced model 405 card reader. The decline of the ubiquitous punched card ("IBM card") had been predicted almost from the start of the computer industry. The punched card had been around since the 1890s! The Unityper was an early effort to replace the punched card as a device for entering data into the computer. Still, in 1963 punched card usage was large and growing rapidly. Because Control Data computers were among the fastest available at that time, they required an input device that could read cards quickly and reliably. The need was met by designing the model 405, which read twenty cards per second. The card reader was the size and shape of a small desk. Cards to be read were placed on edge in a stainless steel tray and held upright by a "bookend" under spring tension. The entire tray, which held four thousand cards, was mounted on rubber shock mounts and was shaken continuously by a vibrator to jiggle the cards into alignment, much like a card player will tap a pack of cards on the table to make a neat deck. An air compressor was mounted inside the card reader, and jets of air were blown through pinholes in the bottom of the input tray to separate the cards from one another slightly. One of the most common problems in reading cards is their tendency to stick together, especially if they are old and dog-eared or if the air is dry and static electricity builds up. Each card to be read was pulled from the deck by a rotating drum with suction holes in it, much like the vacuum capstan in the tape transports. The card grabbed by the suction drum would be pulled through a narrow slit which was just wide enough to allow one card at a time to move to the reading station.

The holes in the card were read by shining a strong light (actually an automobile headlight) on one side of the card and detecting if light came through with a vertical row of photosensitive diodes on the other side of the card. Each card was read twice at two different reading stations and the results were compared instantaneously in the logic circuitry of the card reader. If the two read stations did not agree, the card was routed into a "reject" bin for the operator to examine. (Most rejected cards were crumpled or torn.) To me, the finest aspect of the design was that by flipping two levers the entire card path through the reader could be opened up for servicing or for clearing jammed cards. The model 405 was the finest example of mechanical design that I have ever seen in any peripheral equipment. Its reputation with Control Data customers has won it a unique distinction: Twenty years since it was first announced, it is *still* listed as an active product in the sales manual. I know of no other computer device that even approaches this longevity. The division that now manufactures the model 405 would love to stop production because only a few are sold each year, but some of Control Data's oldest and most valued customers insist on buying it. The model 405 is a good illustration of the quality of design talent that PED had available in those days!

In our lunchtime discussions on the state of the computer industry, optimism was boundless. We openly speculated on how many years it would be before we passed up our parent, Univac, in sales. Some of the real visionaries predicted that within ten years CDC would be neck and neck with the "jolly gray giant," IBM. Nothing seemed impossible, given the great progress made since the company's founding in 1957 and the ambitious plans already in place for newer and better computers and peripherals. Alas, it was not to be!

10

To See or Not to See

My nominal job function at Control Data's Peripheral Equipment Division was to promote the development of militarized peripheral equipment. I was hired to work with the Government Systems Division (GSD) in preparing proposals for and obtaining contracts from our military customers. I duly made contact with the GSD, which was headed by Noel Stone, a former boss from my NTDS days, and I worked with GSD on several proposals, but nothing much came of them. Our customers were by and large skeptical as to the ability of peripheral equipment to survive in the rough environment of ships and aircraft, and the militarized peripherals business never amounted to much. Thus with a good deal of free time on my hands, I became the planning coordinator for PED and got involved in a variety of fascinating projects.

One of the first of these projects was the problem of providing reels of good reliable magnetic tape for the Control Data customers using our tape transports. Customers and sales representatives frequently asked PED which brand of magnetic tape we recommended for use on our tape transports. The testing that engineering had done on different brands of tape with our tape transports indicated that IBM tape had the best overall performance at that time. Tom Kamp was understandably reluctant to recommend that our customers buy tape from our principal competitor, so we set up an evaluation project to write a specification for the ideal magnetic tape. Then we invited the leading manufacturers of magnetic tape to bid on making tape to our specifications. The tape thus manufactured to meet CDC specifications would be "private branded," wound on reels carrying the Control Data name and sold by our sales force from our pricing manual. This was and still is common practice. Control Data had nowhere near the sales volume to justify building our own production facility for magnetic tape. After some testing and negotiating, Control Data settled on Minnesota Mining and Manufacturing, now known as 3M, as our magnetic tape vendor. I was invited to tour the 3M magnetic tape plant at Hutchinson, Minnesota, a small town fifty miles west of Minneapolis.

By this time all manufacturers had abandoned the metal-plated tape that I had first encountered on the Univac I. Magnetic tape was and still is made by coating a clear plastic film with a mixture of magnetic oxides, basically rust! At the 3M plant I was shown the ball mills, huge rotating cylinders filled with steel balls that ground the magnetic mixture into a fine powder, somewhat like giant cement mixers. The Mylar plastic film was not made in the plant but arrived on large wide rolls like newsprint. I did not see the actual coating of the liquid oxide mixture onto the plastic film because of some proprietary features of the coating process and because the coating takes place in a superclean environment. Any small bit of dust can cause a flaw on the finished tape, so extreme care is taken to clean everything that goes into the coating area. As the plastic film, now coated with the brownish oxide, comes out of the coating process, it is dried with heat lamps to evaporate the solvent; it then passes through a row of slitting knives, arranged like the teeth of a comb, which cut the wide roll into the standard half-inch tape width. The tapes are then wound on individual reels and taken to the inspection and test stations. The exact composition of the magnetic oxides and of the binder, or glue, that holds the oxide to the plastic film is proprietary to each tape manufacturer.

PED was particularly interested in 3M's testing procedure for the finished tape. On my visit I saw that they were using to test their tape the same brand of OEM tape transport that Control Data had been buying before PED had developed their own tape transports. PED knew the limitations of this device, so it decided that PED should do its own tape testing if it was going to put the Control Data name on the tape. Engineering was asked to design a tape tester, and 3M agreed to sell their tape untested at a lower price.

PED's tape transport engineering group designed a tester based on a "stretched" tape transport. This device, which was twice as wide as a standard transport, had a microscope station for visual inspection located alongside the magnetic heads. The tester would automatically write a magnetic pattern on the tape, read it back, and compare. If an error was found, the tester would automatically make several attempts to read, moving the tape forward and backward. The tape cleaning devices on the tester would sometimes remove a spot of dirt or oxide with this back-and-forth motion. If they did not, the tape would stop with the bad section located directly under the microscope. The test technician would then look at the bad spot and attempt to clean it with a surgical scalpel. I do not recall any case in which an error could not be attributed to a visible flaw on the tape. In most cases a particle of dirt or a tiny clump of oxide caused the error. Occasionally there was a void or gap in the coating. PED sent the rejected tapes back to 3M with a notation of where the errors were found. In order to check their own test procedures, 3M had tested the reels of tape before they were sent to us, although they were not contractually obligated to do so. It soon became obvious to 3M that the CDC tester was far more effective than the 3M tester, so they asked permission to watch our inspection process. They were so impressed with the tester performance that 3M asked to buy CDC testers for their tape manufacturing plant. Control Data ended up selling some two dozen tape testers to 3M. One engineering development constantly led to another in those days because of our creative engineering group and an extremely aggressive, marketing-oriented attitude throughout the corporation.

In setting up the tape program, I dealt mostly with Bob Hall, who was PED plant manager and reported to the director of manufacturing. Bob was short, balding (although only in his early thirties), quick of speech, and enthusiastic. He was a pleasure to work with and got things done quickly. Bob was soon promoted to head one of the earliest joint-venture companies formed to develop peripherals: a joint effort with the Holley Carburetor Company to design and build medium- and high-speed computer printers. The new venture, Holley Computer Products, was located in the Detroit suburbs. Later, Control Data bought out the Holley Carburetor interest and made the printer facility part of still another joint-venture company. On Bob's return to Minneapolis, he rose rapidly to vice-president and was considered one of the leading contenders for a senior management position. But he surprised everyone by resigning to join the New York Stock Exchange as head of their computer automation efforts. The last I heard, Bob Hall was chairman of Satellite Business Systems.

Throughout this period Bill Norris continued to acquire many small companies by an exchange of stock. To critics who complained about the rate at which he was making acquisitions, he was rumored to have said: "Hell, it's only Chinese money anyway!" I was assigned to investigate and to write a report recommending acquisition of one of these small companies. The controller of PED was assigned to work with me on the financial section of this acquisition report.

Jack Rabinow was the founder and president of Rabinow Engineering, a firm of a hundred or so employees in Rockville, Maryland, just north of Washington, D.C. Jack was a middle-aged Russian-born Jewish man with thinning gray hair and rimless glasses. He was, by my reckoning, the third genius I had met thus far in the computer business (the first two being George Cogar and Seymour Cray; I rank Hi Osofsky and Lloyd Thorndyke as borderline). Jack had over a hundred patents at the time Control Data acquired his firm, and he has added to the total since. Rabinow Engineering had a full-time patent attorney on the staff, the first I had ever met. Joe Genovese had worked for a time in the US Patent Office, and he knew his business. I learned a lot about the patent process when I came to know Joe. Both Univac and Control Data had had a somewhat casual attitude toward patents. Officially, engineers at both companies were encouraged to patent innovative ideas, but no real efforts were made to encourage the time-consuming process. Because engineers joining either company had to sign over in advance any patent rights that they might claim, they had little incentive to patent, other than the prestige of the thing and the fact that a patent or two looked good on an employment résumé. Presumably both Univac and Control Data had patent attorneys buried somewhere on their corporate staffs, but they did not wander around the labs talking to the engineers on a daily basis as Joe did. I believe that the reason why patents were treated somewhat casually in the computer industry was the break-neck pace of innovation. Patenting involves public disclosure, and your competitors, who are keeping an eye on new issues in the Patent Office, would be alerted to your technology. Better to keep an innovative technique secret and build it into your product. By the time a competitor can buy your product, "reverse engineer" it to figure out what you did, and build a copy, you can have a newer and better model on the way.

Jack Rabinow's inventions covered a wide variety of ingenious mecha-nisms: mail sorters, a phonograph turntable, a light-activated keyboard, and a device for picking a single sheet of paper from a loose stack. Jack once told me that his single most profitable patent was for the automatic regulator on automobile clocks (the older mechanical clocks, not the new quartz clocks). When the owner sets the time on the automobile clock, Rabinow's automatic regulator adjusts the clockwork mechanism to run a little faster if the clock is being set forward or to run a little slower if the clock is being set backward. Jack's patent royalty was paying him only one-half cent per clock manufactured, but millions of automobile clocks were made using this invention. As visitors walked from the office area in the front of the Rabinow plant back into the lab area, they would pass a row of tables on which various mechanisms invented by Jack Rabinow were displayed.

The particular field in which Jack Rabinow was an internationally known expert, and the reason for Control Data's interest in his company, was

Optical Character Recognition (OCR). OCR is, to this day, a specialized, esoteric technology. It is a means for converting numbers or letters printed on paper into digital code representations to be processed by computer. It works something like this: An optical system consisting of a bright light, lenses, and mirrors focuses an image of the character to be recognized on an array or matrix of photosensitive elements, each of which passes an electrical current proportional to the amount of light falling on it. The array of photosensitive elements produces a kind of electrical "map" of the character, depending on whether a black or a white portion of the character is focused on each sensing element. This map is then compared electronically against a set of maps that are prestored in the optical character reader. The logic circuitry of the reader then determines which of the prestored maps most closely resembles the character now focused on the photosensitive elements. The reader then sends to its associated computer or stores on magnetic tape or disk the digital code for the prestored character most nearly resembling the character on the paper. If the process sounds complicated, that is because it *is*!

No one has yet built an optical character reader capable of reliably reading handwritten cursive script. Many readers can read hand-printed numbers, fewer can read hand-printed capital letters if they are carefully drawn. Most optical character readers recognize characters printed by a computer printer, typed by an electric typewriter, or embossed on a charge slip by a plastic credit card. The complexity and cost of an optical character reader is proportional to the number of different characters that it must recognize. For example, a reader that has to recognize only the numbers 0 through 9 is much cheaper than one that must recognize letters as well. A reader that must recognize only one type style or font is much simpler than one that must recognize characters in several type fonts. The most complicated reader ever built at Rabinow Engineering was one that read typewritten pages prepared on any one of five different makes of typewriter. This reader sold for $1.5 million.

Two somewhat related technologies are *not* OCR. The highly stylized, almost unreadable numbers on the bottom of every bank check are printed in magnetic ink for magnetic ink character recognition, or MICR (pronounced "mike-er"). These numbers could easily be read optically, but they are not because of something called overprinting. Bankers have a great fondness for stamping every piece of paper that crosses their desks with teller stamps, etc. Any stamp that overlaps the numbers on the bottom of the check would cause an error for an optical reader; however, a MICR reader can pick up the magnetic ink through the nonmagnetic overprinting. Incidently, movie and TV portrayals of computers often show highly stylized alphabetic characters looking much like the MICR numerals. This is artistic license; the official MICR font defines only the numerals 0 through 9 plus a few special symbols.

Bar codes, the zebra stripes that appear on so many grocery packages, might be considered a degraded form of OCR. The black and white vertical bars, known as UPC (for Universal Product Code), represent a twelve-digit number registered to the grocery manufacturer. The number defines the manufacturer, the product, and the size container and is usually printed in arabic numerals under the bar code. The bars, not the arabic numerals, can be read optically because the scanner in the checkout counter can easily pick up the random angles of the bars as the checkout clerk passes the items over the scanner.

Jack Rabinow had many patents in OCR, and Rabinow Engineering had built a number of optical readers for individual customers, but Rabinow had no standard product offering. Jack had worked for years at the National Bureau of Standards; he then built a consulting practice that gradually evolved into Rabinow Engineering. A major customer was the US Post Office. The Post Office had a research and development facility in the Washington, D.C., area that was at the time evaluating optical readers for ZIP code and automatic mail sorters built by Rabinow. I was given a tour of this facility and saw the largest and most impressive of the devices Rabinow had supplied: a thousand-pocket automatic mail sorter. It was an enormous Rube-Goldberg-like machine, perhaps fifty feet long. An endless chain carried a thousand small metal boxes with hinged bottoms, each box carrying one envelope to be dropped off at its proper station.

Jack had surrounded himself with some bright engineers, many of whom had impressive patent collections of their own. He was willing to sell his company to Control Data, Jack told me, because he was worried about the responsibility of keeping a steady stream of contracts coming in to keep all his employees busy. He was eager to design and build a standard OCR product line to be sold by Control Data. Bill Norris had been an early and enthusiastic exponent of OCR, which he saw as a way to replace the ubiquitous IBM keypunch as the primary source of computer input data. It looked like an ideal combination of talents. My acquisition report was glowing. There seemed to be no limit to the peripheral developments that we could undertake, given Rabinow Engineering's electromechanical design talent (a rare commodity) and the design talent at PED. The acquisition of Rabinow Engineering was consummated in late 1963.

Now I had the problem of defining exactly what kind of optical character reader to offer as the first Control Data product. Because the stated goal of the product was to replace the keypunching of cards as the means of entering computer programs and data, a "page reader" was obviously needed. A little explanation is required. Optical character readers are divided into document readers and page readers. You probably handle several optically read "documents" every month. Nearly all utility bills are optically read when they are returned to the utility with your payment. Document readers can read only from one to three lines on a document, and these lines must be positioned in exactly the same locations on a document of standard size. In the case of the utility bill, it is necessary to read only the account number. The name and address need not be read because the utility's computer stores names and addresses by account number. Even the amount paid need not be read (in some systems) because the computer knows the amount outstanding on that account and assumes that payment in full is made unless the clerk opening the payment envelopes makes a notation of partial payment. Another optically read document that you have probably seen is the gasoline credit card charge slip. Virtually all the charge slips of the major oil companies are read optically. Here again, not everything printed on the slip is read. The credit card number imprinted from the embossed letters on your credit card is always read. The dollar amount of the transaction may be imprinted by the station attendant in an optically readable type font, and the station number and date are often preset on the imprinter mechanism.

A page reader is a considerably more complicated device than a document reader because it must be able to read everything on a normal-sized page. The precise location of the information on the page may not be known, so the reader must be able to "look" and locate the first line. A typical use for a page reader is reading the information typed on a form, say, an insurance application form. The necessary information is typed on the form in areas set aside for policyholder's name, address, amount of policy, beneficiary, etc. The completed form would be signed by the applicant and countersigned by the agent. The insurance company could enter this policy information into its computer system by running it through a page reader. The reader, knowing the type of form it is reading, can be programmed to read only the variable information, ignoring the preprinted parts of the form and the signatures (which it cannot read anyway). The application is not changed in any way by being read, and so it can be filed as a legal record.

At the time that Control Data acquired Rabinow Engineering, a number of document readers were in use, mostly by oil companies and airlines, but page readers were uncommon. Most data entered into computer systems were first punched into cards by operators at keypunch stations, virtually an IBM monopoly. Each card could store a maximum of eighty characters, so entering an entire page of information would require twenty-five to thirty cards. Keypunches had to be leased from IBM, and keypunch operators were always in short supply. Computer programs were generally entered from punched cards also, and every programming group would have two or three keypunches so that programmers who wanted to could punch their own cards rather than wait for the regular keypunch operators to get to their jobs. The bundle of cards representing a particular job then had to be kept together in sequence in a "deck" and kept separate from other decks. When the job was to be run on the computer, the deck was read by a punched card reader, such as the model 405 described earlier. A common sight in computer rooms of this period was boxes and boxes of card decks, representing jobs that were about to be run or had just been run.

Those of us who advocated designing an optical page reader as a standard product argued that, with this device available, any secretary with an electric typewriter could prepare data or programs for computer input. Because eighty characters can be typed on a line of ordinary office stationery, with twenty-five to thirty lines per sheet (double-spaced), the savings in punched card stock alone would be considerable. There were two problems: The type style of the typewriters had to be one of the standardized fonts designed to be machine readable, and, to keep the cost of the optical reader down, only the uppercase letters, numbers, and some symbols would be read. This is not to say that the typewriters could not have lowercase letters, but only that documents intended for optical reading must be typed in uppercase only. Out went a decree from Bill Norris that all new typewriters purchased by Control Data must be equipped with the "OCR-A" type font. The decree was obeyed, and even today some of the typewriters still have the rather stylized but not unpleasant uppercase letters and numbers.

Jack Rabinow had a collection of photographic enlargements of actual documents received at Rabinow Engineering to illustrate the difficulty of reading by machine what the human eye can read easily. With some of the type styles designed to be aesthetically pleasing, it is nearly impossible to differentiate between the individual characters 5 and S, 2 and Z, and O and Q. The percentage differences in black area are slight. The human eye and brain are incredibly skillful at extracting the intended meaning from printed material that is misspelled, smudged, or mutilated. The brain apparently reads much more by context than I had appreciated. One of Jack's examples that I remember was a letter delivered to "Rainbow Engineering." Until he points it out, almost all visitors read right over the obvious misspelling.

The first product that I helped to design became the Control Data model 915 Optical Page Reader. It was a sophisticated machine for its time. Its operation was totally controlled by an associated minicomputer, which stored an image of the form to be read and directed the reader where on the page to read. The minicomputer recorded the data read on a standard magnetic tape, which could then be transferred to a Control Data or other computer system. Rabinow later developed document readers, combination page and document readers, and specialized readers, such as the five-font reader mentioned earlier. At one time Control Data had more optical character readers installed than any other manufacturer, including IBM (who never pushed their product offering hard). Nevertheless, sales were always lower than projected and costs to Control Data were always higher, so the program was never a money-maker. What went wrong?

First of all, the OCR technology proved to be more exotic and costly than Control Data had appreciated. Machines required constant "tweaking" and adjustment to operate properly. (See the cartoon (figure 10) that mysteriously appeared on the bulletin board of the Rabinow machine test area.) Second, the installation of OCR required that customers be given a great deal of advice and help in setting up their systems. Design of the forms, color of printing on the forms, paper quality, typewriter adjustment, and even the typewriter ribbons had to be rigorously controlled if the OCR was to read reliably. In a typical case a customer would call the Control Data analyst and complain that the forms, which had read fine last week, now could not be read at all. Investigation would show that some purchasing agent had gotten a deal on cheap typewriter ribbons that did not meet the specifications for optical reading. The typed copy might look all right to a human, but the light sensitivity of the optical reader does not correspond exactly to the sensitivity of the human eye, and the optical reader could not see data typed with the cheap ribbons. Third, and most important, a new technology (or a revival of an old technology), another alternative to keypunching, began to appear shortly after Control Data's entry into OCR.

Direct keyboard-to-magnetic-tape systems were first popularized by Mohawk Data Systems, a small company founded in 1965 in upstate New

York. The vice-president of engineering and the technical cutting edge of Mohawk was my former instructor and friend, George Cogar! The market success of keyboard-to-tape systems depended on achieving a low cost per operator station. George designed a simple, low-cost station, and in so doing, he wiped out a large part of the potential market for optical page readers. Mohawk was soon followed by other small firms specializing in data entry devices. Keyboard-to-tape systems were soon followed by keyboard-to-disk systems, and the use of cards and keypunches gradually faded away.

One of the fringe benefits of my involvement with Rabinow Engineering was a chance to make customer visits with Jack Rabinow. Jack was one of the wittiest men I have ever known, and he probably could have made a good living as a stand-up comedian. He had an endless stock of stories about customers, engineers, and competitors, and he could keep his dinner table companions in stitches. The high point of my association with him was a visit we made, together with Tom Kamp, to talk to Sidney Fernbach of the Livermore Research Laboratory. You will remember that Fernbach was the head of the computer lab at Livermore Laboratory and responsible for purchasing the LARC and STRETCH supercomputers; he now had a Control Data 6600 on order. He was one of the most sophisticated computer users in the world. Eventually the Livermore Laboratory tied all their large and small computers—and there were many—into a gigantic network, known appropriately as OCTOPUS. Sidney Fernbach was reportedly one of the few people in the world from whom Seymour Cray would accept suggestions!

Jack Rabinow's visit came about because Fernbach was interested in a specialized optical scanner that would pick out the tracks of subatomic particles on photographic film and store their digital coordinates for later computer analysis. The work was being done manually at that time, and it was slow and boring. We did not enter the lab itself, which required elaborate security clearance in advance, but we met with Fernbach at a restaurant near the lab for lunch. For two hours I got to enjoy the witty conversation of these two outstanding men. A videotape of that lunch would certainly compare in interest with *My Dinner With Andre*. Jack had no problem in understanding the lab's requirement, for he had bid on other jobs at least as exotic. So far as I know, the scanner was never built by Control Data, but the discussion sure was fun!

After a few years Jack Rabinow grew weary of fighting the increasingly bureaucratic burdens imposed by a large organization. He resigned and returned to the National Bureau of Standards to work until retirement. A succession of general managers followed at what was now called the OCR Division, but none of them had Rabinow's brilliance or his credibility with the senior management of Control Data. The operation drifted downhill, with many of the most creative engineers leaving. In 1976 the plant in Rockville was closed. A few of the remaining engineers transferred to Minneapolis. The OCR business never developed much beyond its original beachhead in the reading of credit card charge slips and utility bills. Today Control Data is out of the OCR business.

11

Project SPIN

Apart from unique opportunities such as the acquisition of Rabinow Engineering, the product development strategy of Peripheral Equipment Division was simple: If IBM announced a computer peripheral, CDC would also develop one, but with a 10 percent higher performance and a 10 percent lower price. This simplistic approach led us down two or three blind alleys, but it was probably the wisest course of action to develop market-accepted products. IBM's market dominance is so great that a Control Data sales representative had only to explain that "our product is like the IBM model XXXX only faster and cheaper," to be granted an immediate hearing. A product having no IBM equivalent, even though technically excellent, would be a long and difficult sell. When Control Data entered the business of selling peripheral subsystems that were directly attachable to IBM mainframes (the so-called end-user business), we carried the process to the logical extreme. We gave the Control Data products model numbers that were the same as the IBM product numbers with an extra digit tacked on, just to remove any confusion about which CDC model was compatible with which IBM model.

This product development strategy failed, of course, when IBM produced a product that was not widely accepted in the marketplace. This happened twice while I was still at PED. I was instrumental in aborting the PED development of a cartridge-loading magnetic tape system compatible with IBM's Hypertape and later with canceling development of a magnetic card recording system compatible with IBM's Data Cell Drive. Both were canceled before much money had been wasted on development. I should point out that PED did not "reverse engineer" and simply copy the IBM devices. We did use IBM product capacities, transfer rates, etc. as specifications to be met or exceeded, but the technologies used at PED were often quite different.

Offering end-user versions of PED peripherals was done primarily to gain greater volume and hence lower manufacturing costs for devices that were needed on CDC computer systems and for sale to OEM customers. Directly competing with IBM was and is extremely precarious. IBM's production volumes are so high and their manufacturing costs accordingly so low that they can always cut prices to regain their market share if they believe it worth the sacrifice in profit margin. Other competitive moves by IBM include frequent announcement of new models and adjustment of the ratios of purchase prices to lease prices to keep competitors off balance. Control Data at this time was compared to a pilot fish, which swims close to a shark to pick up morsels of food while being agile enough to avoid confrontation.

Shortly after the Rabinow acquisition, PED had the opportunity to buy a small company making a line of high-speed card punches. (High-speed card punches are connected to a computer channel and punch cards as fast as the mechanism will allow, in contrast to keypunches, which punch character by character, as keyed in by an operator.) Bridge Incorporated was a machine shop in an industrial section of Philadelphia. PED had not developed a card punch of its own because (1) the internal CDC market was small, as a computer system seldom required more than one card punch; (2) the OEM market, if not actually declining, was not likely to grow much; and (3) the manufacture of the punch dies, the parts that actually cut the holes in the cards, requires a high quality of precision machining not always readily obtainable. The punch dies are high-precision devices, and the dust from the punched cards is surprisingly abrasive; thus a card punch that holds up in heavy use is difficult to manufacture. Control Data had been buying card punches for our computer systems from IBM, even though they offered no discount from retail price. Bridge had a card punch in production that tested well, and it would fit into the Control Data product line with only a change of paint color. (It became the Control Data model 415.) Bridge also had well-developed plans for a complete line of lower-speed, lower-cost card readers, card punches, and combination reader/punch devices. PED bought Bridge Incorporated and moved them from the shabby plant in north Philadelphia to a new plant in an industrial park in Valley Forge, Pennsylvania.

The new model 405 card reader described previously was now in production and was proving reliable. Control Data customers loved it, but, as predicted, no substantial OEM sales were developing; most OEMs were content with lower-speed, lower-cost card readers. The model 405 was now transferred to the new Valley Forge Division, which was to have all responsibility for punched card equipment.

On completion of the first generation (model 60X line) of magnetic tape transports, a new engineering project was started to develop a second generation of cost-reduced transports. Lloyd Thorndyke, who opposed the idea, gave the project the code name PLUTO, because, as he said, "They are both dogs!" Tom Kamp decided to transfer the PLUTO development to Valley Forge also, in order to give the new division a critical mass. The resulting products justified their code name; they were a disaster. Unreliable and accepted by neither Control Data users nor OEM customers, these products were eventually replaced by yet a third generation of tape transports designed at Valley Forge. The third generation was much better, but market momentum had been lost. Control Data never regained the market reputation it had enjoyed in tape transports before the transfer. This was the second example I had witnessed of the dangers of transplanting technology (the first being Univac II). I was shortly to see many more such examples.

The new Valley Forge Division was plagued with management difficulties, and many of the senior people from Bridge resigned. Valley Forge Division was incorporated into a joint-venture company with National Cash Register called Computer Peripherals Incorporated (CPI). Some but not all of the planned card reader and card punch developments were completed and integrated into the Control Data product line, but they never attained the reputation of the model 405 and the model 415. The card equipment business continued to drift downhill, and the last card readers from Valley Forge were based on a design purchased from a much smaller firm. The model 405 lives on to this day despite all efforts to kill it. After a bad start the tape transport business revived and today has a respectable market share. Valley Forge Division did attract some talented engineers.

I mentioned earlier the joint venture with Holley Carburetor, Holley Computer Products. When Holley Carburetor sold out their interest to Control Data, the then wholly owned Printer Division was moved to a new plant in suburban Rochester, Michigan, north of Detroit, and became known as Rochester Division. The new high-speed drum printer designed and put into production at PED was transferred to Rochester Division. The transfer was not nearly as disastrous as the transfer of the PLUTO tape units to Valley Forge, perhaps because the Rochester engineers, already designing printers, were more familiar with the problems, perhaps because the design was sounder, perhaps because of the shorter physical and cultural distance between the transferring and receiving divisions. Based on my observations over the years I had already begun formulating the Lundstrom Laws of Technology Transfer, a sanitized version of which appears here:

Lundstrom Laws of Technology Transfer
1. If possible, don't do it!
2. If you must do it, keep the physical distance short:
    a. If across town, the problems are easily manageable.
    b. If across the country, the problems will be much more difficult and roughly proportional to the distance.
    c. If across the sea, only the most exquisitely detailed and painstaking planning can avert utter disaster!
3. A good social and professional relationship between the transmitting and receiving engineers greatly increases success.
4. The best executed transfer will introduce a six-month delay in any schedule. A poorly executed transfer will cost from eighteen months up.

Rochester Division proceeded to develop a complete line of low-, medium-, and high-speed line printers that were moderately successful. All the Control Data computer system needs for printers were met, and a respectable OEM business was developed. In 1972 the Rochester Division was included along with Valley Forge Division when CPI was formed as a joint venture between Control Data and National Cash Register. The stated purpose of the joint venture was to realize the cost savings possible through increased manufacturing volume by producing for both parent companies as well as for OEM customers. ICL, a British computer firm, was later taken in as a third joint-venture partner. The gains in manufacturing cost savings were apparently offset by the loss of focus and direction, because the competitive position in OEM printers has declined ever since. In 1983 the Rochester Division was sold to Centronics Data Computer Company, a New Hampshire firm specializing in dot-matrix-type printers, in exchange for Centronics stock. Tom Kamp became chairman of the board of Centronics. In 1986 Control Data sold its stock in Centronics; today it has no printer manufacturing capability whatever.

Two more adventures in technology transfer, in opposite directions, will complete the printer saga. In 1973 a joint-venture company was formed between the government of Romania and Control Data to build computer peripherals in Romania. Some punched card products and a medium-speed printer design from Rochester Division were selected to be built in the new plant outside Bucharest. What happened next was never widely publicized, but it eventually became known throughout Control Data that there were five hundred Romanian-built printers in a warehouse in Europe that Control Data could almost literally not give away. "Want to buy a Romanian printer, cheap?" became a favorite one-liner around headquarters. Sometime later the trade paper *Electronic News* carried an article about the government of Romania signing an OEM purchase agreement with Dataproducts, a leading US printer manufacturer. The article went on to point out that the government of Romania was the half-owner with Control Data of a printer manufacturing plant in their own country. The official explanation was that export controls had restricted the designs sent to Romania to obsolescent models. This may well have been true, but in my opinion the intended European customers, who are not stupid, had other reasons for their notable lack of enthusiasm for Romanian printers.

The other printer technology transfer was from Europe to the United States. The Rochester Division had never designed a dot-matrix-type printer. When a market developed for this type printer, Rochester Division bought the manufacturing rights to a design from a French company named Logabax. (A dot matrix printer forms a character at a time from a series of small dots. Printers sold with home computers are most commonly dot matrix printers because they are the cheapest type to build.) By the time that Rochester Division had discovered that they could not build a printer from the French design and had completely redesigned the unit, they had spent $2 million, according to one of my friends among the Rochester engineers. The redesigned Rochester matrix printer, named the Control Data model 755, was particularly disliked by the customer engineers who had to install it because, although advertised as a tabletop printer, it weighed just under a hundred pounds! American manufacturers had in the meantime come out with much smaller and cheaper printers. Technology does not travel well across saltwater.

So far I have described only disasters and modest successes in the peripherals business. How did Control Data become the world's leading supplier of OEM peripherals? The answer begins with a project code-named SPIN.

SPIN was the name given by Lloyd Thorndyke to the development of a large fixed-disk file. You will recall that, at the time that I joined Control Data, there were two disk file projects in development: the large SPIN file, in which the disks were permanently bolted to the spindle and could be removed only with a set of wrenches and a chain hoist (the individual disks were 28 inches in diameter), and the much smaller disk pack, in which the disks were stacked under a plastic cover with a handle on the top. The whole pack of 14-inch diameter disks could be unscrewed and replaced by an operator. Two developments had been started in accordance with the PED general theory of product planning, which stated that, if IBM had a particular peripheral, PED had better have one also. SPIN had been started in response to the large IBM 1301 disk file, and the disk pack had been started in response to the IBM 1311 disk pack drive. SPIN was also driven by a more pressing requirement: the need for a high-capacity, high-transfer-rate disk file to work with Seymour Cray's new 6600 computer. The unprecedented processing speed and input/output capability of the 6600 required a lot of data to be transferred in and out quickly if the computer was to operate to its full potential. Because SPIN was not ready, the first few 6600 computer systems were shipped with large fixed-disk systems supplied by an OEM vendor. Besides being poorly matched to the 6600 performance, these OEM disk files had a tendency to leak hydraulic fluid and an even more disconcerting tendency to "walk" across the computer room floor when the hydraulic head positioners were operating at a high-duty cycle!

Lloyd Thorndyke headed the large disk development from the start and soon had responsibility for all disk development. There were not that many magnetic disk systems in use in 1964. Most computer systems used for their external storage a long row of from ten to twenty magnetic tape transports, with perhaps a magnetic drum or two for short-term, rapid-access storage. It was not at all clear whether the future would show that the large high-performance disk files or the smaller, cheaper disk packs would be the best solution for external storage. Lloyd, with remarkable insight, correctly identified that, no matter which direction the market took, three critical technologies would always be required to build *any* disk files: design and manufacture of magnetic heads, the coating of disks with magnetic material, and quick and reliable positioning of the head over the magnetic track.

Design and manufacture of magnetic heads Because there are many heads in each disk file (a minimum of one per surface or two per individual disk), heads must be reliable and inexpensive to manufacture. Head manufacture is a high-precision process, with assembly done under microscopes.

Coating of disks with magnetic material Computer disks (except floppy disks, a different technology) are made by coating aluminum plates with a magnetic oxide material. The process is somewhat similar to the way magnetic tape is made but far more critical. A single particle of dust on a computer disk is disastrous. Extreme precautions are taken to get a uniformly thick coating, absolutely clean and highly polished.

Positioning of the head over the magnetic track quickly and reliably Information is recorded on magnetic disks in a series of concentric rings spaced only a few thousandths of an inch apart. The heads must be moved along the radius of the disk rapidly for distances up to several inches and then stopped precisely on the center of the narrow track.

Lloyd determined that these three critical technologies must be developed, not bought, and that all manufacturing must remain in-house. Less critical components, such as power supplies, cabinets, and the blank metal disks themselves, were bought from outside suppliers and subcontractors, but the critical technologies remained under tight control, never purchased or subcontracted from outside vendors. Continuing engineering development projects were funded in these three areas, never ceasing but continually defining newer and higher-performance designs and manufacturing techniques. Thus no matter what type of disk file the market demanded, Control Data would always be ready with state-of-the-art designs in magnetic heads, magnetic disks, and head positioners. Because a variety of disk file products of different capacities and costs could be created by varying the diameter and number of disks in a stack and by physical packaging, new product development could be done relatively quickly using technologies researched in advance. In retrospect, the analysis of the critical technologies and the decisions based on this analysis represent one of the shrewdest management decisions that I have seen in thirty years in the computer business. In another chapter we will see how the failure to make such a technology analysis and act on it led to the frittering away of a leading technical position in another rapidly growing market.

Project SPIN was completed, and the large disks with special high-transfer-rate interfaces were used successfully on the Control Data 6600 and later on the 7600 computers. A few SPIN files with a slower interface were sold in the OEM market, but the general use of large disks soon diminished. The market for small disk pack drives, in a wide range of capacities, grew dramatically. Eventually, most of the smaller disks also became nonremovable and were sealed to reduce contamination from room air. Bit densities (the number of bits in a linear inch of track) and track densities (the number of concentric tracks measured in an inch along a radius) have increased so much that today a Control Data disk file about the size of a shoe box containing 5¼-inch diameter disks has a greater capacity than the original SPIN file, which had four stacks of 28-inch diameter disks. Control Data became a world leader in disk file technology, with product offerings in nearly all catagories. In 1980 Tom Kamp, still in charge of Peripheral Products, threw a party for the employees. Sales of peripherals, mostly disk products, had for the first time exceeded $1 *billion* a year.

Even with the tape transports, high-speed printers, and model 405 card reader production transferred to other divisions, the PED plant soon became too small for disk file development and production. It was expanded once when I was working there, and it has been expanded four or five times since. The plant overflowed the building site available in the suburb of Bloomington. An addition, linked by a corridor, was built in the adjacent suburb of Edina. Tom Kamp had the good judgment to keep all the disk activities concentrated in the same location as long as possible. I believe that this stability was the second most important decision contributing to the success of the disk business. Much of the disk development work going on today is within a hundred yards of where it all began, and some of the same people are still working in the same specialized areas. The advantages of developing model after model, generation after generation, of product in the same location with a stable team are hard to quantify, but they are enormous. The tricks of building something as specialized as disk file heads are not taught in universities or in technical trade schools but must be learned by trial and error. Thus a new firm trying to get started in a high technology business has little choice but to pirate some key individuals with experience in the particular specialties needed. These key individuals, like most human beings, tend to remain where they are through inertia, provided that they are reasonably satisfied with their pay and have interesting work to do. Management announcement of the intention to move them across town or across the country and to break up the comfortable working relationships with their peers causes these key individuals to reconsider their career direction. Suddenly job offers from competitors and phone calls from "headhunters" (freelance personnel recruiters) which had previously been ignored begin to get serious consideration. In the computer disk business nearly every new company can be traced through a few key individuals to pioneering work done at a few locations many years ago. These genealogies, often extending through three and four generations of companies, mean that every old-timer has friends at half a dozen competitive companies. This clublike atmosphere in the industry makes retention of key technical personnel difficult. Stability is a major plus in keeping the players on your team.

In 1975 Control Data succumbed to the temptation to form yet another joint venture, this time with Honeywell Incorporated in the disk business. By this time Control Data and Tom Kamp had gotten a good deal smarter about joint ventures. Control Data retained a 70 percent controlling interest in Magnetic Peripherals Incorporated (MPI). Employees noticed little difference beyond the name on their company badges. Tom Kamp continued to call the shots. The former Honeywell disk plant in Oklahoma City was given responsibility for smaller disks while the PED complex of plants concentrated on larger disks. Much later two more partners were taken into MPI: ICL, the British computer firm, and, ironically, Sperry Univac. After so many years Univac had abandoned their own independent disk development and joined a firm that was started by Univac alumni. Control Data retained effective control of MPI despite all the partners.

When I used to take visitors on tours of the PED plant, the high point of the tour was always a visit to the SPIN lab. The device was impressive— about nine feet long, six feet high, and two tons in weight. The rotating stacks of disks on each end of this behemoth were enclosed in transparent cylinders of blue Plexiglas. The thump of the head positioners and the rushing air sound of the rapidly spinning disks gave an impression of both high technology and raw power. The main casting, which was made of aluminum and held the rotating stacks of disks, motors, and head positioners, was so large that changes in its dimensions with room temperature had to be compensated for. Finding a local foundry capable of making the main casting was a problem. The solution was Northern Ordnance, which had specialized in making gun mounts for the US Navy. Visitors always came away with a high opinion of Control Data's technical capability after they had seen SPIN, especially if Lloyd Thorndyke had been available to describe it. Nothing nearly so physically impressive is made by the company today. I miss it.

12

Whatever Became of George Cogar?

In addition to pursuing contracts for militarized peripheral equipment and investigating and recommending acquisitions for PED I was serving as chairman of a group called the Peripheral Equipment Strategy Committee. The committee included in its membership a number of the technical heavyweights interested in peripheral development, including Lloyd Thorndyke, but its accomplishments were not as impressive as its name implies. Because the peripheral products strategy boiled down to following IBM's lead, there was seldom much controversy about product direction. If asked to list my contributions to PED's success as a result of chairing this group, I would have to list mostly negative recommendations: We quickly recognized, for example, that IBM's Hypertape was not going to be a market success and recommended cancellation of the PED development project for a cartridge tape transport.

As a result of my involvement in this peripherals strategy group, I did become acquainted with some of the deep thinkers in the Computer Systems Division, and together we undertook a genuine product planning task. The typical customer for a large Control Data computer was and still is a large scientific or engineering firm, a government laboratory, or a university. The large computer system would be installed in a climate-controlled computer room with a raised false floor to accommodate the interconnecting cables. The computer center was isolated from the remainder of the building and staffed by a variety of computer specialists. It was often surrounded by glass panels, thus being visible but tantalizingly inaccessible to the average engineer or scientist. The only way that a typical user could get a job run was to physically carry a deck of punched cards or reel of magnetic tape to a counter at the computer center. There an attendant would take the job together with such information as name, account number, interplant mail station, and phone number. Depending on the computer center workload that day and the user's priority and/or political influence within the organization, the job would be inserted into the card reader attached to the computer and either run immediately or stored temporarily in a queue of jobs on magnetic drums or disks. Nearly all the computer centers of the 1960s were run "closed shop"; that is, only the computer operator staff was allowed to enter jobs into the computer and to retrieve the results, most usually a stack of printouts from the high-speed printer. The user's results would eventually be printed and returned by interplant mail or by a special courier service run by the computer center, but the elapsed time between submitting a job and receiving the results could often be two or three days. Users complained bitterly about this system with comments such as "What is the use of running my job on a computer that can solve the problem in thirty seconds if it takes me three days to get my results? I can run the job on a desk calculator in three days!" The problem was especially severe if the computer center serviced a number of plants that were widely scattered around a metropolitan area or even around the country.

The problem of distributing access to a computer system had been recognized from the earliest days at Control Data. The model 160 computer, an early minicomputer packaged in an office desk, had been intended from the first as a "satellite" that could be located remotely from the main model 1604 computer, connected to it by telephone lines. Jobs could then be submitted by the user to the nearest satellite computer; the satellite would submit the job to the main computer for solution, receive the results, and print out the report. There were no technical problems in locating the satellite as far from the main computer as necessary, and multiple satellites could be used on the same computer. Why, then, didn't these satellite computers solve the problem? The answer was cost.

In order to be of any use as a remote job entry (RJE) station, the small satellite computer had to be equipped with, at a minimum, a card reader with its associated control logic and a high-speed printer with its associated control logic. Many stations also wanted magnetic tape and some small amount of magnetic drum or disk storage. Connection to the telephone line required a modem (for *mo*dulator/*dem*odulator), a device that converts the digital signals from the computer into tones that the telephone lines are designed to transmit. A modem is needed on each end of the connection: to convert the computer bits into tones and to convert the tones received back into bits for the receiving computer. The lines leased from the telephone company were themselves expensive, especially if high data rates were required. The customer in the early 1960s could easily end up looking at a retail price of $150,000 or more per satellite, a figure that discouraged all but the most determined and best-funded customers.

In the analysis done by the Computer Systems people, a good part of the cost could be eliminated by reducing redundancy in the satellite computer and its associated peripherals. Each piece of equipment had been designed as a freestanding box with its own cabinet, power supply, logic circuitry, and buffer memory. A complete RJE station, therefore, consisted of from three to five separate boxes all cabled together, each capable of performing many more functions than were necessary in that specialized configuration. Dramatic cost reduction appeared possible by designing an integrated station with a single cabinet, a single power supply, and a single set of electronic logic circuitry to act as the central control element for all the peripheral devices. This concept gained the forbidding title RSPPC, for Remote Site Peripheral Processing Controller.

Many Control Data divisions expressed an interest in the RSPPC, and it was soon in danger of being drowned in company politics. One of the smaller divisions specializing in data communications had developed their own minicomputer (it might almost be called an early microcomputer), the 8-bit-word model 8092. This was lower in cost than the 12-bit model 160 and its derivatives. I had previously recommended that Rabinow Engineering use the model 8092 as the control computer for the model 915 optical page reader, and this had been done. Now the Industrial Data Processing Division made the case that their model 8092 should be used to control the RSPPC also. This proposal was discarded after analysis showed that this computer was too slow to perform all the functions of control of the peripherals and of the communications line simultaneously. Another suggestion that complicated the definition of the RSPPC was a proposal to use a simplified OCR scanner instead of a card reader as the primary input device for the station. This suggestion received a lot of attention because of Bill Norris's high interest in promoting OCR. My own view was that adding a new and somewhat exotic technology to the RSPPC development was not the way to go. I discussed the requirements with Jack Rabinow and obtained some rough cost estimates for using a simple OCR as an alternative input device. I also wrote memos to the printer division and the card products division explaining the concept of the RSPPC and the need for simplified, stripped-down printer and card reader mechanisms and requesting confirmation of the feasibility of meeting the mechanism cost goals. I received replies confirming that the proposed cost goals were reasonable from the standpoint of the mechanism suppliers.

Another suggestion, which proved impossible to kill, was to use the new minicomputer now under development by Seymour Cray at the Chippewa

Lab as the processor for the RSPPC. The idea certainly had some appeal. Seymour had completed development of his model 6600, and the first five production models were being built at the Chippewa Lab. He had started on the design of the next generation computer, known at that time as the model 6800. To handle input/output for the model 6800, Seymour was planning to use 12-bit minicomputers, somewhat similar to the model 160 but much smaller and much faster. These new minicomputers were referred to for convenience as the model 680's. I planned to pay my first visit to the Chippewa Lab to discuss the model 680 and the RSPPC concept with Seymour.

The Computer Systems Division was insisting that the integration of the peripheral devices with the model 680 be done at their plant in Arden Hills, a suburb north of St. Paul. The Peripheral Equipment Group (the new name for the organization composed of PED, Rabinow Engineering, and Bridge) saw themselves only as component suppliers. I argued for a much more active role. The RSPPC required major components made by divisions in Valley Forge, Pennsylvania; Rochester, Michigan; Bloomington, Minnesota (PED); Chippewa Falls, Wisconsin; and possibly Rockville, Maryland; all being integrated in Arden Hills, Minnesota. Perhaps a product that required close cooperation between all of those scattered facilities could be designed and built, but a cost-effective product—never! I expressed my concern in a lengthy memo to Tom Kamp in June 1965.

In this memo I argued strongly for setting up a coordinated design team, composed of top designers from each of the participating organizations, working together under one roof. Because the RSPPC was a cost reduction effort, with a goal of performing the same functions as the model 160 satellite computer system at about one-third the cost, a tightly integrated design with "messy" physical and electrical interfaces between devices was required. I drew an analogy between development of the RSPPC and the development of the Univac model 1004, a successful, small computer system that was developed by eight to ten top engineers working together in a former stable on the grounds of Rockledge, the Remington Rand executive headquarters estate outside Norwalk, Connecticut.

The refererence to the Univac 1004 developed in a stable is a clue to what George Cogar had been doing.

I had kept in touch with my friends at Univac, principally through Dick Karpen. He had remained at Univac as manager in charge of the computer development that became the Univac model 1107. Dick saw the need for a successor machine and continued to harangue Univac management for permission to develop the computer that eventually became the model 1108. He finally grew tired of fighting the system, became a wetback, and joined the Government Systems Division of Control Data in April 1964. We had lunch together occasionally and kept up to date on mutual friends. George Cogar, you will recall, had returned to the Philadelphia plant after having helped to get the Univac II on the air. His brilliance was recognized, and he was chosen to head the development of a minimal computer system to compete with the IBM 1401.

The IBM model 1401 was the least that could be called a computer; in fact, some would prefer to call it a "programmable calculator." It was introduced in 1960 and incorporated a punched card reader, an optional card punch, a printer, and logic circuitry to do simple calculations. The 1401, primitive as it was, was priced at $150,000 or more for the most basic system, which was a low price for a computer at that time. IBM eventually sold some 12,000 of them. Univac felt the need for a product to fill the same market niche. Low cost was the primary design goal.

A project was set up at Univac under the code name Bumblebee, and George Cogar was chosen to lead it. Key personnel from both the computer development and peripheral development groups were assembled. They worked together in a building that had actually once been a stable. The project was kept secret while under development, always wise with a new product concept because, besides avoiding alerting the competitors, it keeps your sales force from selling prematurely. Secrecy also cuts down on product sniping by rival product development groups within your own company. The result of Bumblebee was the Univac model 1004, which became one of the more successful Univac products of that time. I have seen it; it was large and rather ugly, but it performed well, and its cost was low. What better possible leader for the RSPPC project than George Cogar?

I discussed Cogar and his qualifications with my boss; then I called George at his home in Pennsylvania. He was happy to hear from me and flattered that we wanted him, but he had made a commitment to some friends that he could not talk about yet. I soon read about his commitment in the trade papers: A group of former Univac employees from the Philadelphia and upstate New York facilities (Remington Rand manufacturing plants were in the Mohawk valley in upstate New York) had founded Mohawk Data Sciences in Herkimer, New York. The new company was just across the river from Ilion, where a major Remington Rand plant was located. (Sound like a familiar scenario?) Their first product was to be a keyboard-to-magnetic-tape station called the Mohawk Data-Recorder. The vice-president for engineering and the chief designer of the data recorder was George Cogar.

The new product incorporated the basic concept of the old Unityper together with some dramatic cost-reduction techniques. It represented a full-scale assault on the keypunch market dominated by IBM. While the Unityper used a minireel of magnetic tape, which was a nuisance, the data recorder used a standard 10½-inch-diameter reel, which held 2400 feet of tape. The Unityper recorded incrementally; that is, it recorded a single character on the tape, then stepped the tape forward a fraction of an inch. The data recorder stored an entire record (eighty characters, or one full IBM punched card) in its memory before writing the record on tape. This not only made correction of wrong keystrokes easier but also made the reading of the recorded tape into the computer much faster because more data was packed into each inch of tape. The data recorder met a market need and was an immediate success. Mohawk stock price soared, and George, who had a lot of stock, became a multimillionaire.

In 1967 George left Mohawk and the next year set up his own company, Cogar Corporation, with the expressed intent of producing some of the early integrated circuits for the computer industry. He hired a number of former IBM employees from the upstate New York area, and as a result Cogar Corporation joined the growing list of companies to be sued by IBM on a charge of stealing trade secrets. The lawsuit was settled quietly, and George turned his talents to the design of early CRT remote terminals. Cogar Corporation was sold in 1975 to Singer Corporation, of sewing machine fame, which was then diversifying into high technology businesses. George became a consultant to Singer Corporation. In the fall of 1983 George Cogar and several friends were flying in a private plane to a wilderness cabin near Prince Rupert in British Columbia, Canada. The plane never arrived. Neither the wreckage of the plane nor the bodies of the occupants has ever been found. All are presumed dead—a sad ending for my first computer instructor and the first genius that I encountered in the computer business.

Another friend was soon involved with Mohawk Data Sciences. After George Cogar left, Mohawk continued to grow and acquire a number of small peripheral equipment companies around the country to complement its primary business of data entry devices. Dick Karpen grew dissatisfied with working under what he described as two really inept senior managers brought into GSD. He got an offer from the president of Mohawk, an old friend from Univac Philadelphia days, and he moved to Herkimer, New

York, as executive vice-president of Mohawk. In the meantime, the Univac model 1108 computer, whose development Dick had urged, became a big success. Univac tried to hire him back.

In the early 1970s Mohawk ran into financial problems and suffered large losses. A coup ousted nearly the entire management of Mohawk, including Dick Karpen. He then returned to Control Data as president of Computing Devices of Canada, a subsidiary in Ottawa doing mostly military work. After a few years Dick returned to Herkimer to head a group of former Univac employees who had bought out a company called The Library Bureau, another part of the old Remington Rand empire in upstate New York. Dick Karpen is today president of The Library Bureau, a company that makes furniture for libraries and has nothing to do with the computer business whatsoever. He professes to be glad to be in a low technology business at last! We still exchange notes at Christmas and see each other occasionally at "Unihog" reunions (an interesting group that I will explain in a later chapter). Mohawk Data Sciences, with headquarters no longer at Herkimer, continues to struggle with management problems.

After my failure to recruit George Cogar to head the RSPPC development, the RSPPC continued to be the subject of much corporate interest, but it lacked overall leadership. One memo from Bill Norris commented on the importance of the effort. A manager on the corporate staff was appointed to coordinate the efforts of the various divisions involved. I met with him, and I was so successful that one of his progress memos quotes almost verbatim my earlier memo to Tom Kamp stressing the need for close physical proximity and administrative control of the design team if cost goals are to be met.

Despite all the good intentions, the project was fragmented. The Terminals Division eventually got responsibility for the product. Coordination of the design efforts for the controller and the peripherals was limited to holding a series of meetings and writing specifications, which proved inadequate. Years later a series of remote job entry products (the models 731, 732, and 733) were produced. They bore only a slight resemblance to the concept of the RSPPC. Individual boxes were still cabled together to form these products. The manufacturing costs proved to be twice the original planning goals. Moreover, during the long time that the products were in gestation, competitors had developed lower-cost remote job entry stations, and it proved impossible to sell the Control Data products at a profit. I was upset at the direction that I saw the RSPPC development taking, but it was no longer my responsibility. I was not part of the peripheral products group anymore. Twenty miles to the northeast I was learning about the large computer business.

13

The Large Computer Business

In the fall of 1965, after working more than two years at the Peripheral Equipment Division, I became aware that Control Data was in financial trouble. As usual, the hallway rumors and the worried expressions on the managers' faces telegraphed the problem long before any formal earnings report. The company had grown large enough by this time that it adopted the usual large-company solution to problems of this sort: It established a task force. The Profitability Improvement Task Force had seven members: two from each of the three operating groups of the company—Peripheral Equipment Group, Computer Group, and Business and Industrial Products Group—and a chairman. My boss, Dick Clarke, was one of the two members from Peripheral Equipment Group, and most of what I learned was gleaned from him.

The core of Control Data's business, and the part contributing most of the profit, was the sale of large computer systems. All large computer development, manufacturing, and programming, including Seymour Cray's Chippewa Lab, reported to Frank Mullaney, vice-president of the Computer Group and the number two man in Control Data. The large computer business had made money from the delivery of the first model 1604, and it was still making money. Recently, improvements by competitors in computer price/performance ratios (IBM had announced the System/360 in 1964) had forced Control Data to reduce retail prices. CDC's large computers were still profitable, but the markups had been cut.

In his eagerness to grow to a "critical mass," Bill Norris had directed a strategy of acquisition and of internal growth of a number of small divisions that provided complete application systems to customers in selected industries. He was particularly convinced of the growth potential of the data services business, and he had directed establishment of a number of data centers around the country. The data services business sells computer time and the use of some computer application programs to customers who either do not have their own computers or do not want to bother developing certain applications for their own computers. Most of these small application system divisions and all but one or two of the data centers were losing money in 1965. The profitability of the large Control Data computer systems had in the past been so high that the losses on these start-up operations could be covered and the corporation would still show earnings growth. This was no longer true.

The final report of the Profitability Improvement Task Force was kept so confidential that even the task force members did not get to keep their own copies! The report recommended that the worst money-losing divisions and many of the data centers be closed in order to concentrate the available funds on the continued growth of the core business—large computer systems. The report split the executive committee of Control Data right down the middle. Frank Mullaney accepted the report as good sense. Bill Norris flatly rejected the report and called for an across-the-board expense reduction by all operations. After some acrimony, Norris's view prevailed.

In the resulting cutback at Peripheral Equipment Group my job position was eliminated, and I was told that I would have to find another job within the company. A major reshuffling of personnel followed. My friend and boss, Dick Clarke, left PEG and became marketing manager for Control Data OCR products. Before I had time to worry about finding another job, I was offered one at the Computer Systems Division in the St. Paul suburb of Arden Hills. My boss would be Jay Kershaw, my old boss from the NTDS project. His boss was Noel Stone, formerly the general manager of the Government Systems Division and another former boss from NTDS. It would be like coming home. I accepted with alacrity.

The plant at Arden Hills was a large white, two-story structure with narrow vertical windows, typical of Control Data construction at that time. Although only a few years old, it already had a comfortable, lived-in feel that recalled in many ways the old Univac plant at 1902 West Minnehaha, of which it was a direct spiritual descendant. Buried in the basement were several classified government project areas to which one could not gain access without a security clearance, a familiar touch to me. The larger part of the plant was partitioned into offices and labs, and behind any door one might find a novel and exciting project. The complex, consisting of two buildings, one behind the other, joined by a corridor, was positioned on half the available site so that space was left for a mirror-image plant to be built next to it. Clearly, unlimited expansion was planned. This was an exciting time to be working with large computers.

The model 6600, designed by Seymour Cray at the Chippewa Lab, was just coming into production at Arden Hills. Seymour had insisted on building the first five computers at Chippewa Falls because he believed in giving his development team the experience of production and because they were the only ones capable of building the machine until the Arden Hills engineers had learned the design thoroughly. Serial numbers six and up were to be assembled at Arden Hills. The model 6600 was a milestone computer, in some ways the finest thing that Seymour ever designed. It was the world's fastest computer in 1966, rated at three million instructions per second (expressed as 3 MIPS). A full-blown computer system with peripherals sold for $6 million. The logical organization, or architecture, was unique. The central processing unit (CPU), which performed the calculations, consisted of ten separate "functional units," each optimized to do only one particular operation—multiply, add, divide, shift, etc. The CPU communicated only with its central memory; it had no input/output instructions whatsoever. The CPU operated on a 60-bit word, which is unusually long. Included in the 6600 computer and communicating with the CPU's central memory were ten independent 12-bit minicomputers, each having its own separate memory as well as access to the CPU's memory. These minicomputers, called Peripheral Processing Units (PPUs), provided the input/output instructions to keep the CPU fed. Thus a model 6600 consisted of eleven (or twenty, if you counted each functional unit separately) discrete programmable computers, all capable of working independently but all capable of communicating with each other through the central memory. This proved to be an extremely powerful organization and one capable of surprising extensions.

The computer had the physical configuration of a plus sign, with each of the four arms being about six feet long. The center, where the four arms joined, was simply a space for interconnecting cabling. The structure stood about seven feet high, was painted battleship gray, and, like all Control Data equipment of that time, was of massive, solid construction. The cooling system was extremely innovative. Instead of the usual cooling air blown through the computer, the machine was cooled by circulating chilled freon gas (the same as used in your home refrigerator) through coils buried in the aluminum structure of the chassis. Chilled metal plates separating the printed circuit cards carried off the heat. There were no blowers; thus no dust was raised, no filters had to be changed, and no noise was produced.

Still another innovation was the elimination of the traditional operator's console with its row upon row of switches and flashing lights. In its place was a desk with two round CRT screens and a keyboard. The console was cabled to a PPU, and a program running in the PPU sent the computer operator status messages in plain English. The console was built for the 6600 by Data

Display Incorporated, the firm started by Malcolm Macaulay from Univac. Because CRTs capable of high resolution were not available in large sizes at that time, two 12-inch-diameter round CRTs were used. They were mounted side by side on a panel rising from the desk top. The twin CRTs looked like a pair of eyes staring at the operator! The tubes' phosphor and hence the messages on the screen were a bright green. A conventional typewriter keyboard was set into the desk top. Given this wonderful new toy, the programmers were not long in inventing video games to run on the PPU. The first that I saw in late 1965 or early 1966 was called Baseball. The program displayed on the CRT screen a baseball diamond with players distributed around the field. The pitcher threw the ball when the "P" key was hit. The ball could be seen moving toward the plate. The batter swung at the ball when the "S" key was pushed. Timing of the swing would determine the movement of the ball out over the field. More sophisticated games were programmed a short time later.

The 6600 was an awe-inspiring machine, and we later found out just how much it worried IBM. Control Data's Arden Hills engineers were also somewhat frightened of the machine at first. Because of the extreme speed of the circuitry, the wires connecting the printed circuit cards had to be "tuned," or cut, to the proper length. The length of time that an electrical signal takes to move through a foot of wire was an appreciable portion of the 6600 cycle time, and the engineers responsible for manufacturing and testing the computer were afraid that any inadvertent change that they might make might cause the computer never to run again! With familiarity the Arden Hills engineers gained confidence, and soon major surgery was being performed on the 6600 without fear. At the same time that the early 6600's were being delivered, an engineering group at Arden Hills was designing a lower-speed, lower-cost version. The concept was to replace the ten functional units forming the heart of the CPU with a single all-purpose unified processor that would operate at about 1 MIPS. The basic architecture and the ten PPUs were retained, and the new model, named the 6400, was completely compatible with the 6600. This modification worked out so well that a machine with *two* of these unified processors, rated at about 2 MIPS, was built next. This model was named the 6500. Then it was suggested that ten PPUs were not enough for a really large configuration; couldn't Control Data design a computer with twenty PPUs? This also proved feasible. The need for more memory was met by designing an external large core memory that communicated directly with the central memory at high data rates without going through the PPUs. While the designers were at it, they designed this Extended Core Storage (ECS) so that up to four 6000 series computers could be connected to, and communicate through, the ECS. The variations possible with the basic 6600 architecture seemed endless, and one modification followed close after another. The true brilliance of the design was proved by its extreme flexibility and longevity. Current Control Data Cyber 180 computers owe a large debt to the architecture of the model 6600.

My first assignment on arriving at Arden Hills was as acting manager of a systems management group. The previous manager, whose office I inherited, had transferred to another facility, and someone was needed to fill the vacancy at a critical time. Eight or ten systems managers reported to me. Systems managers at Control Data usually have an engineering or programming background. They are responsible for pulling together all the parts of a particular customer's system and ensuring that all necessary hardware and software are ordered and delivered on time and for seeing that the contract is handled smoothly and efficiently. Systems managers must work with the sales representative responsible for the account, contract administration, manufacturing, scheduling, software development, and customer engineering to ensure that there are no last-minute surprises when the computer system arrives at the customer's site and that installation and acceptance go rapidly. Such individual attention to each order is expensive for Control Data, but with systems selling for a minimum of $1.5 million, as they did in 1966, the cost is justified if it reduces the time taken to get a system on rental or invoiced for purchase. System managers for the 6000 series computers normally accompanied their computers to the customers' sites and stayed until the machines were operating and formally accepted by their customers.

With the first shipments of a radically new computer such as the 6600, system managers expected a lot of problems—and they were not disappointed! Far and away the greatest problem was SIPROS.

To understand what happened, the reader is going to have to submit to an oversimplified explanation of computer software, the sequences of instructions that make a computer compute. Professional programmers are going to disagree violently with what I have to say. In fairness, my descriptions of computer software bear about the same resemblance to the real thing as a child's stick drawings bear to real people; they give you the main idea with an enormous amount of detail left out.

All computers can ultimately understand instructions written only in their wired-in instruction set, so-called machine language. Machine language, if printed out, appears as a list of numbers and letters, incomprehensible to the average computer user. The designers of the earliest stored-program computers assumed that users wishing to program their problems for computer solution would learn the machine language appropriate to their computers.

The early computer users would have to remember not only the computer instruction set but also the contents of a number of intermediate-storage registers (these change with the execution of each instruction), which memory locations were available to use, the status of input/output instructions in progress, and a great many other details. For average users, programming in this manner was extremely slow. Strangely enough, certain individuals seemed to have no difficulty. I remember watching one programmer on the NTDS project, a former high school mathematics teacher, who could write computer instructions in machine language as rapidly as I can write plain English. The most famous practitioner of this art is Seymour Cray, who is reputed to have written an entire computer operating system in machine language. A special type of mind is required. In my opinion the individual who can play ten simultaneous chess games will have no difficulty programming in machine language. For the rest of us, it was soon recognized that some programming aids would be required.

The first programming aids were called assemblers. Assemblers are essentially translation programs that convert the programmer's instructions written in an artificial assembler language, which is designed to be easy to remember and to use, into machine language instructions. Of course, a new assembler program must be created for each new model computer having a different instruction set. Many different assemblers were written by computer manufacturers and by major computer users. At one time nearly every university that owned a computer also had its own favorite assembler written by a staff member. These programs were usually given names ending in "al" for "assembly language." An assembler does not simply translate one assembler instruction to one machine language instruction. Whole commonly used sequences of machine language instructions can be translated from a single assembler instruction. The contents of memory locations, intermediate-storage registers, etc. can be coordinated automatically by the assembler program. The use of assemblers made programming much easier, but it was not an unmixed blessing. For one thing the running of a program now took two passes through the computer instead of one: the first to translate the assembly language instructions into machine language (sometimes called "object code" as opposed to the assembler "source code") and the second pass to execute the machine instructions. Of course, if the program was to be run more than once, the object code could be saved and the translation step skipped in subsequent runs. A second disadvantage was that seldom could an assembler produce as "tight" (that is, computer-time efficient) a code as could a clever machine-language programmer. This really mattered only when programs were to be run over and over again, as, for example, the central portion of an operating system. However, the savings in programmer time using assemblers were so substantial that only a few brilliant eccentrics continued to program in machine language.

The need for even easier-to-use programming aids was soon recognized, and compilers were developed. Compilers perform much the same functions as assemblers, and the distinction between the two is not always clear. Compilers also provide the programmer with an artificial language and a translation program that converts compiler language to machine language. They differ from assemblers in that the format of the compiler language instructions is optimized for the easy specification of a class of problem; the assemblers tend to be organized so as to make most effective use of the particular computer's architecture. The sequence of instructions written by the programmer using a compiler may be quite independent of the sequence of machine language instructions followed by the computer in actually solving the problem. In other words, the problem to be solved using a compiler may be written in a form that makes the problem easy to state; the compiler translation program then "cracks" the source code and may reorganize the problem to a form most efficient for the computer to solve.

Another goal of compiler development is to standardize the compiler languages so that a source program written in a standard compiler language can be run on any existing or new computer (with different translation programs, of course, to allow for different machine instruction sets). This goal has almost, but not completely, been reached today. Some compilers in common use are Cobol (Common Business-Oriented Language); Fortran (Formula Translation), used mostly for engineering and scientific problems; and Basic (Beginners All-purpose Instruction Code), a sort of minimal subset of Fortran often used by students and home computers users. There are hundreds more, largely for special applications or particular groups of users. Like all good things, the compilers have some disadvantages. The "compile" run itself can be a complex program and can take a lot of computer time. Code written in a compiler language, especially by an inexperienced programmer, can take many times the number of machine instructions to execute as the same problem written in machine language, or even in an assembler language. These factors have become less and less important as compilers have become more sophisticated, the cost of computer hardware has dropped dramatically, and the cost of writing programs (read "programmers' salaries") has increased.

What about operating systems? In the beginning, programs were run on a computer system one at a time by a computer operator. Each job would be read into the computer from punched cards or magnetic tape; the computer would do the computation, and the results would be printed out on a high-speed printer or recorded on magnetic tape for later analysis or printing. It was soon realized that with this sort of operation the computer was idle most of the time. It could just as well be made to overlap three jobs at once—reading in one job while computing on a second job while printing out a third job. In this way all the expensive hardware could be fully utilized. A simple little program often called a monitor was written; the purpose of the program was to monitor the resources of the computer. The monitor ran whenever the computer was in use, scheduling more jobs as fast as they could be accommodated. For accounting purposes it was considered advantageous for the monitor to keep records of which jobs were run, what time of day they were entered, how much computer time they required to run, how many lines of output were printed, and so on. As central memories got larger, several jobs could be contained in memory at the same time, and the CPU could work on a second job when the first job required input or output (multiprogramming), so, of course, the monitor had to keep track of the memory available and assign memory space to new jobs waiting to come in. Large magnetic disks, especially nonremovable disks that could not be dedicated to a particular job, had to be shared among many users, so the monitor had to keep track of available storage space on disks also. Commonly used "utility" programs, such as programs to make copies of tapes or disks, were added to the monitor so that users would not have to provide their own. The functions that would be "nice to have" continued to grow, with each feature added calling for still more functions. Operating systems, as they came to be called, became so large that they could fill the entire central memory of the computer, leaving no room for useful programs to be run! Computer operation came to be controlled by the operating system, which instructs human computer operators when to mount particular magnetic tapes or disks on the tape or disk drives and tells them when to load certain types of forms in the high-speed printer.

Operating systems for major computers today incorporate hundreds of thousands of computer instructions. They have been described as among the most complicated things made by humans. With a few special-purpose exceptions, no operating system is kept entirely in the computer's internal memory; only a small central portion is kept in memory and the remaining capabilities are called in from magnetic tape or disks as needed. Of course, the operating systems for home computers are stripped-down versions of the operating systems for mainframe computers, without the elaborate accounting routines and the scheduling for multiple users, but they are still complicated.

As the numbers of programmers employed by Control Data increased, a pecking order developed. At the top of the pyramid, nearly equal with the top computer designers, were the designers of operating systems. Because design of an effective operating system requires an intimate knowledge of the inner workings of the computer hardware, many of the best were former computer design engineers. Next in status were designers of compilers and assemblers. The programs must interact intimately with the operating system, and so their designers were accepted almost as equals by the operating system designers. A number of the best ones are mathematicians by training. At the bottom of the status heap were those application programmers who worked only in compiler languages. Cobol programmers, probably the largest group, had the lowest status. It should be pointed out that this pecking order applies only to *computer manufacturing* firms. Software companies, whose whole revenue may come from widely accepted application programs, have a quite different view!

With this oversimplified background, we can proceed with the story of the 6600. The operating system planned and contractually committed to the early customers for the 6600 computers was being written by a Control Data division in Los Angeles, the System Sciences Division. SIPROS (for *Simultaneous Processing Operating System*) was a sophisticated, feature-rich operating system for its time. Customers and prospective customers to whom SIPROS was described were invariably impressed, and many customers insisted on writing a requirement for SIPROS into their contracts. Unfortunately, while the 6600 computers were running, SIPROS was not. The first five 6600 computers built at the Chippewa Lab had been delivered with a rudimentary operating system reputedly written in octal for engineering checkout by Seymour Cray. The Chippewa Operating System (or CHOPS) supported only one programming aid, a Fortran compiler also written at the Chippewa Lab. Completed 6600 computers were sitting on the test floor at the Arden Hills plant. Customers were refusing to allow shipment until they could see the promised SIPROS running. Millions of dollars in finished inventory of computers was building up on Control Data's books, and promises, but no software, continued to come from Los Angeles. This was the situation at the time I transferred to the Computer Systems Division. There was worse to come.

One of my first duties in the systems management job was to write a weekly letter describing progress on each of two 6600 computers destined for the Bettis Atomic Power Laboratory (run by Westinghouse and called BAPL (rhymes with "apple")) and for the Knowles Atomic Power Laboratory (run by General Electric and known, logically enough, as KAPL). Both laboratories were subcontractors for the US Navy nuclear propulsion program, whose head was Admiral Hyman Rickover. Among the many requirements in the contract was a stipulation that, if deliveries were delayed, a weekly letter from a senior corporate executive had to be sent to Admiral Rickover personally, explaining the delays and predicting the completion date. Weekly letters to the famous irascible admiral were a minor part of the price that this delay was costing Control Data. A penalty payment of $3000 *per system per day* was required until the two systems were accepted or for 180 days, whichever came first. Unfortunately the 180 days came first! Each week I would draft the letters reporting real or imagined progress on the BAPL and KAPL systems, then drive to headquarters to get Frank Mullaney, vice-president of the Computer Group, to sign them. He was always courteous to me in our doleful weekly meetings.

After some months of agonizing, a decision was finally made. SIPROS would be abandoned, a new operating system based on CHOPS would be written, and existing customer contracts would be renegotiated. What had gone wrong?

In my opinion, based solely on conversations with knowledgeable programmers who had worked on the 6600, three things.

1. Los Angeles is two thousand miles from Chippewa Falls, Wisconsin. Operating system design requires the most intimate, detailed knowledge of hardware idiosyncrasies. By the time a 6600 was shipped to Los Angeles for the programmers to use, a lot of mistakes had already been made.

2. Seymour Cray and Bob Fagan, general manager of the System Sciences Division, reportedly disliked each other and communicated as little as possible.

3. SIPROS had contracted that most malignant of all software diseases, "creeping elegance." When a software product is in the design stage, the temptation to add one more feature, which will "only take a few lines of code," is almost irresistible. If these temptations overcome caution and if more and more sophistication is added to the design *before the basic system is operating,* disaster inevitably follows. This is the case because an operating system is so complex that one logical error ("bug") will mask another; the program will become nearly impossible to troubleshoot as an untested entity. If, however, portions of the operating system have been run on the computer and debugged beforehand, logic errors in additional sections will be comparatively easy to locate.

Right or wrong, the operating system decision was made, and all the 6600 customers (except one who insisted on, and finally got, a truncated version of SIPROS) were unsold on the glories of SIPROS and sold on the classic simplicity of CHOPS. Things were not quite as bad as they might have been. Some of the programmers at the Arden Hills plant, not trusting their California brethren, had already been working on enhancements of CHOPS. Most of the early 6600 customers were government laboratories and universities that had their own staffs of bright programmers. Many of these programmers looked with contempt on software supplied by the computer manufacturer and used it only as a base to which they added their own improvements. Professional pride and rivalry to have the most advanced computer system was always a major factor in selling to these groups. First among equals at this time was, of course, the Livermore Laboratory, which usually ordered the first model of each new computer that Seymour Cray designed.

CHOPS, by default the new standard 6600 operating system, was enhanced and improved by programmers at Arden Hills and was renamed SCOPE (Sequential Control of Processing Executive). SCOPE was a traditional name for Control Data operating systems, having been used for the model 3600 operating system as well. Deliveries of 6600 computers could now resume.

One day Jay Kershaw called his managers into his office and closed the door. He had shocking news—Frank Mullaney had resigned! Mullaney's resignation was followed by those of a number of his principal lieutenants, among them Bob Kisch, another Control Data founder and a longtime collaborator of Seymour Cray. The company held its collective breath. Would Seymour resign, too? Seymour stayed and continued work on the model 6800, now renamed the model 7600. The entire company heaved a sigh of relief.

Frank Mullaney was a great loss to Control Data, not only because of his personal character and ability but also because of his unique position in the power structure. A wealthy man from his stockholdings, Mullaney knew that he would never be number one at Control Data so long as Bill Norris kept his health, but he would never be number three either. Thus he served as a kind of fixed point around which the currents of company politics and ambition swirled, as the ambitious and clever were attracted by the success of Control Data and struggled to extend their power. I always had the feeling that, if an issue could be brought to the attention of Frank Mullaney, he would have only one criterion for making a decision: What would be best for Control Data? Every large company needs a Frank Mullaney.

14

How Hard Is Software?

The history of the electronic computer business, of which this account purports to reveal only a narrow but typical slice, is littered with costly fiascoes. Just as archaeologists form an opinion of the contents of a large man-made mound, or "tell," by cutting a deep, narrow trench through the center and extrapolating from the artifacts that they find, my narrow view of the computer industry, if extrapolated, would conclude that billions of dollars have been expended on development projects that failed to meet their objectives or overran their budgets by several hundred percent or both. A disproportionate number of these dramatic failures have been software projects. Some anecdotes from the next period of my career may suggest factors contributing to the historically high failure rate of software projects.

In the aftershocks resulting from the Mullaney resignation, my boss's boss and old acquaintance, Noel Stone, was replaced by a new vice-president coming from one of the small application divisions. He brought with him his own manager of systems management, and I was transferred to become the first employee of a newly formed group called product management. The job of a product manager at Control Data had little in common with the job function as performed in consumer products companies. The product manager did not manage the product, a computer system, in terms of directing future developments or recommending pricing. Those were the functions of the product *line* manager. The product manager worked with the Control Data sales force, the prospect or customer, and the rest of the Computer Systems Division to configure the best possible combination of hardware and software to solve the customer's problem. Product managers had the authority to recommend modifications to the product line and special development of what sometimes became new products in order to best meet their customer requirements. Appointed to head this new group was Nate Dickinson, whom I had never met before. Nate was transferred from a small computer company that Control Data had bought in La Jolla, California. Because he was not a Univac alumnus and, indeed, because he was completely unknown to me, I was somewhat nervous about this new boss. I need not have worried. Nate proved to have an infectious, irreverent sense of humor; he was more fun than anybody I have ever worked for. He arrived from California, tall, blond, and ruddy-complexioned, wearing only a light topcoat in the middle of the coldest, snowiest January in some years. As his only employee when he arrived, I had to listen to his jokes about the mental deficiencies of anyone who would choose to live in Minnesota in the winter. I could hardly argue with him; it really was a brutal winter.

As another result of the reorganization following Frank Mullaney's resignation, work on a major enhancement of the SCOPE 2.0 operating system for the 6600 was ordered to be transferred to a Control Data programming group in Palo Alto, California. Operating systems, and other software packages, are commonly designated by a name and a number indicating the revision level. A change in the *integer* number of the revision level (that is, from SCOPE 1.0 to SCOPE 2.0) indicates a major rewrite with increased capabilities. A change in the number *following* the decimal point (that is, from SCOPE 2.0 to SCOPE 2.1) indicates a minor enhancement. In either case, the highest number is always the most recent version. The Los Angeles operation of the System Sciences Division had not long survived the SIPROS debacle, but Control Data had a second programming group in California, unsullied by the previous disaster. The programmers at the Arden Hills plant raised understandable objections to this transfer: "Surely it is not wise to move the operating system development two thousand miles from the hardware expertise again?" The countering argument was: "It is much easier to hire good programmers in California." This is true. There are many good programmers in California, and many good programmers will refuse to live anywhere except in California. The reverse side of the coin is that it is also easy for programmers to job-hop in California. Rumor had it that computer-related companies were so thick in Silicon Valley that a programmer could get a better-paying job without even changing car pools! Programmer turnover became a major problem at Palo Alto. The structure of an operating system is so complex that even experienced programmers take months to learn it before they can write any useful code.

Another problem was productivity. Programmers from Arden Hills were fond of pointing out the presence of two Ping-Pong tables on the lower level of the Palo Alto facility. They also liked to remark that, when visiting Palo Alto when the weather was good, which was most of the time, they could seldom find any of the programmers at their desks. The half-humorous suggestion was made that both of these problems, turnover and productivity, could be solved by establishing a programming facility at Brainerd, in northern Minnesota. This facility, which would be abbreviated BRAIN-FAC, would be assured of at least nine months of productive programming every year because the winter is nine months long in Brainerd! I myself suggested Duluth, Minnesota (although this could be abbreviated DUL-FAC), on the grounds that winter is ten months long there!

As the reader may have guessed from this buildup, the first version of the 6600 operating system to come out of Palo Alto, named SCOPE 3.0, was a disaster. Palo Alto programmers had not only added a lot of features but also made fundamental changes in the file structures, etc., making the conversion from programs running under SCOPE 2.0 to those running under SCOPE 3.0 a major effort. The new system was so full of errors that a number of customers underwent the painful conversion process *back* to SCOPE 2.0 so they could get their jobs to run. Eventually SCOPE 3.0 was cleaned up, and it became quite a good operating system, but the period was difficult for those of us who had to explain to customers why Control Data had had *two* operating system fiascoes with the 6600.

About this time I became aware of a quiet bootleg activity taking place in the dead of night in the Arden Hills plant. A single dedicated engineer-turned-programmer was developing what amounted to his own operating system competitive with SCOPE! He worked at night when free computer time was available on machines undergoing checkout on the assembly floor. Like an owl, he would disappear with the sunrise. The test engineers and technicians working on the assembly floor were aware of Greg Mansfield's activity and welcomed it. If a computer in test failed while Greg was working on it, he would fix it. The computers that he worked on would always end up in better condition than when he started. This shadowy development gradually came to have a name—MACE. I caught Greg one morning before he went home to sleep. When asked the meaning of MACE, Greg replied that it had two meanings: the commonly accepted one of *M*ansfield *a*nd *C*ahlander *E*xecutive (Dave Cahlander was another brilliant engineer who sometimes helped Greg) and the real meaning—a large spiked club with which to beat SCOPE over the head!

Greg Mansfield's method of working was classic. He worked totally alone except for occasional consultation with Dave Cahlander and one or two others whom he respected. He started with an enhanced version of CHOPS, similar to SCOPE 2.0, and improved it on a cautious, step-by-step basis. Convinced that the developers of SCOPE 3.0 were going in the wrong direction, he took great pains to keep his operating system lean, finely tuned, and fast, adding only modest feature and performance improvements. I once drank coffee with Mansfield and Cahlander in the Arden Hills cafeteria while they argued the best possible sequence of instructions to perform a simple function in the operating system—determining a count and setting it into a storage register. Mansfield's sequence of instructions to do the job took eighteen minor cycles of computer time. Cahlander's entirely different approach required only seventeen minor cycles. They agreed to use Cahlander's sequence. A minor cycle of the model 6600 is one ten-millionth of a second!

Greg did all his programming from the CRT console of the 6600 under test. To avoid having to leave the console to punch cards and thus break his chain of thought, he had written a small program (called 029 after a popular model of IBM keypunch) that effectively converted the entire 6600 computer system into a keypunch. He would key in the program modifications from the console keyboard and cause the 6600 to punch out the cards on its attached model 415 high-speed card punch. Greg would select a small portion of the base operating system that he thought could be speeded up or enhanced. He would then recode this section and test it. If it worked as planned, he would integrate it into the operating system replacing the old routine and test again. To verify that he had not introduced "bugs" that would affect the operation of the unmodified portions of the operating system, he would run a set of programs he called his "garbage dump," using the newly modified operating system. The garbage dump was a collection on magnetic tape of all the programs he could find that had caused earlier versions of the operating system to fail. Greg was always on the lookout for more garbage, and he urged any user having problems with MACE to save the failing routines for him to add to his dump. The garbage dump would be run using the modified operating system for some hours or days until Greg was convinced that the new system was as stable as the old. He would then select a new section to improve.

MACE, while lacking some of the features of SCOPE, ran customers' jobs substantially faster. It was often used to run customer benchmark programs. Many prospective customers visited the Arden Hills plant, accompanied by their Control Data sales representative and a programmer analyst from their local sales office. Usually they brought with them their most important production programs, mostly written in Fortran, on magnetic tape or cards. Engineering and scientific users have an insatiable appetite for computer speed, and the stopwatch timing of these important programs was a major factor in deciding which computer to buy. If the initial run of these programs using the SCOPE operating system did not time out fast enough, the benchmark lab people had available tapes of MACE. The problem was, if the customer impressed by the benchmark performance bought a computer system, the sales rep had to tell the customer that only SCOPE was a standard operating system supported by Control Data. MACE had no official standing whatsoever. Inevitably, sophisticated customers demanded and got tapes of MACE, standard product or no. This problem was soon to be corrected.

In an attempt to reduce the high cost associated with the system manager functions, Control Data now split the rapidly growing Computer Systems Division into two divisions. The Standard Systems Division was to handle most of the 6000 series computer orders that utilized only standard, off-the-shelf hardware and software products. Standard systems were to be handled on more or less of a production line basis with minimum system manager involvement. Standard systems ranged in selling price from $1.5 million to perhaps $5 million. "Special" systems, which to be so classified had to include major new or modified products, were to be handled by system managers as before, with the extra handholding believed necessary for these more complex and usually higher-dollar-value systems. Special systems ranged in selling price from $2 million to a three-mainframe complex selling for $20 million. Nate Dickinson and I were to be part of the Special Systems Division, as our product management function was not considered necessary for the standard computer systems.

Each month the sales force had to submit a prospect report through the marketing organization chain of command. This report listed each prospect for a 6000 series computer system, the likely configuration and selling price, the projected date of order, the probability of closing the order, and the primary application for which the system would be used. These prospect reports would go to the two systems divisions, and the two general managers would sort out which systems were to be assigned to which division. There were many borderline cases, and a lively competition between divisions soon developed. Nate's group, which had now added several senior engineers and programmers, gained a reputation for aggressive sales support. The field sales reps, who had an excellent grapevine and who wanted all the free sales help they could get, soon learned to bend the ground rules in order to get their customers assigned to Special Systems Division. After jurisdiction was established, I would call the sales rep long distance to discuss the customer's application and the best configuration to solve it. Sooner or later a face-to-face visit with the customer was required. Some customers would want to come to Arden Hills with their benchmark programs, and in these cases I would coordinate their visits and line up the appropriate technical specialists to talk with them. More often, visits to the customer site and presentations of our proposed hardware and software configurations were called for.

Field sales had three levels of technical support available to help close a sale. The first level was the local field analyst force. These were programmers and computer system analysts who worked in the same local office as the sales rep. They were available to do programming under contract to the customers and to support the rep's presales efforts. The next level of support was the division product manager. As a product manager I was expected to have a good general knowledge not only of the current hardware and software products but also of those products under development and those special products being custom designed for other customers in similar industries or with similar applications. Through the product manager the sales rep had access to the ultimate technical resource, the engineers and programmers who actually designed the products. The latter resource was used with great care. Not only was it undesirable to take them away from their projects often, but also highly technical people tend to be honest in the extreme. Horror stories abound of design engineers who, in front of the customer, voluntarily detailed all the shortcomings of their equipment, contradicted what the sales representative had just said, and told the customer that he didn't know what he was talking about! Selection of technical people to make customer presentations was wisely left to a product manager who knows the people. The product manager would brief the engineers and programmers on what to say and stay with them in the customer's presence, prepared to kick them under the table if necessary!

After a few months at Special Systems Division I had picked up enough knowledge of the 6000 series product line to handle the hardware portion of nearly any sales presentation. I already knew the peripheral products, but my knowledge of software was weak. When visiting customer sites, I would either depend on a strong local programmer analyst to handle the software questions or bring along a senior programmer or a programming manager to handle the software part of the sales presentation. The 6000 series was selling well, and I often traveled to customer sites: BAPL in Pittsburgh, Goodyear Tire and Rubber in Akron, Combustion Engineering in Hartford, Rome Air Development in Rome, New York, and Battelle Memorial Institute in Columbus. This period was pleasant. The customers were always technically sharp and asked hard questions, but they were never hostile. I learned all sorts of interesting things in discussing their applications, for instance, how a computer is used to calculate the neutron flux density in a nuclear reactor and why a computer is useful in designing a tire tread pattern.

Customer objections to the Control Data systems proposed almost always centered on deficiencies in our software. Usually the customer wanted a compiler or a file management system that IBM offered and CDC did not yet have. The hardware came in for little criticism, so I had the easy part of the presentation. I came to have a respect and even a liking for most of the customer personnel that I dealt with.

One exception is instructive, however. I was once called on to make a presentation in lower Manhattan to a prospect who was considering a large 6000 system for processing brokerage transactions. Without much more information than this to go on, I arranged a visit, taking with me a programming manager from Special Systems Division to handle the software questions. No sooner had we sat down in the customer's office that I sensed that we were in trouble. The customer, a vice-president, was himself quite savvy technically, and he had with him in the meeting a senior programmer from his organization who had thoroughly studied all the Control Data programming manuals. They were not only primed for our visit but hostile. I got off comparatively easily describing the hardware, but the customers asked incredibly detailed questions about the software. They wanted to know *exactly* how certain routines operated, and they were sarcastic when the programming manager could not explain. At a post-mortem meeting with the salesman after this ordeal we decided that the MACE system was needed for this application and that we had better throw in the first team, that is, Greg Mansfield and Dave Cahlander, if the situation was to be saved.

Back at Arden Hills I had some misgivings about bringing two of the most technically oriented men in the division into this customer's office. They would have the answers, I was sure, but how would they react to this customer's aggressive style of questioning? I need not have worried.

I sat down with Greg and Dave over coffee in the cafeteria and explained the application and the fact that the customer was technically sharp but disagreeable. Dave Cahlander was of medium height, with blond hair and rimless glasses, a somewhat pudgy face, and a cherubic smile. I had known him for several months before I learned that he had a Ph.D. in electrical engineering. I had always thought of him as a programmer, which indeed he was—the best in the division in the area of input/output programs. Dave had a bad reputation with the secretaries, some of whom refused to enter his office. He had a great interest in bats and had written his thesis on the bats' echo-location abilities. Several specimens of long-dead bats hung on the walls of his office, which accounted for the reluctance of the secretaries to enter. At one time we had a "bat alert" when a bat somehow found its way into the Arden Hills plant; Dave rushed out of his office urging people not to kill it. Later Dave Cahlander became Control Data's chief guru on computer chess. An expert player himself, Dave worked with Control Data customers who had written computer programs to calculate chess moves in games that were played against other computer chess programs and against human players. The best computer chess programs can easily defeat 90-odd percent of all human chess players, but no computer program has yet been able to defeat the top-rated chess masters. As a leading expert on computer chess, Dave has taken part in matches against such world champions as Boris Spasky.

Dave told me not to worry; he and Greg knew how to handle this type of customer. The next week Greg and Dave packed up their documentation, consisting largely of a computer printout of MACE, and we left for New York City. In the customer's office, Greg and Dave displayed a skill that reminded me of an experienced vaudevillian handling a heckler. They had worked together long enough to have perfected the Tweedledum and Tweedledee routine. For those who have never seen it in action, it works like this: Tweedledum, in this case Greg, who gave most of the presentation, would be at the blackboard explaining a point. Suddenly the customer would interrupt with a question designed to throw the presentor off balance. Instantly Tweedledee, Dave, would interrupt the interruptor, amplifying or clarifying the question, while Tweedledum thought of the answer. They could play this back and forth indefinitely, never allowing the customer to sidetrack the presentation or, indeed, to gain control of the conversation. It was fun to watch. I leaned back in my chair and enjoyed the show.

Greg's command of his subject was most impressive. He could go to any level of detail, explaining exactly how the operating system worked and how every routine interacted with every other routine. He seldom looked at the MACE listings. His performance reminded me of George Cogar, although I do not think that Greg has a truly photographic mind. The customer finally ran out of questions and was forced to admit that, yes, MACE would be suitable for his application and Control Data people really did understand how their operating system functioned. To my knowledge this customer never did buy any system; his funding was not approved!

The presentation in New York gave me just that sort of satisfaction that I imagine a master carpenter feels when he selects just the right tool from his workbench and forms a piece of rough wood into a piece of fine furniture. Analyzing the customer application and situation and selecting just the right individuals to work on it was as much fun as the computer business has ever been. I was soon to need this ability to select just the right talented people in a much, much more difficult situation.

The story of MACE continues. Some time after the New York visit a data services company in Kansas City approached Control Data about using the model 6400 computer for time-sharing applications. Time sharing, or time slicing, is a technique whereby a large computer is used to work on a large number of small jobs at once. The concept was originally developed at Dartmouth University for running student computer programs. The key requirement is that the system must be able to switch from working on one job to working on another job every few thousandths of a second with minimum wasted "overhead" time. The time-sharing computer works on multiple small jobs in a round robin fashion, giving each job its attention for a preset number of milliseconds (thousandths of a second) before moving on to the next job, whether or not the first job is completed. This is necessary to prevent one long job from tying up the computer. The length of the compute interval, or "slice," is set such that the majority of small jobs can be completed in one time slice. Longer jobs, which are not completed in one slice, are suspended and their parameters stored until their turn on the processor comes around again. Computer systems into which remote users dial commonly utilize some version of a time-sharing operating system.

In 1967 Control Data had never thought of the 6000 series as suitable for time sharing. The machines were conceived and sold as "number crunch-ers," computers of great power for solving complex problems that can require hours of computing time. When the Kansas City customer called it to our attention, we took a second look and decided that the 6000 series did have the hardware features that would allow a rapid switchover from one program to another. The computers were suitable for time-sharing appli-cations. That these computers should be suitable for such widely differing applications illustrated once again the brilliance of Seymour Cray's design. The operating system presented another problem. The current version of SCOPE was deemed totally unsuitable. It was simply too slow in switching between jobs. MACE, which had been kept fast and lean, looked adaptable to time sharing. A contract was signed. A programming group, which included Greg Mansfield, was established, and the product manager handling the account coined the name KRONOS, for the Greek god of time. The KRONOS operating system worked well, the customer bought additional Control Data computers, and the KRONOS operating system became a standard product supported on a level equal with SCOPE. I found a fiberglass replica of a mace at a decorator supply shop. It was presented to Greg Mansfield with appropriate ceremony. He had scored one victory over SCOPE. He was to have another.

For some years both SCOPE and KRONOS were supported and enhanced equally. Control Data's own Cybernet data services centers offered SCOPE for batch, large-job customers and KRONOS for time-sharing customers. Finally it was decided that, coincident with the announcement of a new computer product line, the two operating systems would be merged into a single one combining the best features of both. The new operating system was to be called NOS, for Network Operating System. Because it was determined that it was easier to add SCOPE features to KRONOS than to add KRONOS features to SCOPE, the base product for developing NOS would be KRONOS. After some time the effort to combine the two systems was abandoned. The two operating systems had diverged so far that they could not be combined. NOS could not be designed so that it satisfied both existing SCOPE users and existing KRONOS users. Because the SCOPE users refused to go through the difficult and expensive process of converting their applications to run under NOS, SCOPE would have to be retained as a secondary operating system. Because Control Data had advertised that NOS was *the* operating system of the future, the embarassment had to be ameliorated by *renaming* SCOPE as NOS/BE for Network Operating System/Batch Environment. Greg had succeeded in destroying SCOPE in name even if he had not ended its use completely! Once again the dedicated product champion had triumphed over his committee-designed rival.

15

Visits to Chippewa Falls

If the Control Data sales force was doing its job well, it would determine the customers' requirements for new computer systems long before the prospects had formalized their requirements in written documents, Requests for Proposal, or RFPs. When we at Special Systems Division received an RFP from a customer with whom we were not already working, we referred to it as a "cold" RFP, and we assigned a low probability to a sale to that customer. Writing a formal RFP is a tedious and time-consuming task. Almost always the customer will accept the eagerly proffered assistance of a friendly computer sales representative in drafting the RFP. The sales rep, being no fool, will try to write into the "requirements" section of the RFP a number of hardware and software functions that *his* product line offers, ones that his competitors' product lines do not have. A favorite tactic of the IBM sales force was to write a requirement for a compiler known as PL/1, a compiler that IBM had developed and was promoting and one that most competitors did not have. Another trick was to require delivery in such a short time that only a manufacturer who happened to have the exact configuration in inventory could meet the required date of installation. An RFP that has been written with the aid of a computer sales rep is said to be "wired" for that manufacturer. It is not impossible to upset a wired RFP with a clever and competitive proposal, but it is difficult.

The desired situation, therefore, is to have the Control Data sales force doing the wiring or, better still, to persuade the prospect to dispense with an RFP altogether (which no one really wants to write anyway) and simply to negotiate a contract with Control Data. In theory all US government agencies are required to issue RFPs and to get competitive bids. In practice there are a number of loopholes that allow a "sole source" contract: urgent schedule requirements, compatibility with the customer's existing software programs, and national security considerations, for example. Control Data has always had close ties with the government agencies involved with cryptography, going back to the founding of Engineering Research Associates, and we sold many systems for these applications. The Control Data salesman having account responsibility for one of these agencies, a short, curly-haired man of Italian heritage named Chuck Puglisi, sold system after system without the expense and uncertainty of writing proposals. "Pug," as he was universally known, reputedly made more money every year than anyone else in Control Data, including Bill Norris. I worked with him briefly. He was worth it.

If a proposal had to be written, it might consist of anything from a two- or three-page letter detailing the configuration and price, to a set of four or five volumes and thousands of pages. A great part of the bulk of a thick proposal will consist of non-customer-specific information about Control Data, its product lines, its major customers, its financial stability, its quality and reliability standards, its maintenance organization, and so on. This general information, which is used repeatedly in successive proposals, is referred to somewhat contemptuously as boilerplate. One apocryphal story about the derivation of the term is that a number of years ago a government agency required more and more such information in proposals submitted until the resulting documents became of obviously unreadable length. One smart product manager, concluding that the agency must be selecting the winning proposal by weight, bound a sheet of iron boilerplate between the pages of his proposals and thereafter won every competition! The Control Data marketing staff at one time assigned a man to research successful and unsuccessful proposals in order to come up with tips for improving proposal writing. I sent him a stack of winning and losing proposals prepared by Special Systems Division, together with Lundstom's Law of Proposal Probability. This law reflected my experience: The thinner the proposal, the higher the probability of an order. The reasoning behind this is that the sales rep who really knows the customer's concerns will address only those issues in the proposal. All the boilerplate will be left out because it is unnecessary.

Control Data was usually competing with IBM and Univac. IBM had a fairly competitive product line in its System/360 when bidding against the lower models of the 6000 series, but nothing to match the power of a fully configured 6600 system. To compete at this upper end, IBM kept announcing new models at the top of the System/360 line (series 90 models), some of which were built in ones and twos and some of which were never built at all. Many people at Control Data, certainly including Bill Norris, strongly suspected that IBM was announcing these machines solely to dissuade customers from ordering 6600's. Another IBM competitive maneuver was to offer large "educational discounts" to colleges and universities buying IBM systems.

Stories that had leaked out indicated that IBM had suffered worse birth pangs with their Operating System/360 than Control Data had with the SIPROS and SCOPE 3.0 fiascoes. With their almost unlimited financial resources, IBM had simply kept pouring money and programmers into the development while offering interim operating systems to retain their customers. Eventually they made the Operating System/360 work. In my analogy of the development wedge, even the dullest, poorest directed wedge can be made to crack granite if it is hit long enough with a large enough hammer.

In 1968 Control Data filed a lawsuit against IBM claiming unfair competitive practices. I was one of the majority of Control Data employees who believed that IBM was probably guilty of some sharp practices all right but that they were much too clever to leave any evidence lying around where competitors' lawyers could find it. Besides, they could afford to outlawyer us by a ratio of ten to one! I expected that nothing would come of this lawsuit other than the enrichment of a great many lawyers. I was wrong.

Univac's competitive offering was the model 1108. I have already explained how Dick Karpen became a hero at Univac in absentia when the model 1108 became a big success. In bidding against either IBM or Univac, Control Data developed an effective strategy of stressing an "upward migration path." All computer system customers are convinced that their application is going to grow, that its usefulness is not fully appreciated, and that in three or four years they are going to need a much larger computer than the one they are currently buying. Control Data could not only offer them the powerful 6600 but also could show them the next generation, the new computer being developed by Seymour Cray at the Chippewa Lab, the incredible model 7600. True, the model 7600, earlier identified as the model 6800, was not completely compatible with the 6600 (some would claim that "almost compatible" is a logical absurdity; compatibility is a binary condition—either it is or it isn't), but the 7600 was more nearly compatible with the 6600 than, say, an IBM System/360 or a Univac 1108. The effectiveness of this strategy was much heightened by the eagerness of our prospective customers to visit the Chippewa Lab and meet Seymour Cray. Seymour was already famous among computer cognoscenti, and Control Data customers included the most sophisticated users in the industry. If everyone that wanted to visit Chippewa Lab had been accommodated, little work would have gotten done there, so Seymour had imposed a strict procedure for authorizing visits. It was said that Bill Norris himself could not visit the Chippewa Lab without first clearing the visit with Seymour!

For visitors other than Bill Norris, the procedure for getting approval for a visit required convincing the vice-president for marketing that the customer was seriously considering buying a large system (that is, the customer was not just sightseeing) and that the probability of an order would be significantly improved by a visit to the Chippewa Lab. If the vice-president gave his approval, then Seymour or his right-hand man, Les Davis, could be called to schedule a visit. Seymour usually came in around noon and worked until late at night, so visits were scheduled in the afternoons only. I made the trip myself only three times: once with a group of product planners to discuss the RSPPC controller, once with a group of US Army brass considering a large computer system, and once with the technical staff of Trans World Airlines, of which I have more to say in a later chapter.

Many visitors assumed that Seymour would have a full beard, shoulder-length hair, or some visible sign of strong individuality, not to say eccentricity. I recall one visitor to Arden Hills from Bell Telephone Labs asking if he "could visit Chippewa and meet your bearded genius?" He was disappointed to learn that Seymour is clean-shaven and the most average-looking man in any group. No one was disappointed in the approach to the lab, however. The ninety miles or so from Minneapolis could be driven in about two hours, or, if the visitors were short of time, a small commuter plane could fly us to the Eau Claire, Wisconsin, airport. The road to the lab branched off the two-lane road connecting the small towns of Eau Claire and Chippewa Falls, both of which are located on the Chippewa River. The approach road ran literally through a cornfield and narrowed to a single-lane driveway through the thick woods bordering the banks of the Chippewa River.

The lab building was a modest, single-story structure of concrete block and brick set slightly back from the steep bank of the river. Seymour's house was invisible in the thick woods on the other side of the road. The choicest view from the lab, on the side overlooking the river, was given over to a lunchroom for the employees. There was no food service in the lunchroom. Everyone brought sack lunches, but a refrigerator and a stove were provided, as well as a great view through the picture windows. A row of modest private offices ran along one side of the building. The remainder of the space was partitioned into a few large rooms where the design, assembly, and testing of the world's fastest computers took place.

Seymour, dressed in a sport shirt and slacks like the rest of the lab employees, would greet the visitors, then we would all sit down for a discussion of the new machine. No formal presentations were ever given when I was present, no slide projectors or charts were used, and Seymour's comments were so understated as to be almost comic. I remember an Army colonel asking what would be the performance of the model 7600 as compared to the 6600. Seymour replied that he would be happy if it just ran! Somehow the quiet, low-key discussions were terribly impressive. The image of a man who knew *exactly* what he was doing came across clearly to the visitors, as they told me afterward.

The visit to the lab concluded with a short tour of the facility and a look at the first computer under construction. Few employees were in evidence, just two or three working in each lab area or at their desks in silence. The total number of employees at the Chippewa Lab never exceeded thirty-five or so. One of the funniest documents in my collection of computer memorabilia is an internal IBM memo, which surfaced during the discovery phase of the various IBM lawsuits (figure 12). T. J. Watson, Jr., questions with acerbity just why such a small, low-budget operation as the Chippewa Lab developed the fastest computer in the world, while IBM's vast research establishment cannot. I believe that Seymour would say that Mr. Watson answered his own question.

The model 7600 was a physically beautiful machine. About six feet high, it had the shape of a hollow rectangle, with an open doorway in the center of one long side, startlingly similar to the Univac I and II, but the 7600 was slightly smaller and it was open at the top. It was also much better looking than the early Univac machines. The outside of the computer was composed of hinged doors of blue glass, matching the then-current Control Data styling theme, set off by panels of wood-grained vinyl. The center of the machine was totally open, forming a small room. The model 7600 was cooled by freon, as the 6600 was, so the computer was totally silent. One joke at the time was that, if a customer was really short of floor space, he could place the customer engineer's desk in the center of the computer, thus making him readily available if the machine failed!

The Seymour Cray of legend is somewhat different from the quiet, understated individual I met. While courteous with those seeking information, he could be brutal in rebuking what he considered technical ineptitude. Engineers who worked with him told of being "Seymourized" or "Scrayed" when their work fell short of his expectations. "Scraying" was the more serious dressing down that could leave even the strongest shaken. In deflating pomposity, Seymour had a gift for the scathingly sarcastic reply. Several "Seymour stories" give the flavor. I cannot personally attest to the truth of any of these. I can say only that they were recounted with laughter in the hallways by engineers at the time.

The first story goes back to Univac days, to the beginnings of the early transistorized computer, the M-460, which evolved into the NTDS computer. The Naval Electronics Laboratory (NEL) in San Diego dearly wanted to design this prototype NTDS computer. However, the Navy had wisely awarded the initial development contract to Univac, to a design group that included Seymour. At a meeting, the NEL technical staff, all pumped up with the latest buzz words in computer architecture, presented their ideas on features that the new computer should incorporate. All through the presentation Seymour sat in stony silence, not saying a word. When the last of the NEL presenters sat down, Seymour walked up to the blackboard. "I am sure that when you build your computer it will have all of these nice features," he said. "However, *my* machine is going to be very simple." And then he proceeded to tell them exactly how it was going to be.

The second story is the one that I have heard most often quoted. At the time that the model 6600 computer was under development, a feature called memory parity was much in vogue. Memory parity requires the addition of an extra bit to each word stored in memory. This added bit, called a parity bit, with related checking circuitry, serves to detect certain types of memory failure. Use of parity bits was, and is, universal in writing magnetic tape. Seymour did not believe it useful in his 6600 memory. When a visitor asked why the 6600 memory did not include parity, Seymour replied: "Parity is for farmers!"

The third story, my particular favorite, concerns a former vice-president of Control Data. This vice-president, having at the time only few and vaguely defined duties, decided one afternoon to drive out to Chippewa Falls to see the 7600 then under development. Without calling Seymour, this dignitary walked in past the receptionist to the computer room where the first 7600 was being assembled. As luck would have it, Seymour himself was working on the computer, his back to the door. "That is nice-looking mahogany paneling you have on the machine, Seymour," says the vice-president. *Without turning around*, Seymour replied, "You don't know your wood either!" (The vinyl is walnut patterned.)

The fourth story is of more recent vintage. A new semiconductor material, gallium arsenide, is coming into use as a replacement for silicon in some high-speed computer applications. Seymour was asked in an interview if he anticipated any design problems in using gallium arsenide components. Keep in mind that this is the foremost computer designer in the world being asked a serious technical question. "Well, once you learn to spell it," Seymour replied, "I don't anticipate any particular problems!"

I once had the opportunity to have a long lunch with a friend, an engineer who had worked for six years at the Chippewa Lab under Seymour. I got a vivid impression of what it was like to work in that environment. Seymour was a technical dictator, making all but the most insignificant decisions himself. He was unique among computer designers in the great personal attention that he paid to the physical packaging of the computer. He strove for the utmost in compactness, not for handsome appearance or low cost but because the ultimate limitation on speed is the length of interconnecting wires between the circuit elements. The 6600, you will recall, was shaped like a plus sign, the 7600, a hollow rectangle, the Cray Research model 1 (of which more later) is a capital letter C, the newest Cray Reasearch model 2 resembles nothing so much as a tropical fish aquarium also in the shape of a capital letter C.

Complementing Seymour's dictatorial direction of the design project was his willingness to admit his mistakes. Typically he would work a technical problem doggedly until he reached a dead end and slowly became convinced that the basic design direction was wrong. He would go home and sleep on the problem. The next day he would call the designers together and tell them: "I have decided that this approach is wrong. From now on we will do it this way," and he would proceed to outline the new design approach. That was the sum total said—no apologies, no rationalizing of an approach that may have cost months of time and hundreds of thousands of dollars—just: "That way was wrong; from now on we go this way."

In my opinion, that single character trait, the willingness to admit a mistake and get on with the job, would have ensured Seymour's success even if he were not a genius. The number of reports written to prove that "the engineering approach was right; it was the laws of physics that were wrong" would fill volumes. Every year hundreds of millions of dollars are wasted on development projects that are clearly and unmistakably doomed to failure because of the leader's ego and refusal to admit that a mistake was made. To my knowledge Seymour has never accepted a contract to design a computer to specifications written by someone else. He believes that people smart enough to write detailed specifications and to get them correct in advance of completing the design ought to design the computer themselves. His design approach is totally pragmatic. Whatever works best *is* the right way.

Seymour's dislike of what he considered unnecessary paperwork is also legendary. At one time Control Data held annual or semiannual planning meetings. At these meetings, which took several days and were held in a hotel ballroom, each division would make a presentation. Each would define its business areas, its goals for the coming year, new products under development, staffing levels, financial results, etc. These presentations, typically running from twenty to thirty pages per division, would be printed, bound in a large loose-leaf notebook, and handed out to meeting attendees. In the notebook for the December 1964 planning meeting, which I attended, was a tab labeled "Chippewa Laboratory." Behind the tab, a single page contained Seymour's contribution to the planning meeting: "Activity is progressing satisfactorily as outlined under the June plan. There have been no significant changes or deviations from the outlined June plan." That was all.

Although Seymour hated and refused to do unnecessary paperwork, he could and did write when he considered it necessary. I had for many years a copy of the reference manual for the 7600, an extremely detailed document filling a four-inch-thick loose-leaf notebook. This manual was, according to reports from Chippewa, written by Seymour personally, a few pages every night. He believed that this manual was necessary and that it was good discipline for him to document the computer as he designed it.

Figure 8
Control Data model 606 magnetic tape transport. Photograph courtesy of
Control Data Corporation.

Figure 9
Lloyd M. Thorndyke. Photograph courtesy of Control Data Corporation.

Phase 1. Engineering.

Phase 2. Production.

Phase 3. Test.

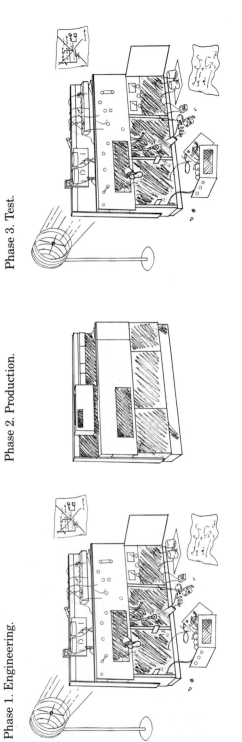

Figure 10
Cartoon: "Life cycle of the 915 Page Reader."

Figure 11
Seymour R. Cray at the console of the 6600 computer. Photograph courtesy of
Control Data Corporation.

MEMORANDUM

August 28, 1963

Memorandum To: Messrs. A. L. Williams
        T. V. Learson
        H. W. Miller, Jr.
        E. R. Piore
        O. M. Scott
        M. B. Smith
        A. K. Watson

   Last week CDC had a press conference during which they officially announced their 6600 system. I understand that in the laboratory developing this system there are only 34 people, "including the janitor." Of these, 14 are engineers and 4 are programmers, and only one person has a Ph.D., a relatively junior programmer. To the outsider, the laboratory appeared to be cost conscious, hard working and highly motivated.

   Contrasting this modest effort with our own vast development activities, I fail to understand why we have lost our industry leadership position by letting someone else offer the world's most powerful computer. At Jenny Lake, I think top priority should be given to a discussion as to what we are doing wrong and how we should go about changing it immediately.

                T. J. Watson, Jr.

TJW,Jr:jmc
cc: Mr. W. B. McWhirter

Figure 12
Memorandum from T. J. Watson, Jr.

Figure 13
Control Data 7600 computer. Photograph
courtesy of Control Data Corporation.

Figure 14
Control Data IATA ticket printer. Photograph
courtesy of Control Data Corporation.

Figure 15
CDC IATA ticket printer promotional cartoon.

16

Up, Up, and Away!

I would now like to lead you through the details of the longest, costliest, most technically challenging, most fun-filled, and ultimately the most heartbreaking technical proposal effort that I ever directed. It had a severe negative impact on my own career, and in reviewing the story, I cannot see where I could have done anything differently. It all began with a personal friendship.

Bud Feely, a senior member of the Control Data home office marketing staff, had once worked at Martin Marietta with Warren Koch, another computer specialist. Koch was now senior director (a title that corresponded with general manager at Control Data) of the computer center of Trans World Airlines. Koch called his friend Bud Feely and asked him if Control Data, as maker of the world's largest computers (the model 7600 had recently been announced), was interested in working with TWA in a study of an advanced passenger reservation system. When this request was forwarded to Special Systems Division, I was skeptical. Airline reservation systems take a lot of computer power all right, but they are a specialized application with which only IBM and Univac had any experience. Control Data had never implemented a system that even resembled an airline passenger reservation system. Why did TWA want to work with us?

Control Data had employees who had worked on the early Univac passenger reservation systems for Eastern, Capitol, and Northwest Airlines utilizing the Univac File Computer, a vacuum tube contemporary of the Univac II. These systems had kept only a seat inventory, a relatively simple task. I knew that the software for a modern passenger reservation system was unique and highly complex. According to computer industry gossip, IBM had spent eight years and tens of millions of dollars to develop the prototype of modern airline passenger reservation systems—the SABRE system for American Airlines. Only IBM's unwillingness to admit defeat and their unlimited financial resources had averted another classic software development disaster. Later, IBM generalized the SABRE software, named it PARS (for *Programmed Airline Reservation System*,) and sold it to most large American airlines. Univac had maintained a toehold in the market with a few US airline systems and had sold passenger reservation systems to several international airlines. No other US computer manufacturer was even in the game, so I believed at the time.

I met with Bud Feely. I told him that I was afraid a joint study with TWA would be a waste of time and money. CDC knew nothing about modern airline reservation systems, and that fact would become embarrassingly obvious once we started serious discussions with TWA. Bud assured me that his old friend Warren Koch understood our position. TWA had worked for years with Burroughs Corporation developing a reservation system using a one-of-a-kind large computer system called a D-830 built by Burroughs military division. The system was still not wholly operational, and TWA had some doubts about the ability of the Burroughs processors to handle the future growth of passenger traffic. Burroughs had no logical follow-up product to the D-830, and TWA had begun to realize that they had chosen to go down a blind alley. Koch's concern was to establish an ongoing relationship with a major computer manufacturer who would always have a newer and faster computer on the drawing board. TWA wanted powerful computers. We were soon to understand why.

Reassured by Bud, I began recruiting a technical team to make the first call at TWA's new computer center at Rockleigh, in northern New Jersey. A carnival atmosphere soon developed. With the scent of a large system order in the wind (a single 7600 sold for about $8 million at that time), every organization wanted to participate. The eastern marketing region having sales responsibility sent six representatives, home office marketing staff sent three, divisions responsible for remote terminals and printers sent one or two each, and Special Systems Division contributed hardware and software specialists. When we all met as arranged for breakfast at the Fort Lee, New Jersey, Holiday Inn, the delegation numbered twenty! This tendency to jump on the bandwagon when a 7600 sale was in prospect was later celebrated in a little ditty called the "TWA Flight Song" set to the tune of "Seventy-Six Trombones" from Meredith Willson's *The Music Man*:

7600 trombones led the big parade, With 110 marketeers close behind.

Todd Murphy, the eastern region manager, and I got this huge group somewhat organized, and we drove the few miles to Rockleigh. The computer center was housed in a new spacious building in a beautiful suburban industrial park. The TWA people, a little taken aback at the size of the CDC delegation, were cordial. They set up a number of separate discussion groups. TWA specialists in reservation software, communications, terminals, and nonreservation programs such as flight planning gave informal lectures on their plans and problems to the CDC people, who were broken up into corresponding groups.

Todd Murphy and I met with Warren Koch, senior director in charge of the entire computer facility. He was straightforward in telling us what he expected. He had instructed his people, he said, to give us all the information we wanted about TWA's present and planned computer system requirements. He even offered us office space in his facility if we wished to work there. In return he expected CDC to give him in four to six weeks a proposal telling him how CDC could solve TWA's advanced system problems using our largest computers. He was more interested in CDC's commitment and demonstrated understanding of TWA's problem than in specifics of configuration and pricing. An immediate system order was not in the cards, but TWA did want to make an early decision as to which computer vendor to work with over the long haul. TWA was also talking to IBM and Burroughs on the same terms. This was the essence of what Koch told me. Time proved that he was telling the truth as he saw it.

I met Koch's chief technical staff aide, John Hitch. Hitch, a large, balding man with piercing eyes, appeared to be another borderline genius. He was an engineer by training with a number of patents to his credit. He had worked for Burroughs before joining TWA. His particular area of interest was the reservation terminals and ticket-printing terminals, but he seemed to understand the entire computer system hardware and software. I was to spend many hours talking with him.

We toured the computer room, and I met "George," the name given to the entire Burroughs reservation system. I never did learn the derivation of that name. The computers—there were three to allow for continued operation in case of failure—looked like military machines. They were in plain gray metal cabinets. Most impressive was the row upon row of large disk files, dozens of them. They were of the type known as head-per-track, or fixed-head, faster in access time and more expensive than the more common moving-head disk files. Total storage capacity of all the disk files on George was two billion characters. The entire system was running, but only a few reservation terminals were hooked up for software debugging. TWA was not yet using the system for passenger reservations. Some smaller Burroughs computers in the computer center were in use for nonreservation applications. The computer center was equipped with an elaborate standby power generating system for use in case of power company failure. A power outage could otherwise shut down the entire airline reservation system, which could nearly shut down the airline. The whole installation at Rockleigh was first class; it was obvious that no expense had been spared. I began to feel more optimistic about the prospect.

At the suggestion of Warren Koch and John Hitch, our group also toured the TWA telephone reservation center in Manhattan before returning to Minneapolis. Because the George system was not operational, TWA reservations were made using a simple seat inventory system, not so different from that implemented by Univac for Northwest Airlines many years before.

The reservations agents, a large room full of them, answered telephone calls from customers and travel agents. In front of each reservations agent was a small special-purpose seat inventory terminal. The agent, wearing a lightweight telephone headset, would indicate the TWA flight desired by pulling a small plastic punched card from a box of flight cards and inserting it into the reservations terminal. The seat inventory computer would then respond with a green or a red light indicating "seats available" or "flight full," respectively. If the passenger decided to book that flight, the agent would push keys indicating "sell" and the number of seats wanted. The inventory computer would then decrement the "seats available" count. The passenger's name, phone number, etc. were written out by hand and filed by flight number and date. These cards were collected before flight time and a passenger list was typed up. Processing passenger reservations in this way required a lot of employees in the several TWA reservations centers and was particularly troublesome if a passenger called back at the last minute wanting to change reservations.

In order to shift more of the clerical burden from the reservation agents to the computer, The IBM PARS system, and the George system when operational, used a much more sophisticated PNR (for Passenger Name Record) system. With a PNR system, the reservations agent used a typewriterlike keyboard and a CRT display. (Some early systems used a keyboard and a printer, which was cheaper than a CRT in 1968.) Now the agent could make an "availability" inquiry by typing in the cities of origin and destination. The computer responded by displaying all flights between these cities on which seats were available, listed with the earliest time of departure first. When the passenger picked a flight, the agent typed in the name, phone number, connecting flights, etc.; the computer would automatically file the PNR according to initial flight number and date. If the passenger called back to change the reservations, the computer would retrieve and display the PNR to the agent. The passenger list for a flight would be typed automatically just before flight departure time. The time spent by an agent with each passenger inquiry was reduced, and more accurate records could be kept.

An interesting sidelight of our reservation center tour illustrated the competitive nature of the airline business in those days of airline regulation. The phone number listed for TWA reservations in the New York City telephone directory would connect the caller with the General Reservations area, where the majority of the agents worked. VIPs and major business travelers were given a different phone number, which connected them to Ambassador Service. A separate group of senior agents would give preferential treatment to the customers calling on this number. The really cute part is that TWA had a *third* telephone number, called Super Ambassador Service, the existence of which was carefully concealed from both the General Reservations and Ambassador Service customers. This number was given out only to the *really* important customers, who were given individualized services by a small group of the most senior agents.

The competitive factor, as our TWA contacts continually pointed out, was especially important on certain heavily traveled routes, because all the airlines were flying the same types of aircraft, with the same fares, on similar schedules. Certain straightforward competitive measures that would have attracted more customers, such as offering free drinks in tourist class, were forbidden by CAB regulations, so the airlines were spending a lot of money advertising what seemed like trivial advantages over their competition. The classic high-competition route, always used as an example, was New York to Chicago. Three major carriers, TWA, American, and United, competed head to head with hourly flights. Because each passenger lured from the competition represented almost pure profit (the cost of the meal, if any, was the only incremental expense), the three airlines were always searching for gimmicks to appeal to business travelers on this route.

After we left the TWA people at the reservations center, the Control Data group held a postmortem on the TWA visit. If we were to conduct a long-term study and write a proposal as TWA wished, we had to reduce our unwieldy group to a small nucleus dedicated to the TWA proposal and call in technical specialists as appropriate. I agreed with Todd Murphy, the eastern regional manager, that I should work closely with his assigned account salesman, Fred Bandierini, and that he in turn would call off the rest of his marketing people. We were lucky in the salesman assigned. Fred Bandierini was competent, hard working, and absolutely honest in his dealings with us, in contrast to some of the other New York area sales reps that I had encountered. As the chief technical coordinator, I had one overwhelming problem: where to find one or two really sharp software specialists who could intelligently discuss programming of the 7600 computer to perform passenger reservations. The programmers that I had taken with me from Special Systems Division confessed to being baffled by the problems of implementing a PNR system as described by the TWA specialists. In addition, the 7600 was so new that few in the division knew its inner workings well, and little standard software had been written to run on the 7600 thus far.

An airline PNR system is one of a class of computer applications known as transaction processing. Transaction processing systems have become commonplace, particularly in banks and other financial institutions, but the airline PNR systems were one of the earliest and certainly one of the most difficult for the computer system designer. A few illustrations will make clear just why it is so difficult. A major airline will have thousands of agent CRT terminals scattered around the country, all connected to the same computer system. TWA in 1968 was planning three to four thousand terminals on the George system; American Airlines was reported to have over fifty thousand terminals on their SABRE system in 1986. Because the airlines reservations agent has the customer either on the phone or standing there at the counter, the answers to computer inquiries must be rapid. An absolute maximum delay of three seconds from inquiry to response is acceptable. An enormous volume of information must be stored in PNR records, amounting to billions of characters. Reservations can be made up to one year in advance, and they are kept in the computer system until after the flight has actually departed. Each PNR contains many pieces of information: name, phone number, complete travel itinerary, persons traveling together, fare quoted to the customer, dietary requirements, and special needs, such as a wheelchair, car rental, etc. The files containing the PNRs, the flight availability information, and fare data are all stored on magnetic disks.

Magnetic disk files provide a lot of storage capacity at a relatively low cost, but compared to the speed of the computer central processor, they are painfully slow. A large disk file might require only 50 milliseconds, 50 one-thousandths of a second, to fetch a particular record. The processor of the 7600 was rated at twelve million instructions per second, which is twelve thousand instructions per millisecond. Thus the processor is capable of performing 600,000 instructions in the 50 milliseconds that the disk file requires just to fetch one record. This great discrepancy in speed is the source of many complications. Imagine that reservation agent A makes a flight availability inquiry. The processor analyzes the inquiry, determines which records on disk files must be looked up, and commands the disk system to fetch the proper files (there may be several files needed for this one inquiry). All this processing requires only a few millionths of a second. The processor cannot simply wait until the files for A are available; agents B, C, and D are requesting information. The processor suspends operation on job A, stores away the inquiry and the partially completed answer, and works on the next inquiry, sending another request to the disk system for B's files. Hundreds of inquiries later, the files requested for agent A are delivered by the disk system. The processor again suspends whatever it is working on and completes the transaction for A. The process resembles a master juggler, who can keep a whole set of dishes in the air at once while balancing a pencil on his nose! Adding to the complexity is the requirement that a computer failure at any time cannot cause the whole system to stop or to lose reservations already made. This is a little like requiring the juggler to skip rope while performing his other feats! This last requirement is met by having at least two processors operating all the time, with provision for one of them to take over the whole load automatically if the other processor fails. Duplicate copies of all vital records are also kept on separate disk files.

The thoughtful reader may ask why the PNR files were not kept in the computer's high-speed internal memory so that the computer could simply process each transaction through to completion without the need to constantly switch between jobs. The answer is cost. Memories of the size needed were, and still are, prohibitively expensive. Semiconductor memories are now dropping in cost so rapidly that we may soon see internal memories used for all but the largest files, with a resulting simplification of transaction systems.

At the end of the three-day visit, our Special Systems Division group returned to Minneapolis. I realized that the TWA proposal effort was going to be lengthy, expensive, and political. Still, I was excited and wanted to lead this challenging program. Accordingly I wrote my trip report with great care and extraordinary detail, and I sent copies to Special Systems Division management, our vice-president, and his boss, the group executive. The group executive was Paul Miller, who had been general manager of Nate Dickinson's division in La Jolla. Paul Miller was of medium height, with brown hair and piercing blue eyes. He was a graduate of the US Naval Academy, a former test pilot, and the finest executive that I have ever worked with. The action of his mind I would liken to a zoom lens: He could zoom in on the smallest detail of a job, ask probing questions, and then seemingly without effort zoom back to see the big picture of overall corporate strategy. I was careful to keep Paul Miller well informed of each step of the study, as I could foresee a time when I would need his approval to submit a proposal that would commit Control Data to a large development program indeed.

I started making the rounds of my contacts among the sharpest software people in Control Data, looking for the best person to take on the PNR system design. My old friends Greg Mansfield and Dave Cahlander could not help; they did not know how to approach the problem. I visited a project within Special Systems, which was working on a classified, large dual-computer system for Chuck Puglisi's customer. There I found a friend from my Univac days. Vic Benda was not a Control Data employee but was working as a consultant on this project. Vic was vice-president of a (then) small software company called Analysts International Corporation (AIC), another spin-off from Univac St. Paul. AIC had specialized in hiring only top, experienced programmers, who they then contracted out to companies that needed their particular talents. Vic and I had worked together briefly in attempting to sell military computers in the post-NTDS days.

Vic Benda is tall, with black curly hair and an easy-going manner. His hobby is collecting Chevrolet Corvettes. He usually has one or two for driving and eight or ten, of different model years, in various stages of reconstruction. On weekends he attends swap meets where he trades hard-to-find parts with other Corvette collectors. Of all the software experts I have known, Vic has the widest range of knowledge. Others may be stronger in one specialty or another, but no one seems to have such a grasp of *all* software. As soon as I described the PNR application as I was just beginning to understand it, Vic picked up the key problem areas and started hypothesizing solutions. Vic had been working with a senior CDC programmer named Stu Rogers, who immediately chimed in with his suggestions. Their thinking aloud seemed to stimulate each other. I realized that I had found my team!

Vic and Stu proved to be not only sharp software designers but another Tweedledum and Tweedledee pair expert at making presentations, even more skillful than Mansfield and Cahlander, if that's possible. Their minds ran along parallel tracks at the same speed, so that one could almost finish the other's sentences. I begged their services from the project manager, who owed me a favor anyway, and set up the next trip to TWA.

Another stroke of luck favored my staffing effort. A young engineer named Ken Bach was assigned to the study proposal by the division having responsibility for the reservations terminals. Because of the large numbers involved, the potential terminals business exceeded the value of even a dual 7600 computer system. Ken was eager, technically sharp, and much impressed by John Hitch. The two of them soon fell into a natural disciple and master relationship. Hitch was pleased to have an attentive and admiring listener, and he spent hours giving Ken the benefit of his experience and thinking on advanced terminal systems. Ken then faithfully reflected John Hitch's thinking in the series of terminal proposals and sketches that he prepared. Vic and Stu were well received by the TWA software designers, and soon had their respect. The five of us—Vic, Stu, Ken, Fred Bandierini, and I—formed the nucleus of the study team. We all got along fine. It was just as well; we were to work together for month after frustrating month!

We began a series of weekly routine visits to Rockleigh. Typically our nucleus team, augmented by CDC specialists in communications, 7600 hardware, terminals, and programming languages, would spend three days a week at Rockleigh; then we would return to Minneapolis to get answers and to develop technical position papers. I have never worked harder in my life, nor have I had more fun. Our time at TWA was a continuous learning process with a lot to absorb. In Minneapolis I had to search out technical specialists, brief them on the system to be proposed, persuade their organizations to make them available, and work out jurisdictional disputes among divisions. I wrote my detailed trip reports on weekends.

Working so closely with the TWA people, we developed personal friendships, some of which have lasted to the present. We learned more and more about the airline business and about the lifestyle of the airline people. One thing I found hard to get used to was their attitude toward travel. The TWA pass privilege policy at that time was generous. Even the lower-ranking professional employees could go anywhere on the TWA system free or for a nominal charge. One of the programmers traveled nearly every weekend to London to see a play or a musical; he claimed it was cheaper than going to Broadway! All of the more senior people seemed to know their counterparts at the other airlines on a first-name basis. A lot of job-hopping took place. Industry conferences were held frequently—in such places as Bermuda and Hawaii. Why not, since the attendees traveled free? A clublike atmosphere seemed to exist even among bitter competitors.

As each week went by, our team felt more confident about the PNR application and about our system design, which was beginning to take shape. We discovered just why TWA was looking for the fastest computers in the world for their advanced reservation system. They really intended to make a leap beyond the PNR systems, which most of their competitors had already implemented, to a new, sketchily defined concept called PSS, for *Passenger Services System*. PSS had been outlined by a working committee of the International Air Transport Association (IATA), the leading industry trade group. It involved several steps in computer processing starting from the PNR: automatic calculation of fares, computer printing of tickets, automated passenger check-in, and automated post-flight-departure processing of tickets.

As every frequent air traveler knows, airline fares were then, and are still, a confusing mess. They change constantly, and on a trip of any complexity the traveler is likely to be quoted three or four different fares by different airlines or travel agents. What is more logical, then, than storing all fares as they are filed in a computer and letting the computer calculate the correct fare given the passenger itinerary in the PNR? Then, with the fare added to the PNR, why not have the computer print the ticket and do away with illegible handwritten tickets? IATA had defined two new ticket formats: (1) The "transitional" ticket is printed with the use of carbon paper between multipart forms. It includes four flight coupons and is fed through the printer on continuous-form stock. (2) The "full IATA" or "machinable" ticket is a dramatically different document, unfamiliar to most travelers. The flight coupons are not flimsy paper but cards, similar to punched card stock. On the back of each coupon is a magnetic stripe, similar in appearance and purpose to the stripes on the backs of most national credit cards. All the key information printed on the ticket is also magnetically recorded on the stripe. An IATA ticket must be printed and magnetically recorded one at a time, without carbon paper. A number of IATA flight coupons are then stapled or glued into a ticket booklet.

Only the full IATA ticket gave the promise of implementing automated check-in and automated post-flight-departure ticket processing because the magnetic stripe is computer readable using cheap, reliable technology.

We had earlier noticed on many of the desks at Rockleigh a miniature flagstaff. On the flag was the legend "TWA Innovates." What our friends at TWA had in mind was to leapfrog their competitors and be the first airline to implement a full PSS system. That was the reason Warren Koch wanted to discuss using only our largest computers and why he was concerned with

CDC's willingness to devote the time and talent necessary to pioneering new software and a whole range of ticket printers and terminal devices. A challenge more to the liking of our technical team could not be imagined. Each man worked like ten as we approached the six-week deadline for producing our study report. I had to give up my congenial role as technical coordinator and become a serious author. While Vic, Stu, Ken, and the rest were preparing drafts on their portions of the system design, it was up to me to write the connective material to turn the pieces into a unified document, edit the whole, get it printed, and obtain management approval to submit it. Fortunately I had been through this type of task a time or two, and so I knew where to place my priorities. The most important part of a proposal or study report is the cover! Customers love to see their name and corporate logo beautifully printed in color. A proposal with a handsome cover gets left out on a lot of desks to be admired and perhaps picked up by senior management.

As soon as I knew that we would be submitting a study report, I contacted a magician named Ed Schraut, our division technical publications manager. Ed was a genius at transforming a disorderly pile of draft material into a beautifully finished proposal on an impossible schedule. He started an artist working on the TWA name and globe logo, which was to be silk-screened onto a white vinyl loose-leaf notebook. In checking the progress of the cover I found that the artist had added the silhouette of a jet aircraft with its following contrail, very pretty. However, the silhouette was that of a type of aircraft that TWA did not fly! The customer would have spotted that in an instant. The silhouette was changed to that of a TWA type aircraft. You have to watch every detail in the proposal business!

Because I knew that some technical sections would be submitted late, I had lined up several typists to work overtime and a drafter to draw bar charts, organization charts, and system configuration diagrams. I took my phone off the hook, chased all visitors away, and in three days had a draft ready to go to the printers. There remained only the problem of getting management approval to submit the report. Here my careful preparation in distributing trip reports paid off—our two levels of vice-presidents were well briefed in advance and needed only to review a summary of commitments that I abstracted from the 200-odd-page report. A 45-minute presentation served to get Paul Miller's approval. Our study team loaded up two large cardboard cartons with copies of the printed report in its vinyl notebook and took off for Rockleigh.

If I had thought that submitting our study report would cause a change in our method of operating, I was soon enlightened. Warren Koch was pleased with our responsiveness but told us no recommendation to his management could be made until IBM and Burroughs had submitted their reports as well. Both were running far behind CDC in schedule. In the meantime we were asked to give a series of presentations elaborating on our study and to consider some new alternatives for reservation terminals, including using the existing Burroughs CRT terminals on our Control Data computer system. Things went on much as before.

17

We Shall Never Surrender!

The TWA study report had estimated that 2½ to 3 years would be required to implement an advanced reservation system on dual 7600 computers, so an interim system solution had also been proposed. The concept was that the George system would continue to process reservation transactions while a dual 6000 series computer system wired directly into George would calculate fares and print tickets. The 7600 system would eventually perform all PNR and PSS functions in the final system. The terminal equipment and many of the computer peripherals would be the same for both the interim and the final systems. Although the majority of the TWA staff at Rockleigh continued to struggle to get the George programs operational, the advanced planners turned to a detailed study of the fare-quotation and ticket-printing problems.

Control Data had a leg up on the airline fare-quotation problem, which was horrendously complex. Long before the TWA involvement, Control Data had bought a small company called SAFIR, Incorporated, which was doing small-scale airline fare construction on a data services basis. Our study team added Ken Haeberle, a programmer analyst who had worked on SAFIR, to the nuclear group. Design of the ticket printers presented another personnel staffing problem. TWA had decided to bypass the transitional ticket altogether and to go from the then-current handwritten tickets to the full IATA tickets. Technical representatives from the Control Data Printer Division in Rochester, Michigan, confessed to being baffled by the problems of handling and magnetically recording on card stock. They suggested that we contact the Magnetic Tape and Card Products Division in Valley Forge, Pennsylvania. My telephoned request brought Bob Oslin, an engineering manager from Valley Forge, to our next meeting at TWA.

Bob Oslin, a short, curly-haired, soft-spoken Virginian with the courteous manners of a Southern gentleman, was a mechanical engineer by training and a wizard at designing ingenious mechanisms; he was also extremely persistent in seeking solutions. He and Ken Bach immediately recognized each other's complementary talents, Bob in mechanisms and Ken in electronics. John Hitch, recognizing that he had some extraordinary talent to call on, began adding more and more constraints to the requirements for the design of the IATA ticket printer. Meeting all eight of his constraints would require an ingenious design.

1. The ticket printer must fit into a standard TWA ticket counter, with the same height and depth as the counter and absolute minimum width. The top of the printer should be usable as working space for the ticket agent.

2. The printer must use individual card stock, not a continuous roll or Z-folded stock. The reasoning behind this requirement is that any type of continuous form must be used up before it can be replaced. Because the number of coupons in the next customer's ticket cannot be predicted (it depends on the number of flight segments), a printer using continuous forms will most likely run out of stock in the middle of printing a customer's ticket. This is irritating to both the customer and the agent.

3. The printer must hold enough stock under lock and key to last for a typical eight-hour shift at an airport ticket counter. This is desirable because access to unprinted stock could be limited to a few supervisory personnel; this would reduce the risk of blank ticket stock being stolen for ticket counterfeiting.

4. The ticket agent or supervisor must be able to add more ticket stock without stopping the printing of tickets.

5. Tickets with magnetic recording errors must be detected and retained in the printer, not issued to the agent.

6. The printer must bond any number of individual coupons up to fifteen into a booklet inside the printer without agent intervention. There was a legal requirement for not delivering the loose coupons to the agent to be stapled. As I understand it, there are cases in which a shuffling of the sequence of the flight coupons could result in a different legal fare. The fare as computed applies to only one particular sequence of flight coupons.

7. The printer must have a provision for an optional magnetic credit card reader. Credit card reading is an entirely separate function from ticket printing, but it would be convenient to combine the two devices for the agent's use. If a passenger pays by credit card, the credit card number is captured by the computer and printed in the "form of payment" block on the ticket.

8. All normal servicing of the ticket printer must be done from the agent side of the ticket counter without having to pull the printer out into the working space behind the counter.

These requirements were not thought of all at once. As John Hitch thought up more requirements, Bob Oslin would return to Valley Forge, make more mechanical drawings, and take them back to Hitch for further give-and-take discussion. At one meeting, Bob arrived with what looked like a large cardboard box. It proved to be a mock-up of the ticket printer mechanism. Although mostly made of cardboard and tape, it did contain some actual components. It was ingenious, the finest mechanism design that I had seen since the model 405 card reader. The card stock was stacked in the bottom of the printer. The cards were picked one at a time from the bottom of the stack, wrapped around a large-diameter rotating drum, and moved vertically past the magnetic recording head, the read-back head, the printer mechanism, and the coupon-bonding station; the finished tickets then popped up through the top of the printer like a piece of toast. Every one of Hitch's design requirements was met. We had a workable design concept for an IATA ticket printer!

About this time I was asked to make a formal presentation on the proposed TWA system at the Control Data Annual Planning Meeting. Planning meetings had grown to be large affairs with several hundred executives, including Bill Norris, attending for two or three days. Our TWA friends contributed a set of 35 mm slides illustrating the concepts of PNR and PSS. With Ed Schraut's help, I had additional slides made up, showing the background of our involvement with TWA, the George system, and the proposed Control Data 7600 system. The presentation seemed to go over well. I heard afterward that Bill Norris had liked it. In any case I had little trouble getting cooperation from other divisions after the presentation.

Another organizational tremor struck! The entire Special Systems Division was to be moved to a new plant in Sunnyvale, California, near Palo Alto. The story told at the time was that Control Data top management had decided that the computer systems divisions should be spread around the country rather than concentrated in Minneapolis–St. Paul. A small company acquired in Arlington, Virginia, was to serve as the nucleus of an East Coast systems division, Special Systems at Sunnyvale would become the West Coast systems division, and Standard Systems at the Arden Hills plant would remain as the Midwest systems division.

Special Systems Division had grown into a powerhouse in its short existence, two years or so. It included a small but competent design engineering group, a programming group, several special-project groups, systems management, product management, accounting, and other support groups. Morale was high, and the system order backlog was rising dramatically. It is easy to judge when the morale of an engineering group is high. Just listen to the conversations in the hallways and in the lunchroom. If the engineers are talking about their projects, morale is high. If they are talking about fishing or baseball scores, morale is so-so. If they are talking about company management and organization, look out—morale is poor. In Special Systems Division all the engineers were talking about their projects.

I had noticed at Special Systems Division, as on the NTDS project at Univac, the extreme ease of formulating solutions to customer problems when the engineers and programmers are in adjacent offices. If the engineers and the programmers drink coffee together, then each looks on the other group as teammates rather than as rivals for R&D funding. Many a design problem was solved without even a formal meeting; it was only necessary to collar a key programmer and an engineer, drag them to the nearest blackboard, and let them work out a solution. One suggestion led to another, compromise was soon reached, the programmer would change her code a little bit, the engineer would change his logic circuitry a little bit, and the problem would melt away with nary a trace. Quite a number of hardware and software products that had been developed in this way as specials for particular customers had proved to be so cost effective that they replaced standard products in the Control Data product set. Special Systems had proved to be particularly effective at designing the hardware and software used to connect multiple remote satellite computer terminals and CRT terminals over telephone lines to Control Data 6000 series computers.

In the last full year of operation at the Arden Hills plant, Special Systems Division had booked system orders totaling $70.1 million, a figure that worked out to nearly $1 million per month per product manager. We thought that this called for a celebration, and so we held a Product Management banquet at a fine restaurant in Minneapolis. A large cake with the legend "$70.1" was the featured attraction.

The TWA effort, still operating without a contract, was to be continued, based in Minneapolis as a new operation that later became known as Airline Systems Division. A new general manager, a man who had recently headed a large project for the US Post Office, was appointed to head Airline Systems. Vic, Stu, Ken Haeberle, and I were to report to him; Ken Bach and Bob Oslin continued to report to their own divisions. Work was to proceed as before except that we were severed from the Special Systems organization. In retrospect, this was a serious mistake.

The corporation made every effort to encourage all the Special Systems Division professional employees to move. For some reason it proved almost as difficult to get Minnesotans to move to California as it is to get Californians to move to Minnesota. Greg Mansfield and Dave Cahlander were among the key employees who refused to move. Nearly the entire Special Systems engineering group resigned. They started a small company named Astrocom, which was to design and build communications equipment. The Special Systems people who did move were installed in a fine new plant in Sunnyvale, but the drive and momentum of the group had been lost. Eventually the general manager and a number of the other senior employees drifted back to the Twin Cities one by one. The organization never recovered its former vitality.

The new general manager of Airline Systems brought with him two colleagues to serve as programming managers (Vic Benda could not serve as a manager because he was not a CDC employee) and a senior electrical engineer named Jack Keilsohn. Jack was a specialist in communications, and so he was sorely needed. He had wild hair like a haystack, a florid complexion, a loud voice, and an excitable manner. A more unlike pair than Jack and Bob Oslin could not be imagined, yet they immediately respected each other and worked in harmony. Ken Bach also instantly discerned Jack's technical competence, and soon all three worked as a team on the terminal and ticket-printer designs.

Our design team had long since exhausted the restaurant possibilities in the vicinity of our first headquarters motel in Fort Lee, New Jersey, so we were now staying in Manhattan. We had to have a rental car in any case, and our commute from Manhattan to Rockleigh was against the prevailing traffic and not too time consuming. The TWA staff and Fred Bandierini were homebodies who left us visitors to our own devices by 6:00 P.M. every night. Our usual routine was to return to the hotel to clean up and change clothes, then meet for cocktails and a leisurely dinner at which we would talk over the events of the day and plan our strategy for the next day's meetings. We had to be back at Rockleigh by 8:30 or 9:00 A.M., so we would break up by 11:30 at night.

A local New York district programmer analyst named Vince Pasquale had been assigned to work with us and to learn about the TWA system which he would eventually support. Vince Pasquale and Vic Benda are both of Italian heritage, both Corvette owners, and both big eaters. They got to joking one day about who could put away more food at a single sitting. The result was a challenge that entered company legend as "the great eat-off." The two agreed to have dinner at the famous Mama Leone's restaurant just off Broadway. The one eating the most, as judged by impartial observers, was to have his dinner paid for by the loser. I was one of the observers, there to eat and to judge but not to compete!

Mama Leone's is a large, rambling Italian restaurant that occupies room after room in the basement and first floor of a connected group of buildings in the heart of the theatrical district. It is popular with out-of-towners and New Yorkers alike for the great number of courses and the quantity of food served. The meal began with a big block of cheese, at least two pounds, a loaf of Italian bread, and a large dish containing iced celery, olives, radishes, and the small pickled peppers—pepperoncini. We hadn't even ordered yet! Vic and I are particularly fond of pepperoncini, and soon we ate all those on the table. Vince Pasquale called the waiter over and asked him to bring more pepperoncini. The waiter went off muttering to himself in Italian. Unfortunately for him, Vince understands and speaks Italian, and he answered the waiter in Italian. He had called us pigs! He hadn't seen anything yet!

Vic put on a virtuoso performance. As I recall, he ate three pasta courses in addition to all the other courses. After eating everything on his plate, Vic would mop the plate with the Italian bread, then eat the bread. He literally ate poor Vince under the table. Vince paid the bill, and we all waddled out into the night air, leaving the waiter shaking his head. I still talk to Vince from time to time. He has never forgotten that evening and always insists that he wants a rematch!

Finally the long-awaited letter of intent from TWA arrived. Letters of intent are commonplace when contracts for complex systems have to be negotiated and the customer wants the vendor to start work before the contract is completed and signed. This letter, a copy of which I still have, was gold plated. It was signed by Charles C. Tillinghast, Jr., chairman of the board of TWA, and was addressed to Bill Norris. It expressed TWA's desire to proceed with the development of the interim automated ticketing system with Control Data. The letter guaranteed payment of CDC's costs incurred up to $300,000 if a contract was not signed. We had an official go-ahead at last. It had been eleven months since I first walked through the doors at Rockleigh. The whole Airline Systems group adjourned for the afternoon to a local bar to celebrate. I felt a strange letdown, possibly a premonition. My personal prestige soared. I received a nice letter of congratulations for my personnel file from our group executive, Paul Miller, commending me on my efforts and promising to put my name in for another stock option. The complement that I treasured most, though, was a rather backhanded one from Ken Bach. He had told his manager, who repeated it to me, "Dave Lundstrom is in charge of this project, and he never seems to be doing anything, but the proposals get submitted on time and presentations get made to the customer, and TWA thinks that we are the most responsive vendor that they ever have worked with."

Airline Systems Division hired more programmers and dug into the writing of detailed program specifications for fare quotation and ticketing. TWA complicated the effort by deciding that they wanted to do on-line credit checks of passengers' credit cards, which proved to be far more difficult than it sounds. Organizational changes continued to impede our progress. Shortly before this time, nearly the entire management of the Data Display Division, our CRT terminal supplier, had resigned to start a new company called Data 100. This was the same management group that, when led by Malcolm Macaulay, had left Univac years before. In the reshuffle of personnel and the combination of divisions that followed, Ken Bach became disgusted and resigned to join a small local company. Ken continued to keep in touch for years afterward, always asking about Bob Oslin and the ticket printer. Luckily, Airline Systems had Jack Keilsohn to take over the engineering for the division.

In the midst of all of this activity I was stricken with a perforated appendix and spent three weeks in the hospital. I was much cheered to receive a get-well card signed by nearly the entire TWA staff that we had worked with at Rockleigh. When I recovered, I got even more disturbing news of reorganization. TWA's vice-president of systems and data services, Warren Koch's boss, had resigned. He was replaced by Robert Crandall from the treasurer's office. Crandall, much younger and more aggressive than his predecessor, was determined to get the status of the George system resolved one way or another. He must have been under intense pressure from the TWA marketing organization, which was beginning to suffer competitively from having only a crude seat inventory system while their rivals were using PNR systems. Crandall brought in outside consultants to evaluate George and resumed talks with IBM about installing a PARS system. All of a sudden the TWA staff, with the exception of John Hitch, became much more circumspect about telling us what was going on. Up to this time they had been open about their troubles with George, and they had indeed hired a CDC consultant to aid them in evaluating its performance. John Hitch, who I believe had an independent income and who certainly had an independent cast of mind, continued to speak to us as openly as before.

The end came quickly. Within a month after Crandall arrived, Control Data received a telegram telling us to cease the work authorized by the letter of intent. Fred Bandierini and I huddled to develop a strategy to stay in the game. Crandall was considering abandoning George altogether because, it now appeared, it would never be able to carry the full transaction load of TWA's passenger traffic. This would be a major decision indeed. TWA had invested a reported $37 million in Burroughs computers and terminals. If George was abandoned, TWA would surely buy an IBM PARS system. Control Data would have virtually no chance at all to sell a fare-quotation and ticketing system attached to an IBM system, given IBM's account control and TWA's management running scared. Our only hope was to keep George alive.

I preempted the services of Vic, Stu, and five of the top Airline Systems programmers, some of whom had reservations experience, and requested a formal meeting with Crandall. In one week we put together a polished presentation, proposing to do a study, to be funded by TWA, that would show in detail how the George system could be off-loaded by performing some of the reservations functions in an attached dual Control Data 6000 system. By taking some of the computational burden off George, we hoped to give it a useful life long enough to allow development of our advanced 7600 system.

The presentation took about two hours and was well received. Control Data soon was given a contract for the $90,000 we had requested to do the study. It was my last success at TWA. Before the study was completed, TWA had filed a lawsuit against Burroughs Corporation, charging that the capabilities of the George system had been misrepresented. The George system was turned off. The Rockleigh facility was closed and later sold. TWA installed an IBM PARS system in their new administrative building at the Kansas City International Airport (promptly dubbed KCAC, pronounced "casey-acey"). Warren Koch and John Hitch both resigned. TWA promptly paid Control Data the $300,000 due under their letter of intent and the $90,000 for the off-load study. I never received my Control Data stock option. Crandall did not stay long at TWA but moved on to American Express and is today chairman of the board of the parent company of American Airlines. The lawsuit against Burroughs was eventually settled, reportedly on terms favorable to TWA. Burroughs never again attempted an airlines reservation system.

Meanwhile, back at Control Data in Minneapolis, strange things were happening.

18

Reprise

Just when it seemed that the probability of Control Data selling anything to the airlines industry had dropped to zero, the corporation did a strange thing—it raised the stakes. Control Data bought a data service bureau located near the Atlanta airport from a firm called CCN. CCN offered full PNR reservations services to several of the smaller regional airlines on a per-transaction basis. The computers used by CCN for reservations were not Control Data computers or even the quasi–industry standard IBM System/360 computers. They were Univac model 494's. These machines, identified by Univac as real-time computers, were direct architectural descendants of the Univac model 490, which, in turn, was a commercial version of the long-ago NTDS computer. This acquisition was rumored to be highly controversial within the corporation; a story had it that Paul Miller, now head of all Control Data marketing, refused to attend the meeting at which the acquisition was ratified.

Shortly before the collapse of the TWA proposal, Control Data had hired a former vice-president of Eastern Airlines to be director of airline marketing. Now he was to move to Atlanta to spearhead the marketing effort for the CCN reservation service. I was offered a job working for him in Atlanta. My options were limited because my former division, Special Systems, had moved out from under me. I accepted the offer and set about trying to sell my house in Minneapolis. The remainder of Airline Systems Division was swiftly broken up. The general manager was to move to Atlanta to head the new acquisition there. He proposed to take with him some but not all of the key team members. Ken Haeberle was to move. Vic Benda returned to work at his own company, Analysts International. He was soon involved in a new project, about which the reader will learn more later. Stu Rogers was not asked to move and soon left Control Data. I protested vigorously to my management chain that a breakup of this team was most unwise. Vic and Stu were the heart and soul of our software capability, and if Control Data wanted to continue to pursue airline business, these two should be involved. I was overruled.

Once again Control Data increased its investment in airlines capability, buying a small consulting firm in Connecticut called Greenwich Data Systems. The staff of this company, all IBM veterans, claimed to be the original developers of the IBM PARS software. Whether or not this claim was true, I cannot say; I do know that the few people I dealt with were technically keen. The Greenwich group was not to be moved to Atlanta nor combined administratively with the remnants of the TWA project and the former CCN staff, now known collectively as Airline Systems Division. Greenwich Data Systems was to report to a different vice-president, also a former IBM employee, one who had joined Control Data when the small data services company he founded in Texas had been acquired. By these two acquisitions, Control Data had managed to create three airline-oriented groups, each somewhat suspicious of the other two and each partial to a different manufacturer's computers: Greenwich Data Systems to IBM, CCN to Univac, and the TWA veterans to CDC.

The Greenwich Data Systems (GDS) staff was soon launched on a proposal effort that was even longer and, I suspect, more costly than the TWA proposal. ASTA, the American Society of Travel Agents, is a trade group to which most US travel agents belong. GDS proposed to establish a central airlines reservation system, owned by Control Data, that would provide airline reservation and ticketing service to travel agents on a subscription basis. Agents signing up for this service would have one or more CRT terminals installed in their offices, connected to Control Data's central reservation computer. They would be able to see flight availability and to book reservations in the same way as airline reservations agents with PNR systems. Up to this time, travel agents had to telephone airline reservations agents to get flight availability and to book passengers, a time-consuming process. Automatic ticket printing was another time-saving option to be offered to the travel agents. In short, GDS would provide to the members of ASTA the same sort of service that CCN was providing to the small regional airlines. The pursuit of ASTA was by any standard a mink-lined effort. The ASTA executives were wined and dined; they lunched with Bill Norris in the boardroom, and they were given an elaborate multimedia presentation at the travel agent convention in Acapulco. The GDS people proposed to implement their reservation system on the IBM computers with which they were comfortable. Had they succeeded, the result would have been that Control Data offered airline reservations on the computers of our two principal competitors—IBM and Univac—but not on our own CDC computers!

Back in Minneapolis I was having trouble selling my house after a prospective buyer backed out of a deal. A budget crunch hit the group in Atlanta, and my job offer there was withdrawn. I was "between assignments" once again. The corporation had suffered several budget crunches during this "airlines" period. Twice the pay of all employees had been reduced by 10 percent for several months to save cash. At the same time a new fourteen-story headquarters tower was being built on the site near the old headquarters building. The new tower was sometimes referred to by employees, bitter at having their pay cut, as Norris's Last Erection. The building, sheathed in gold glass, turned out to be both beautiful and pleasant to work in, and it was probably wisely built during a period of recession. I visited with Paul Miller, and he immediately arranged for me to take a job as airlines industry manager in the Industry Marketing group, a staff planning function.

I traveled back and forth to Atlanta frequently as I tried to understand and coordinate the several airline efforts. On one visit Bob Oslin showed up in Atlanta with a surprise for us. Somehow he had managed to bootleg the funds to complete a working prototype of his IATA ticket printer—metal this time, not cardboard! Because the printer weighed four hundred pounds, rather than bring it to Atlanta, he had made a home movie, a super-8 mm film of the operation of the printer inside and out, complete with a magnetic credit card reader. It was a beautiful design and fully realized the promise of the design concept worked out with John Hitch. I fell in love with it and took every opportunity to promote it.

Bob and I, together with the airline marketing people from Atlanta, visited United Airlines in Chicago, Pan American and American Airlines in New York City, and TWA in Kansas City to promote the sale of the IATA ticket printer. Sometimes we took just the film and a brochure we had printed up; sometimes we shipped the prototype printer and arranged for connection over telephone lines to a Control Data computer for a live ticket-printing demonstration. Visiting TWA was interesting. Crandall, Koch, and Hitch were no longer there, but a number of other old friends were, including two former CDC programmers with the Airline Systems Division staff who had chosen to move to Kansas City rather than Atlanta. The Kansas City Administrative Center was thoroughly in keeping with TWA's tradition of first-class office buildings. It was a handsome, large, four-story structure, with an enormous atrium that extended to the roof. Behind the receptionist area was a large decorative pool; in the pool was an artificial island, and on the island, a full-grown palm tree. I offered to buy

TWA a monkey for their palm tree if they would sign up to buy IATA ticket printers!

Reactions of all the major airlines were similar. They admired the printer but did not want to be the first airline to implement IATA ticket printing. Everyone in the industry was keenly aware of the TWA–Burroughs debacle and of a United Airlines–Univac reservation system failure that had immediately preceded it. The financial performance of the airlines had deteriorated. No one wanted to pioneer a new concept. An applicable saying heard at the time was, "You can always tell a pioneer; he is the one with all the arrows stuck in him !" Because of interairline fare transfers, it is true that the full benefit of IATA computer-readable tickets cannot be realized until the majority of airlines are issuing them. No one wanted to accept the higher cost and risk of being first. Printing of transitional tickets, easier to justify costwise by the saving of ticketing agents' time, was beginning to be implemented. A number of small companies were offering low-cost printers for these nonmagnetic, multi-part-form tickets.

I approached the GDS group, hoping to persuade them to promote the IATA tickets with the travel agents as an option to their ASTA proposal. I was snubbed. The attitude of all the former IBM people involved in this proposal seemed to be, "IBM has studied the problem of ticket printing, and IBM has decided against the IATA ticket. IBM is always right. Who do you bush-leaguers think you are to try to advise us?" Greenwich Data Systems planned to bid transitional ticket printing.

Breakthrough came unexpectedly. Bill Norris had met with Donald Nyrop, then president of Northwest Airlines. The subject of their meeting was ways in which the two companies, whose headquarters are only a couple of miles apart, might do more business. Nyrop was given a demonstration of the IATA ticket printer. He was reported to have remarked, "Say, you can read this thing." Remember that IATA tickets are all original impressions; no carbon paper is used. Nyrop left the door open for Control Data to make a proposal to Northwest's vice-president of computer services, Bill Huskins.

I was not present at the Norris-Nyrop meeting, but I was part of the team that first called on Bill Huskins at the Northwest Airlines headquarters at the Minneapolis–St. Paul International Airport. In 1971, Northwest had the reputation of being the most frugal and one of the most profitable of the major airlines. The image of frugality was certainly confirmed by a visit to their headquarters. The facility was spartan. The floors were uncarpeted, the walls were bare of decoration, and there were few private offices. No four-story atrium with a palm tree at Northwest!

Northwest was one of the few US airlines that did not have an IBM PARS system. They had a PNR system using Univac 494 computers, the same model CCN used in Atlanta. Bill Huskins proved to be another one of those customers with whom it was a delight to work. He was technically competent, quiet and gentlemanly, and in complete command of everything in his area of computers and communications. His staff was much smaller than the data processing staffs at the other airlines we had visited, and all seemed to know their jobs well. After some months of negotiation an agreement was worked out between our two companies to test the IATA ticketing. Control Data would supply, at no cost to Northwest, two ticket printers and a controller to allow connection of the printers to the Univac 494 computers. Northwest would install the two printers at their main ticket counter in the Minneapolis–St. Paul International Airport. Northwest would program their computers, at no cost to Control Data, to calculate fares and format the IATA tickets. The magnetic credit card reader was not to be tested. Both organizations would publicize this test and would encourage tours by other airlines.

I had never considered Northwest high on the list of prospects for IATA ticketing because of their reputation for frugality and because they were not a PARS user. The IATA ticket printer, at that time projected to sell for about $15,000 each in large numbers, was two to three times more expensive than the much simpler transitional ticket printers. All of us at Control Data would have much preferred that the first ticket-printer customer be a PARS user because it would then be easier to sell other PARS-using airlines. I frankly did not understand why Northwest was willing to be the first to try the expensive and sophisticated IATA ticketing. After some months of working with Bill Huskins and his staff, I think that I began to understand his motivation.

Like his colleagues in the airline industry, he regularly attended conferences where representatives of the major air carriers gave presentations on their latest innovations in reservations and ticketing systems. I think the Northwest people felt somewhat like poor relations at the family reunion. They had to sit in the back row and listen while their more fortunate relatives boasted. Northwest's reservation system was comparatively modest, and the other airlines were not much interested in it anyway because the others were all PARS users. Many of the larger airlines were now in financial trouble, but Northwest remained profitable. The worm was about to turn. I believe that Bill really looked forward to standing before his peers and announcing that Northwest had scooped the industry, bypassing the transitional ticket and proceeding toward a full PSS system. He proceeded in a methodical and cautious way. Certainly he was aware of the disadvantages of being a pioneer. He brought up at every meeting problems that we had not yet thought of.

A controller device was needed to connect the ticket printers to the telephone lines, which in turn connected to the Univac 494 computers. The controller needed memory to store ticket formats, and it had to be capable of performing simple calculations. We elected to use a 16-bit-word minicomputer, the Control Data model SC1700. This computer was somewhat more powerful than needed, but it was the smallest, least expensive model in the Control Data product line. The SC1700 was mounted in a 19-inch-wide rack cabinet about six feet high. The size was no problem at the Minneapolis–St. Paul airport where Northwest had plenty of space, but it could be a problem at some of the smaller ticket counters around the Northwest system. The printers themselves, you will recall, were designed to fit into a ticket counter and not subtract from the available working counter space. The tops of the printers, at counter height and made of stainless steel, could be used as working space by the agent, except for the slot through which the completed ticket was delivered. This slot was surrounded by a raised collar, the purpose of which was to prevent coffee or any other liquid spilled on the countertop from dripping into the printer, another example of Bob Oslin's thoroughness. Two ticket printers were built at Valley Forge Division and integrated with the minicomputer at the Northwest ticket counter. IATA tickets were printed and sold to real paying passengers beginning in January 1973. Over 300,000 tickets were eventually produced by these prototype printers.

In March 1972 an appalling rumor swept through the hallways at Control Data—Seymour Cray had resigned! The rumor was quickly confirmed by a press release. The press release was worded carefully to soothe investor fears. Seymour was reported to be "phasing out" of full-time employment with Control Data. It was emphasized that development would continue at the Chippewa Lab. Trading in Control Data stock was briefly suspended.

Old-timers who had followed Seymour's career since his Univac days, many of whom had worked with him at Chippewa, were skeptical of the official statements. What could have caused Seymour to resign? He was, of course, a wealthy man from his stock holdings and could do what he wished. But because he had always done just exactly what he pleased at Chippewa, why should he resign to seek more freedom as his own boss? The statement in the press release simply did not make sense. Two rumors told to me at the time may have no truth whatsoever, but they do capture the flavor of the suspicions of many employees.

The first story concerns a Control Data senior financial executive who one day reportedly called Seymour at Chippewa Falls and told him that the lab budget would have to be cut by 10 percent. The Chippewa Lab, with its thirty-odd employees was certainly the most cost-effective computer development facility in the world. Certainly it was the envy of IBM, as attested to by the Watson memo described earlier. Seymour reportedly replied, "Fine, cut me and Les Davis out of the budget," and hung up the phone. This rumor was given credibility by the continuing budget crunches and by the fact that Les Davis, Seymour's chief assistant, did resign and join Seymour in his new venture.

The second story was told to me by a friend who had worked at the Chippewa Lab. He met Seymour in the hallway at headquarters one day. Knowing that Seymour hated being away from his work at Chippewa, he asked him what he was doing at headquarters. Seymour replied that he had been asked to serve on a senior technical task force that had been convened to recommend the future direction of computer development at Control Data. Seymour intensely disliked meetings and task forces, but he agreed to serve because he had been personally assured by a very senior executive that the recommendation of the task force was vital to the future of the corporation. The task force of seven members met for some weeks and concluded that the design direction being taken by the model 8600 (the newest machine under development at Chippewa, successor to the model 7600) was indeed the best architecture for future CDC computers. Just before the final report was submitted, the members of the task force received memos from a second senior executive thanking them for their efforts and stating that the corporation had elected to go in a different design direction. Seymour immediately resigned.

The further history of the Chippewa Lab is revealing. The same press release that announced Seymour's departure announced that the Chippewa Lab would now be headed by Jim Thornton, the number two computer designer at Control Data in terms of experience and prestige. Thornton had just completed design of the STAR 100 supercomputer under contract to the Livermore Laboratory. He stayed at Chippewa only a short time; then he resigned to found his own company, Network Systems Corporation. Chippewa Lab was then assigned to yet a third manager, who had a short tenure. The Chippewa Lab closed in 1974, and the plant on the bank of the Chippewa River was sold. The model 8600 was never completed. Engineers who saw an incomplete prototype told me that it had the shape of a derby hat with a blue Plexiglas dome over the center, dramatic and space-age in appearance.

Seymour Cray and some of his longtime friends soon founded Cray Research, Incorporated. It was privately financed for the first several years. The first chairman of the board of Cray Research was Seymour's former boss, Frank Mullaney. Seymour built a small lab in, guess where, Chippewa Falls and started work on design of, guess what, the world's fastest computer. It was named, appropriately enough, the CRAY 1. When Cray Research went public with a stock offering, the treasurer of Cray Research handling the sale was Noel Stone, my old boss from both Univac and Control Data. I was lucky enough to buy some stock shortly after the public issue. It proved to be a very good investment.

The CRAY 1 computer, first delivered in 1976 with a price of about $8 million, is surprisingly small. It has the cross section of a capital letter C, stands about six feet high, and is open in the center. It is freon cooled, as the models 6600 and 7600 were. A knee-high bank of power supplies surrounds the outer side like the brim of a hat. For the comfort of the service engineers these were upholstered in vinyl. This treatment resulted in a humorous nickname, The World's Most Expensive Wrap-Around Love Seat! The whole computer would fit in an average-sized room. The center of the C is a little too small to use as a customer engineering office! As happened at Control Data with the model 6600, the engineering group at Cray Research has broadened Seymour's original design of a single model computer into a complete family of computers of differing performance and price ranges. Apparently a Seymour Cray design remains so architecturally "clean" that it can be extensively modified without destroying its cost effectiveness. The CRAY 1 and its later derivatives dominate the world supercomputer market today, with an estimated 70 percent share.

The first model CRAY 2 supercomputer was delivered in 1985. Once again Seymour has pioneered a dramatic new cooling technique. The CRAY 2, built of logic circuits assembled in three dimensions, is completely immersed in an inert cooling liquid, which is circulated by a pump. The coolant, which was originally developed as a substitute for blood plasma, is so pure and inert that it could be drunk, inhaled, or injected into the veins without harm. I recently saw my first CRAY 2 at the Minnesota Super-computer Institute near the University of Minnesota. It has the same C shape as the CRAY 1, but it is dramatically smaller, about four feet high and three feet in diameter. The power supplies have been incorporated into the base of the C and are cooled by the same liquid as the rest of the computer. The outer skins of the CRAY 2 are made up of transparent panels, bolted in place with gaskets to retain the coolant. The circuitry can be seen immersed in liquid behind the panels. The CRAY 2 has a nearly incredible 256-million-word (not byte) memory included in this small package. It has already gained the nickname, The World's Most Expensive Aquarium!

Today Seymour's position is peculiar. After serving first as president and then as chairman of the board of Cray Research, he gave up all offices and administrative duties. He now serves as an independent consultant with a contract to supply computer designs to Cray Research. He is working on design of the CRAY 3, which will undoubtedly have still more surprises for the computer industry.

19

A Terminal Situation

My industry marketing group was one of the first to move from the old headquarters complex into CDC's new gold-glass tower in October 1971. I was just beginning to enjoy my fine view of the Minneapolis–St. Paul International Airport when the corporation decided that we could not effectively pursue so many priority industries. Airlines was to be one of those industries dropped, and my job with it. I was immediately offered another job as assistant to the general manager of terminals marketing, another staff job. I was quite knowledgeable about terminal equipment from all my proposal work with the Terminals Division, and this job would still allow me to keep involved with progress of the airline ticket printer, so I accepted. Because the general manager had a window office on the opposite side of the tower and my new office was across the aisle from him, I lost my view of the airport.

The term "remote terminal" as used in the computer industry can mean just about any device connected by means of telephone line, microwave link, satellite link, or what have you to a computer at a different location. A terminal is in some ways the most interesting hardware in a computer system because it is the interface between the user and the computer, often the only thing that the user sees, and it represents "the computer" to her. At Control Data in the early 1970s we catagorized remote terminals primarily as general purpose or application specialized. A general-purpose terminal was listed in the Control Data sales manual and was available for sale to any customer. General-purpose terminals were further divided into conversational, batch, and graphics terminals.

A conversational terminal is what most people think of when "computer terminal" is mentioned. Most have a typewriter keyboard and a CRT display (or in older systems a keyboard and a character-at-a-time printer). The operator "converses" with the computer by typing in an inquiry or command and receiving a computer reply on the screen within seconds. Airline reservation (PNR) terminals are conversational terminals, as are the time-sharing computer terminals used by students. Most conversational terminals use a so-called asynchronous communications protocol, a standardized sequence of bits sent over the telephone line to make up each character. The asynchronous communications protocol was developed years before the invention of the computer to send telegraphic messages between Teletype machines, which replaced the original Morse code "keys." When computers came into widespread use, there were tens of thousands of Teletype machines in use, and their owners quite naturally wanted these message devices to communicate with their new computers. The computer manufacturers all complied, and the "Teletype-compatible" (TTY-compatible), or asynchronous, communications format became a de facto standard. The capabilities have since been expanded far beyond that possible using Teletype machines, but the basic method of communication remains unchanged. The advantage of the asychronous communications format is that it is simple and inexpensive to implement and every computer manufacturer has software to communicate with it. Virtually all home computers that have dial-up communications options use asynchronous line discipline.

When I started working in terminals marketing, Control Data had just announced a new low price for a conversational CRT terminal—$1995. Prices had dropped dramatically since the first conversational CRTs were introduced. The earliest one that I saw when I first arrived at the Arden Hills plant in 1965 sold for $12,000. The high price of a CRT was one reason why almost all the first time-sharing terminals were Teletype machines, one model of which could be bought for less than $1000. CRT terminals are now available for under $400.

More sophisticated "synchronous" line control procedures allow for higher data transfer rates and for options such as "clusters" of conversational terminals, which share a single communications line. By far the most common synchronous conversational terminals are the IBM 3270 series of CRTs. Many smaller manufacturers also sell their plug-compatible versions of the IBM 3270 terminals.

Batch terminals, or remote job entry terminals, in contrast to conversational terminals, are designed to transmit comparatively large amounts of data to a remotely located computer that does the calculations and returns the results minutes, or even hours, later. Minicomputers have now become so low priced that they have replaced dedicated batch terminal devices. A minicomputer with its peripherals can solve small problems locally and obtain solutions to larger problems, or access to data required from large central files, by communicating with a larger mainframe computer, an arrangement known as distributed processing.

Graphics terminals are CRT terminals that have the capability of drawing high-quality pictures on the screen. They are used for computer-aided design (CAD) of everything from integrated circuit chips to skyscrapers. Sophisticated graphics terminals include a "light pen," which allows a designer to "draw" on the screen while the computer records the line. Control Data had pioneered this class of terminal and offered in the early 1970s a top-of-the-line model. The Cybergraphics terminal could change the scale of a drawing, zoom in on a particular detail, "pick" a detail and move it around the screen following the light pen, and label the drawing with four different character sizes. The lettering could be either horizontal or rotated 90 degrees so as to be readable from the right-hand side, as is normal with engineering drawings. This terminal sold for $100,000, which somewhat limited its market, but quite a few were sold to large aerospace companies and to automotive manufacturers. It was fun to demonstrate this terminal and to watch the customer's astonishment at the tricks it could perform.

Application-specialized terminals most familiar to readers are the automated teller machines. These terminals, connected over telephone lines to the bank computers, perform the specialized functions of reading the customer's magnetic credit card, dispensing cash, and transferring funds between accounts. The IATA ticket printer was, of course, another application-specialized terminal, of no use unless connected to a reservation and fare-quotation computer.

Another specialized terminal still built by Control Data in large quantity is the Ticketron ticket vending terminal. Control Data had first bought an interest in and, later, acquired the entire New York company once known as Ticket Reservation Services (TRS). Ticketron uses seat inventory computers and remote terminals to sell tickets to Broadway shows, sporting events, rock concerts, and even campsites in state parks. The terminals originally designed and built for Ticketron used a specialized keyboard with buttons to select ticket event, date, number of seats, price range, etc., together with a custom-designed printer for the long, narrow "theatrical" type tickets. I was to learn a lot about Ticketron's business, particularly because an old colleague from my TWA days, Fred Bandierini, had joined Ticketron.

As an interesting aside, one of the big problems faced by Ticketron in what they call the S & E (for sports and entertainment) ticketing is ticket counterfeiting. A confidence man would buy a pair of tickets to an event that was sure to sell out, usually a popular rock concert, and then make, say, fifty copies. He would scalp these tickets just before the concert and leave town. When fifty people would show up at the concert with the same seat number, a riot would result, and Ticketron would be blamed for selling duplicate tickets. Ticketron had to learn quickly all the tricks of making hard-to-counterfeit tickets.

Later, Ticketron entered the business of providing wagering tickets, first offering off-track horse race wagering tickets and then, as state lotteries were authorized, state lottery tickets. Fred Bandierini became the head of the automated wagering section of the Ticketron business, which has been very successful. Ticketron is, I believe, the leading supplier of state lottery systems in the United States. Each state lottery requires thousands of application-specialized terminals.

Requests for new types of application-specialized terminals arose constantly. Each request had to be evaluated for its market potential, as Control Data could not possibly develop all the specialized types requested by the sales force for their customers. Some thousands of application-specialized terminals were designed and built for the Internal Revenue Service and for the US Army, among others.

My duties in the new terminals marketing job involved giving presentations and tours for sales representatives and their customers, recommending the development of new terminals, pricing or repricing older terminals, drafting plans for sales promotions, data sheets and sales brochures, monitoring the terminals that competitors were offering, and tracking and reporting the orders for terminals against the established sales quotas. One of the fringe benefits was the opportunity to watch Paul Miller in action at close range.

I attended Paul Miller's Monday morning staff meetings in place of my boss, who had a conflicting meeting. Once a month I also made a formal presentation, complete with charts and graphs, on terminal-order performance by category, large orders that were imminent, problem areas, etc. Paul's technique in handling his sales force was fun to watch. He never pounded the table or threatened, but anyone whose performance was not up to par certainly knew it from the sharp questions and the jocular needling. If Paul thought that a sales rep or a sales manager was promising more than could be delivered, he would ask, "Want to bet?" Paul had only two categories of wager. The standard bet was $100. He wrote each wager in a notebook, and, if the order was not closed, the quota not met, etc., he would collect. For smaller fry who could not easily afford to lose $100, he offered a $50 bet. Only once did I ever hear of higher stakes being proposed.

Larry Jodsaas, vice-president in charge of computer development at Arden Hills, once made a presentation to Paul and his staff on a new computer line under development. Paul questioned whether the schedule that Larry presented could be met, and he offered his usual $100 bet. Larry reportedly replied, "I will bet more than that," and he removed his employee identification badge and laid it on the table in front of Paul Miller. For once Paul backed away from a wager!

Paul had an incredible memory, a grasp of detail, and a sarcastic wit that made it perilous indeed to try to bluff him. I recall one meeting that I attended with him and a senior vice-president. Control Data had delivered a number of application-specialized terminals to a major New York City airline (not TWA). The equipment was not working well. Customer engineers were constantly having to replace portions of the terminals, and the customer was getting angry. This happened at a time when several lawsuits were being won by companies claiming that computer equipment they had bought had been misrepresented. Paul was afraid that this airline was considering a lawsuit against Control Data. He called a meeting with the senior vice-president to whom the Terminals Division reported. I was asked to prepare a short presentation on the contractual commitments made to this customer, and other attendees were to report on problems encountered and corrective measures planned. I made my short presentation and sat back in my chair to listen for the rest of the meeting. The discussion proceeded rapidly, as was the usual case with Paul's meetings. The system manager, who had visited the customer installation several times, reported on the problems encountered. It soon became evident that the senior vice-president was not really following the discussion. He was a large, pompous, impressive man, with iron gray hair. He obviously felt that he had to say something; after all, he was in charge of a number of divisions, including the one whose product was under discussion. He tried a safe question: "Uh, what is the ROI [return on investment] on this?"

Paul jumped him. "What has ROI got to do with it? We are talking about whether or not they are going to sue us!" He proceeded to chew the pompous senior vice-president into little pieces—one of the most brutal yet funniest performances I have ever seen. I had to struggle to keep a smile off my face. The senior vice-president subsided for the remainder of the meeting, and Paul Miller took charge of the plans for controlling the damage done to our reputation.

It was safe to joke with Paul so long as you did not try to bluff or hoodwink him. I remember that I took quite a bit of needling when I projected that a large terminal order—$1.5 million worth of batch terminals—would close in the next month. For two months the order did not arrive because it was hung up in the customer's administrative process. Paul, who never forgot anything that anyone had promised, pointedly asked about the order each month. Finally the order arrived. I got a copy, rolled it into a scroll, and tied it with a large pink ribbon. At the appropriate time in my monthly presentation, I pulled it out of my briefcase and presented it to him, with laughs all around the room.

One Monday morning in January 1973, I was informed that the usual 9:30 A.M. Paul Miller staff meeting would be held early—an unusual change from routine. When the twenty or so members of the marketing staff arrived in the large marketing conference room, we were directed without explanation to take the elevator down to the lunchroom on the second floor. There we were met by a smiling Norb Berg. Norb, Bill Norris's right-hand man, announced with a grin that the IBM lawsuit had been settled out of court, on terms favorable to Control Data. The lawsuit had been filed, the reader may remember, in 1968, with Control Data charging unfair marketing practices being used by IBM against the 6600. As one of the terms of the settlement the Service Bureau Corporation, IBM's wholly owned data services subsidiary, was to be sold to Control Data at its book value, and IBM was to stay out of the data services business for six years. There were other concessions, including IBM funding for Control Data research and development and patent cross-licensing agreements between the two companies. All in all the settlement was a great personal triumph for Bill Norris, who had insisted on pursuing the lawsuit in the face of skepticism from many of his own employees. Norb Berg then invited all of us to a victory cocktail party and reception that evening at the nearby Decathlon Athletic Club.

One condition of this settlement caused a good deal of comment. The lawyers for Control Data, working with a group of Control Data programmers experienced in database management systems, had created a computerized index of the millions of IBM documents examined by the lawyers. A database management system is a method of organizing computer files such that a person can search for all documents by subject or by author without knowing exactly what he is looking for, an elaborate cross-indexing system. This computerized index, together with the lawyers' notes, the programmers' coding sheets, and everything connected with the index (but not the original IBM documents themselves) were required to be destroyed, and indeed they had already been destroyed over the weekend before the settlement was announced on Monday morning. Curiously, the magnetic tapes containing this information were reportedly physically destroyed using acid. The usual method of wiping out information on magnetic tapes is to erase the tapes magnetically and then rewrite them with random-pattern information. However, it is sometimes possible, using sophisticated equipment, to recover information previously written and erased from magnetic tapes, although the process is time consuming, expensive, and chancy.

The US government had filed an antitrust suit against IBM just after Control Data filed its suit. According to reports in the trade press at the time, the government lawyers were upset over the destruction of the Control Data document index. It was too late; the information was already gone. Control Data had paid to develop the index, and the government lawyers had access to all the same original IBM documents that Control Data had used. I followed reports of the government lawsuit in the trade press for years afterward. The contrast between the outcome of the two suits, filed within a month of each other, is certainly striking. Billions of pages of IBM documents were demanded and copied by the government. The suits and countersuits stretched out for *thirteen years*. The case was finally dropped by the government after accomplishing nothing except the waste of millions of taxpayer dollars and the enrichment of dozens of lawyers.

The Decathlon Athletic Club is a two-story, brick, U-shaped building just a mile down the freeway from the Control Data corporate headquarters. I was a charter member, as were Bill Norris and a number of the CDC old-timers, so I felt confident in entering the lobby and checking for the victory party after work. The Control Data party had taken over half of the main Olympia dining room on the second floor. Tables of hors d'oeuvres and an open bar had been set up. Perhaps a hundred Control Data executives were milling around with plates of hors d'oeuvres and drinks in their hands. I knew maybe two-thirds of them well enough to say hello; the corporation still had something of a small-company atmosphere in 1973, at least for a Univac veteran. A group was standing around Bill Norris near the doorway. I drifted over to hear what he had to say. One of the executives was complementing Bill on his persistence in pressing the lawsuit. "There are some things a man has just got to do; those bastards deserved it," was his reply.

Another story of the lawsuit settlement is apocryphal. I did not hear Bill Norris say it, but it certainly sounds like him. Supposedly Vincent Learson, then president of IBM, suggested a personal meeting with Bill Norris to discuss the terms of settlement. The locations he suggested were all resort areas—Bermuda, the Virgin Islands, etc. "Hell, tell them we will meet in Omaha!" Bill, a former Nebraskan, is said to have replied. The meeting actually took place in Minneapolis.

All through this period I had kept in touch with Vic Benda. We would have lunch every month or so and swap the latest industry gossip. Benda was involved on a part-time basis with another large Control Data computer system—one so infamous that its very name became the punch line of many an in-house joke. The computer system for the Union Bank of Switzerland, universally known as the UBS project, was a large multicomputer complex to be installed in the bank's headquarters in Zurich. A new Transaction Oriented Operating System (TOOS) was to be developed for the UBS project and used on some other large systems as well. Development work was being done primarily at a plant in the Minneapolis suburb of Plymouth, with a project office also being set up in Zurich.

Vic, while not working on UBS in the same full-time dedicated manner that he had worked on TWA, did have one of his AIC senior programmers, another Univac veteran, working full time at the project in Plymouth. Early in the project it became obvious to nearly all the programmers that TOOS was in deep trouble. TOOS became the subject of jokes whenever two or three programmers would gather over coffee. Two samples of programmer humor appeared on various desks and were pinned to department bulletin boards. No one claimed credit for them, and they are reproduced here (figures 18 and 19). The psuedo-horror-movie advertisement lists the real names of some of the programmers working on the UBS project. TOOS certainly does sound like a horror movie. I particularly like the caption: "See Switzerland Beg for Foreign Aid!" The parable written in Biblical language goes a long way toward explaining what I believe went wrong with UBS. The truth about the project, obvious to everyone actually working on it, was being filtered through a large, increasingly hierarchical organization, each level of which was subtly altering the message passed on to the next higher level. The AIC programmer working at Plymouth became so upset about his involvement with a project that was sure to be a disaster that he begged Vic to assign him to another project.

Vic made a serious effort to inform Control Data management of the TOOS problems. As he explained it to me, he felt that, as a conscientious contractor, Analysts International had a duty to tell their customer about problems on a project for which they were hired as consultants. After failing to get any response from the management of the project, Vic persuaded his boss, the president of Analysts International, to call an old friend from Univac who was now a senior executive of Control Data. This executive, himself about to leave town, arranged for Vic and his boss to have lunch with the Control Data vice-president directly responsible for the UBS project. For two hours Vic outlined in detail the problems with the project and possible solutions. The vice-president said little. He later made a half-hearted attempt to look into the problem by setting up a task force to investigate. The task force concluded that everything was under control.

Some months later in the fall of 1974, the final blowup came. The customer ordered the UBS project halted. The Control Data vice-president responsible had by this time left the company. Reportedly, the first that Bill Norris understood the depth of the problems with UBS was when he met in Europe with the president of the bank, who told him, "I am not here to negotiate; take your equipment out!" Lawsuit and countersuit followed, and Control Data carried a $30 million contingency loss reserve until a settlement with the bank was finally reached. If any formal postmortem was done to discover just why the project failed, I never heard about it, and I had many contacts among the workers both in Plymouth and in Zurich.

In my opinion, the saddest result of the great UBS fiasco was a dramatic change in attitude at Control Data: a newfound reluctance to accept *any* large system orders that included considerable new hardware and/or new software development. The company reacted rather like a small child who, having once burned his hand on the stove, now refuses to go into the kitchen.

20

Oops, I Lost the Computer!

In 1972 Bob Oslin had another surprise for me. He and a general manager at the Valley Forge Division had been working for some time on a proposal for the Washington Metropolitan Area Transit Authority (WMATA). It seemed that WMATA was planning a state-of-the-art subway system for the Washington, D.C., metropolitan area and wanted to use a sophisticated fare card system similar to that used by the Bay Area Rapid Transit (BART) in San Francisco.

For the reader who has never traveled on either subway system, a fare card is a magnetic ticket. The size of a standard plastic credit card with a brown magnetic stripe like many credit cards, the fare card is made of cardboard rather than plastic. Instead of the raised numbers on a credit card, the fare card has a blank space on which its dollars and cents value can be printed (figure 20). Fare cards are useful only on transit systems where the fare charged is based on the distance traveled. The cards are used like this: A passenger buys a fare card from an automatic vending machine before entering the subway. One can buy a fare card for any amount from the minimum fare for the shortest ride, say 80 cents, up to a maximum of $20. The value of the fare card is both printed on the face of the card and magnetically recorded on the stripe. The passenger opens the access gate to the subway by inserting the fare card. The electronic circuitry of the gate reads the magnetic stripe and determines the value recorded on the card. If the value is enough for a minimum ride, the gate opens for the passenger. The circuitry in the gate records on the magnetic stripe the station number of the gate where the passenger entered the system and returns the fare card to the passenger. At the destination the passenger must again use the fare card to get out through the exit gate. The circuitry in the exit gate reads the station of entry and calculates the fare between the stations of entry and exit. It then subtracts the amount of this fare from the value of the fare card and rewrites, both magnetically and in printed numbers on the face of the card, the residual value of the card. The exit gate opens and returns the fare card to the passenger, unless the value of the card has gone to zero, in which case the gate "eats" the card. What happens if the fare card does not have enough value to cover the fare for the distance traveled? The gate does not open. The card is returned to the passenger with the warning "insufficient value." For this eventuality "add-fare" machines are provided into which the passenger can insert the fare card and coins or currency to build up the value remaining on the card. What happens if the passenger has no more money? Presumably she remains trapped in the system forever. As a practical matter there is always at least one human attendant at each station. Use of the automatic equipment saves having to have a large number of ticket sellers on duty during rush hour periods.

What Bob Oslin and his general manager had done was to win the preliminary competition to provide the entire fare card subsystem for WMATA! This would include the fare card vending machines, entrance and exit gates, and add-fare machines. IBM had developed the fare card system for BART, but IBM did not bid on WMATA. Bob told me that he had been able to prepare the winning bid only because of his experience with the IATA ticket printer. Indeed, there were striking similarities in the technology involved. Both systems required magnetic recording and printing on small cardboard documents. The possible fallout from the WMATA development in implementing an airline PSS was also exciting. There was no reason why an entry gate mechanism could not be adapted to read an IATA magnetic ticket, verify flight number and date on the ticket, check the passenger's name against a boarding list, and open to admit the passenger into the aircraft boarding area, all functions that were part of the original PSS concept.

WMATA required that a substantial portion of the work be done in the Washington, D.C., area. Control Data already had an assembly plant, the Capitol Facility, in the District of Columbia. It was decided that Bob Oslin and the development engineering for the fare card system should move to the former Rabinow Engineering plant in Rockville, Maryland, just north of Washington. (Jack Rabinow had left Control Data by this time; the plant was now officially the OCR Division, but old-timers still referred to it as "Rabinow.") Bob was talking big bucks for the WMATA project. The production contract was likely to run $50 to $100 million in value.

I met Bob at Control Data headquarters when he came to brief senior management on the contract and to be annointed officially as head of the WMATA project. By this time, early 1973, Northwest Airlines had decided that the two prototype IATA ticket printers were working well enough so that they would proceed with a contract for twenty production ticket printers to be distributed in ones and twos at their ticket counters in various

cities. Bob was going to take the ticket-printer project with him from Valley
Forge to Rockville. The project engineer in charge of the IATA ticket
printers was to be Jack Keilsohn! My cup of happiness overflowed. I could
see in my imagination the complete scenario for a long-delayed triumph of
Control Data's new technology for the airlines industry.

The first step would be successful completion of the twenty ticket
printers for the Northwest ticket counters in various cities, then completion
of the WMATA project with its access-control gates, then another pilot
project with Bill Huskins at Northwest, this time to install a passenger-
operated self-check-in gate at a Northwest concourse, then widespread
publicity as the traveling public notices the automation at Northwest
Airlines, and finally competitive pressure driving other airlines to implement the IATA magnetic ticket and full PSS. Once the majority of airline
tickets issued were machine-readable IATA tickets, pressure to make
accounting reconciliation of interline tickets easier would drive the
hold-out airlines to adopt IATA ticketing also. (Interline tickets are those
that include travel on two or more airlines. The first carrier, which receives
payment from the passenger, must credit the other airlines with a pro rata
portion of the ticket price.) It was a beautiful vision, satisfying to
engineering instincts. We had already managed to get some national
publicity for the ticket printer. *Aviation Week and Space Technology*, the
leading weekly of the airlines industry, had mentioned the pioneering
efforts of Northwest Airlines and Control Data, and *ABC Airways*, an
international monthly magazine, had run a photograph featuring the IATA
ticket printer on the front cover.

Bob Oslin and Jack Keilsohn settled into the Rockville plant, where OCR
work was still continuing without Jack Rabinow. We kept in touch every few
weeks. One day Jack called me in great excitement. He had just received his
first "microprocessor" chip, an 8-bit-word Intel model 8080. This astonishing chip, he related, performed just like the manual said it would, all the
functions of a computer! More precisely, the large chip, the size of a small
snack cracker, performed the arithmetic and control functions of an 8-bit
minicomputer. The other two functions of the traditional computer
organization, memory and input/output, required additional chips. Even so,
Jack foresaw providing all the functions, if not the speed, of the Control
Data model SC1700 on a single printed circuit board, which he proposed to
mount inside the printer cabinet. He would overcome the comparatively
slow speed of the Intel 8080 microprocessor by providing a microprocessor
to control each ticket printer rather than having a single SC1700 control

two or more ticket printers. It sounded great to me. The cost of a ticket-printing subsystem and the floor space required would both be reduced by eliminating the need for a freestanding minicomputer at each airport.

Other engineers at Control Data had been tracking the invention and remarkable growth of the microprocessor, soon to be the driving force for the next great revolution in computer technology. The process of implementing digital computer logic on chips of semiconductor material had begun with the invention of the transistor, and the end is nowhere in sight. The original transistor, invented at Bell Telephone Laboratories in 1947, packaged a single logic element or "gate" in a cylinder about the size of the eraser on a lead pencil. Three wire leads coming out of the transistor case could be connected to other logic elements. Computers as recent as the model 7600 had been designed with "discrete" logic, or individual transistors. Soon it was discovered that it was easy to deposit several transistor gates on a single chip of material—four, eight, sixteen, or even more. The limitation, it seemed, might be the number of leads that could be brought out of a small "integrated circuit" package, typically about the size of a paper clip. In the usual configuration, the leads come out of the long sides of the chip, then are bent 90 degrees downward so as to be inserted into a printed-wiring board. The resultant chip has the appearance of a flattened centipede. The actual silicon chip, the working part of an integrated circuit, is much smaller, smaller than the nail on your little finger. Most of the integrated circuit package is inert plastic, which protects the silicon chip and provides support to the delicate lead connections.

As the possibilities expanded to include dozens or even hundreds of gates on a single chip, one solution to the problem of the growing number of external leads was to connect the transistor gates *internally* within the chip. This could result, depending on the connections made, in a chip that could serve as an entire module of logic—a counter or a storage register, for example. This reduced the number of external connections that had to be made and, incidentally, greatly improved the reliability over the same module of logic made of discrete components. As the techniques of microminiaturization became more refined, thousands of gates on a single chip became possible. How can one make full use of all of this logic power contained in a small package with only a limited number of external connections? In 1971 a genius at Intel Corporation named Ted Hoff came up with the answer: connect these gates internally to create the logic structure of a simple programmable computer on a single chip. The microprocessor was born!

The first microprocessors were 4-bit-word computers. Because four bits can represent only sixteen possible characters, an initial use for microprocessors was in calculators, which need to handle only the ten decimal digits. As the technology improved, 8-bit-word microprocessors were introduced by Intel and other semiconductor manufacturers. Using eight bits, a standard byte or alphanumeric character can be represented in the same bit coding format as used in large mainframe computers. The world opened up! A small, cheap, programmable microcomputer that can process standard 8-bit bytes has literally hundreds of uses in a computer system. Jack Keilsohn was one of the first to recognize the potential. Control Data's Terminals Division was not long behind. Intel model 8080's began to be designed into the next generation of terminal products. I cannot think of a single terminal device built today by Control Data that does not incorporate at least one microprocessor. Designers of peripheral equipment control logic were next to seize this new tool. A favorite use of microcomputers allows the peripheral controllers to run diagnostic maintenance tests off-line, that is, without the participation of the mainframe computer, which may be doing useful work while the microprocessor is testing the peripheral's condition.

The home computer business is based on the low-cost microprocessor. When Jack Keilsohn bought his first Intel model 8080, the price was relatively high, about $200 for a single chip. Today a comparable 8-bit microprocessor chip can be bought for about $2! Eight-bit microprocessors are used in such home computers as the Apple II, the Atari 800, and the Commodore 64. The semiconductor manufacturers continued to squeeze more logic gates on a single chip of silicon, and 16-bit-word microprocessors became commonplace. The IBM Personal Computer and its compatibles use 16-bit microprocessors. Thirty-two-bit microprocessors are available, and I believe that the only reason why 64-bit microprocessors (which would be the same word length as Control Data's largest scientific computers) have not been announced is the limited market for such a word length. The sales volume of microprocessors is heavily weighted toward the low-end products. Invention of the 8-bit microprocessor did not make the 4-bit models obsolete. Millions of 4-bit microprocessors are sold for use in calculators, toys, household appliances, and automobiles. Fewer 8-bit micoprocessors are sold than 4-bit ones, and fewer 16-bit than 8-bit. The number of new uses being found for these devices is astonishing.

I managed to schedule a trip to Rockville during the WMATA development project. Bob Oslin was cordial but preoccupied. I was given a tour of the development lab and saw prototypes of the fare card vending machines and the access gates. I was given a fare card, and I used it to walk through the access gate. The "money room" was especially interesting. Because the fare card vending machines and the add-fare machines accepted currency in payment, they had to be tested with counterfeit bills to see if they could discriminate good from bad currency. With special permission, a supply of counterfeit bills had been obtained from the Treasury Department. Kept in a safe in a locked room within the lab was a sizable stack of counterfeit bills of various denominations. They were being fed by a technician through the currency acceptor mechanisms. He kept a log of the number of passes and whether or not each bogus bill fooled the mechanism. The information gathered was, of course, highly confidential. I looked at the phony bills closely. Some were pretty crude, but some certainly would have fooled me!

Bob and I got away from the plant for a late lunch together. He confided that he was worried. The project was going well technically, and he had recruited a strong development team, but he was having some personnel problems in dealing with the customer.

Back in Minneapolis reorganization struck again. Constant reorganizing had been the pattern for many years, ever since the first financial crisis back in 1965. By and large the employees hated it. They expressed their view of reorganization by saying, "Management has banged on the bird cage again." The analogy here was that of a large bird cage with many perches and free-flying tropical birds. Every few months management pounds on the side of the bird cage with a two-by-four. All the birds fly up with much squawking, and a few feathers come loose, but gradually the birds settle down again on different perches. Same cage, same birds, same perches, just a different arrangement of who sits where. Certainly the most commonly seen bit of sarcastic humor at Control Data was the quotation from Petronius (figure 22). There must have been hundreds of copies posted over desks and on local department bulletin boards. Most engineers and programmers heartily agreed with the sentiments of the ancient satirical author, who was a nobleman at the court of the Emperor Nero. The WMATA project, when first organized, had been part of the Computer Group. Now it was reassigned to the Peripheral Products Group. Organizational entities that did not clearly fit into one catagory or the other were often tossed back and forth with each corporate reorganization. As I recall, the Terminals Division was passed back and forth three or four times among Peripheral Products Group, Computer Group, and even Data Services Group, always with an explanation that purported to be logical. Next, a new general manager was hired for Rockville from outside Control Data. He was installed as Bob Oslin's boss. I only met the man once, but Jack Keilsohn described him as "a boy scout," whatever that meant.

Northwest Airlines also reorganized. Our customer and friend, Bill Huskins, was promoted to vice-president of maintenance and engineering, a step up in the organization. His replacement was a man we had never met before from the accounting department. Collapse of both the WMATA project and the Northwest Airlines ticketing project came almost simultaneously in 1975. WMATA rejected the Control Data bid for the final and critical production phase of the fare-collection system and awarded the contract to a small California firm. Northwest Airlines claimed that Control Data had defaulted on the ticket-printer project, and they canceled delivery of the production ticket printers. Both actions were immediately enveloped in the dust of lawsuits and countersuits. I have only Bob Oslin's and Jack Keilsohn's versions of what actually happened at WMATA. According to them, the catastrophe really began when BART went out for bids on an addition to their fare-collection system. Bob and his group prepared a bid and sent it to the Control Data sales representative in Oakland, California. The new Rockville general manager forbade them to submit the bid. The only other bidder, a small California firm, subsequently won the BART contract. When the WMATA final phase bid was prepared, the new Peripheral Products management insisted on adding a large contingency cost to Bob's estimate, thus greatly increasing the price to the customer. The same small California firm, now given credibility by the BART contract, then won the WMATA production contract with a price considerably lower than that submitted by Control Data. The whole WMATA operation was disbanded. Bob Oslin and Jack Keilsohn left Control Data. A job was found at Minneapolis headquarters for the Rockville general manager.

I was to play a leading role in the resolution of the Northwest Airlines lawsuit, which did not come to trial until 1979. Long after the collapse, when I was in a new assignment at the Terminals Division, I received a letter from Control Data's outside law firm asking if I had any documents relating to the Northwest Airlines contract. I replied in a long memo that I certainly had. I enclosed a stack of documents and suggested that the lawyer contact Bob Oslin and Jack Keilsohn for more detail. At a meeting in the offices of the St. Paul law firm, I showed the lawyer a copy of Bob Oslin's old super-8 mm home movie of the IATA ticket printer. He was delighted with the film, and he scheduled me to be the lead-off witness for Control Data in our suit to collect money allegedly owed us by Northwest Airlines.

We met in the Hennepin County Court House building the morning that the trial began. I would have been more nervous if I had known that the lawyer representing Northwest was a senior partner in the largest law firm in Minneapolis and a specialist in cases involving high technology. Bill Huskins and a number of the people I knew from Northwest were present in the courtroom as witnesses. We greeted each other in friendly, if guarded, fashion. No executive from Control Data was present in the courtroom, but Donald Nyrop was there. He sat behind the Northwest Airlines witnesses waiting to be called and chatted with them. This was the first time that I had ever seen the controversial president of Northwest Airlines. The judge entered, and we all rose. There was to be no jury. I climbed up into the lonely witness box and was sworn in. After bringing out my educational background and experience in the computer industry, the Control Data lawyer asked me to show the movie and to give the judge an explanation of exactly what an IATA ticket printer was and did. The lights were dimmed, and I narrated while the silent movie showed the outside and inside of the ticket printer in operation. I then reentered the witness box, and the Control Data lawyer questioned me on the background of the development of the ticket printer and on Control Data's initial negotiations with Northwest Airlines to evaluate the ticket printers. Then it was the turn of the lawyer for Northwest to cross-examine. The lawyer, an older man, was courtly and polite, but his questions were tricky. I developed the habit of taking a long breath before answering each one. One of the points that he seemed to be trying to make was that Control Data had substituted the less expensive Intel model 8080 microprocessors in the ticket printers in place of the freestanding minicomputer in order to save money. I tried to make the point that Control Data was trying to give Northwest the benefit of a newer technology that had not been available at the time the contract was signed. I buttressed the position by pointing out the use of the same microprocessor in many current Control Data products. I spent about five hours on the witness stand altogether, with a break for lunch. I stayed in the courtroom for the remainder of the afternoon to hear Bill Huskins's testimony; then I had to return to work.

The lawyer for Control Data had taken my suggestion and had contacted Jack Keilsohn, who was now working for a small modem manufacturer in the Washington, D.C., area. Jack was being flown in at Control Data's expense as an expert witness for our side. I was not able to be in court the day that he testified, and I was surprised to get a phone call from him as I was preparing for dinner. "Jack, I thought that you would be on a plane for home by now," I said. Jack was jubilant. He explained that he had demolished any Northwest case while on the witness stand. What made him even happier was that on returning to the airport to fly back to Washington, he found that Northwest had overbooked his return flight. Northwest had to pay him denied boarding compensation—double the price of his return fare, which was first class—and then provide him space on a later flight! Jack said that he made sure that the unhappy Northwest ticket agent who had to write him out a check for several hundred dollars knew why he had been in Minneapolis— to testify against Northwest in a lawsuit! Jack invited me to join him for cocktails and steaks at Murray's, a popular downtown Minneapolis steak house, "all on Northwest Airlines." We spent a delightful evening drinking, eating, and recalling the past. The only sad note was the waste of the production ticket printers, which were to be scrapped. Jack claimed that they had been working perfectly, with many design improvements over the two prototypes used for the ticketing test. He was particularly proud of the self-diagnostic capability that he had programmed into the Intel 8080's. Any problem in the ticket-printer mechanism would be identified by the lighting of the appropriate one of a row of LEDs (light emitting diodes, a kind of low-power indicator light much used with electronic circuitry) located inside the printer door.

I drove Jack to the airport to catch his midnight flight. Shortly afterward, Northwest agreed to pay up, not as much as Control Data had asked for, but the suit was settled. I had a chance to read the judge's preliminary finding. He had concluded that Control Data had not defaulted in any serious sense and that Northwest's desire to cancel was the result of the change in personnel and the realization that the rest of the airlines industry was buying the less-expensive transitional ticket printers. Shortly thereafter, Northwest did install transitional ticket printers, which are universal in the industry now. No airline has ever revived the IATA ticket to this day.

The Atlanta operation of Airline Systems Division never became successful despite a determined professional effort to sell its services. The problem was that many of the major airlines had reservation systems with greater capacity than needed, so they were selling reservation services to the smaller regional airlines in competition with the former CCN operation. The price per transaction kept getting lower and lower. Eventually the Atlanta center with its Univac 494 computer system was sold to SITA (Societe Internationale de Telecommunications Aeronautique), an airline-owned cooperative that provides communication service mainly to international airlines. Some of the Airline Systems Division personnel chose to go with SITA; some, including our fares expert, Ken Haeberle, transferred to other Control Data facilities; still others, including the general manager of Airline Systems Division, left Control Data.

In the meantime the effort by the Greenwich Data Systems group to conclude a reservations services agreement with the travel agents of ASTA had also collapsed. ASTA was unwilling or unable to make a firm commitment to use the service. The GDS people drifted away, and today none of those with whom I dealt is still at Control Data. The need for an automated reservation system for travel agents was real, and the gap was filled by the larger airlines. American and United Airlines in particular have installed reservation CRT terminals and transitional ticket printers in the offices of thousands of travel agents. The practice has been criticized as unfair competition and lawsuits have been threatened by some of the airlines that do *not* offer this service to travel agents. It seems that if a travel agent requests availability of flights from A to B, the flights of all airlines with seats available will be shown, but the display is biased to show the flights of the airline providing the reservation service at the top of the list. Because a busy travel agent will usually pick the first available flight, this results in extra bookings for the airlines offering the service. These airlines are not stupid! Of course they list their own flights first on availability displays for their own reservations agents, and they quite naturally carry the practice over when providing the same service to independent travel agents.

There is a half-humorous epilogue to this story of dashed hopes in the airlines industry. In 1978, long after the collapse of the projects described, a news item appeared in the Minneapolis paper. A former Control Data employee was suing Control Data Corporation and three CDC executives personally for several million dollars. He claimed that promises made to him of promotion to a higher executive position had not been kept and that his career had been damaged to this extent. I knew the man, who had come to CDC from IBM. I knew the defendants also. They had been involved in marketing to the transportation industry but had given me little cooperation in promoting the IATA ticket printer. Along with most of Control Data, I looked on the lawsuit as a joke. After all, who had not suffered career damage when a market had failed to develop? Then the bombshell struck. A jury awarded the plaintiff $4.2 million! The judgments against the three CDC executives were several hundred thousand dollars each! The head-quarters tower rocked on its foundations. The judge later voided the award, and a settlement was reached, the terms of which were kept secret, but the executives certainly had a scare. Should I ever decide to sue my employer for ruining my career, I know just the lawyer to represent me. I still have his name in my newspaper clipping file!

21

Oink, Oink, Oink

While the Control Data ticket-printer sales efforts were collapsing, general terminal sales remained healthy. I had a new boss and once again an office with a view of the airport. My job remained the same: to support the sales of remote terminals of all kinds. We were having a good year, with over $25 million in terminal orders booked. In due course I received an invitation from Paul Miller to attend the 1974 100 Percent Club.

The Control Data 100 Percent Club is an annual three- or four-day party thrown by the marketing organization for the sales reps, the sales managers, and favored sales support people who have made 100 percent of their previous year's sales quota. This club was to be one of the best ever—to be held at the Acapulco Princess Hotel in Mexico.

The Acapulco Princess is a large, beautiful hotel with a distinctive stepped-pyramid profile on a not-very-good beach several miles outside the city of Acapulco. It is the same hotel where the late billionaire Howard Hughes lived out the last months of his life in guarded seclusion on the top floor. The beach, usable but not very pleasant for swimming, does not really matter because guests have their choice of five swimming pools, both fresh and saltwater, complete with waterfall, body slide, and swim-in bar. The grounds are extensive and beautifully landscaped. The convention facilities are superb, with large meeting halls, stages, and giant screens with multimedia projection. The Control Data sales reps, arriving from all over North America (the European sales reps had their own 100 Percent Club to save transatlantic airfares), were handed complimentary margaritas in the open-air lobby, with its enormous atrium extending to the top floor. We all changed into shorts and loud shirts and prepared to enjoy ourselves. Generally the agenda called for half-day meetings devoted to reviewing sales quota performance, awards ceremonies, new product announcements, and pep rallies; the remainder of the time was devoted to recreation. The highlights of the club were two superbly organized cocktail parties— the first hosted by Paul Miller, as president of marketing, and the second hosted on the final night by Bill Norris, as chairman of the board. Both parties were held outdoors under the clear Mexican sky. Many open bars

and tables of hors d'oeuvres were set up around the five pools. Strolling
musicians played. Everyone had a chance to meet Bill Norris and the senior
executives of the company. The last party culminated in a fireworks display;
the last burst to light up the sky was a replica of the Control Data logo. It was
a gorgeous evening.

Control Data organizations outside of marketing frequently criticized
the extravagance of the 100 Percent Clubs. The Acapulco club, one of the
most lavish, was reputed to have cost $2 million. In my opinion the top sales
reps attending the clubs are near miracle workers, and the benefits in
increased person-to-person communications and morale justify the cost.

Ironically, not long after the big blowout at Acapulco, another financial
crunch hit Control Data. This time the pay of employees was not cut by 10
percent, but a number of job positions were eliminated throughout the
company. My job was one of those eliminated! Once again I had to scramble
to remain employed. By now I was used to this sort of thing, but this time I
had to call on all my contacts to find another job. Budgets had been cut in all
organizations. With the help of a recommendation from Paul Miller I was
offered a job at the Terminals Division at Roseville, a suburb of St. Paul some
fifteen miles north of headquarters. I accepted. I would be doing pretty
much what I had been doing before; my title was Manager of Marketing
Liaison. I found my new boss and co-workers congenial, and I settled in to
promote the sale of terminals for the division that designed and built them.

Terminals Division was in the process of bringing to the market a whole
new product line of asynchronous conversational CRT terminals, including
two associated character-at-a-time printers and a magnetic tape cassette
storage system. These were the first Control Data standard products to be
designed using the new Intel 8080 microprocessor. I had not been in my
new job long before I was invited to join my former colleagues from
marketing in a "flying squad" visiting the European sales offices to brief the
sales reps on upcoming new products. Marketing would pay our travel
expenses, so my new boss had no objection. I put together a slide
presentation describing the new terminal product line and took off for
Amsterdam, where I was to join the other team members. I knew all the
others from the home office marketing staff, who were to give presentations
on the latest large computers, communications, peripherals, and software
packages. We visited the country offices in The Netherlands, West
Germany, France, and Great Britain. The country managers had arranged
for selected sales personnel and programmer analysts to attend our
presentations, which lasted, depending on their requests, from one to three

days. We were made most welcome. For the sales reps, remote from the divisions where products are designed and built, accurate current and future product information is like water in the desert. The more remote geographically, the drier the desert! We were greeted like Gunga Din on a hot day on the Northwest Frontier!

I managed to stay over for a long weekend in London, our last stop; then I flew back to the problems of the Terminals Division.

One of the largest customers of the Terminals Division always has been the Ticketron organization, a CDC subsidiary. When I joined the division, a development project was underway to provide Ticketron with a modular set of terminal devices for selling wagering tickets. I enjoyed visiting the Ticketron headquarters in midtown Manhattan because it gave me a chance to visit with my old friend, Fred Bandierini, and to catch a Broadway show. It was there that I met Larry Littwin.

Larry was the technical guru at Ticketron, having a position somewhat similar to that of Lloyd Thorndyke in the early days at Peripheral Equipment Division. No decision on computer systems, terminals, or software could be made without Larry's blessing. He is a short, dark-haired, native New Yorker with thick glasses and a positive manner of speaking. Larry intensely dislikes writing or reading formal documentation. I have seen him toss into his wastebasket unread memos from the corporate vice-president in charge of systems and procedures. "He keeps sending me these things," was his complaint. Larry's frequent negotiations with the Terminals Division over new product development for Ticketron are largely conducted by telephone with occasional visits to see the prototype hardware. His negotiating technique is a combination of demand, threat, and ridicule. He usually has several feuds going on with other Control Data organizations. His favorite term for the Engineering Services (customer engineering) organization is Engineering Circuses. He is incredibly persistent and almost always gets his way in the end.

Larry's abrasive manner may have made him unpopular, but the systems he implemented using computers and terminals from other Control Data divisions and the unique software written by Ticketron have been enormously successful. It is hard to dislike a customer who keeps on ordering thousands and thousands of terminals. The first dealings that I had with him were when he became dissatisfied with the design approach being taken by Terminals Division in building a modular set of component parts that could be plugged together in different combinations to provide wagering terminals. The modular approach was too costly and occupied too much valuable counter space, he said. Couldn't the division package the CRT display, the unique Ticketron microcomputer, and the specialized wagering keyboard the same as the standard product model 751 conversational CRT terminal? Larry cajoled, threatened, and browbeat the division into a crash redesign effort to give him the terminal he wanted. The result became the staple terminal for all Ticketron business for some years.

I watched a demonstration that Larry put on for me using this terminal during a later visit to New York. In order to understand the significance of the demonstration, the reader must learn a little about how Ticketron bids for state-operated lotteries. Typically Ticketron supplies the computer system, the programs, the lottery terminals, and the maintenance for all equipment. Computer system and terminals, typically several thousand per state, are not sold but remain the property of Ticketron. Ticketron gets paid a certain percentage, depending on their bid, of the total amount wagered, the so-called handle. Lottery tickets are sold, not by Ticketron employees or by state employees, but by independent small business owners—drugstore owners, bar owners, pizza parlor owners—wherever the terminals are installed. The ticket sellers also get a percentage of the value of the tickets sold at their locations. The lottery terminals are therefore scattered all over the state in the establishments of owners who know nothing about either computer terminals or lottery operations but who do have an incentive to sell tickets. Great care must be taken by Ticketron to make the selling transactions foolproof.

The terminal designed for Larry included a high-quality CRT screen and a complete microcomputer system in one cabinet, attached to a specialized keyboard by a two-foot cord. The keys were labeled with legends appropriate to the lottery, with dollar amount, date, type of wager, etc. The microcomputer was based on the Intel 8080 microprocessor chip and included random-access memory (RAM), read-only memory (ROM), and four input/output channels. One input/output channel was normally connected by a phone line to the Ticketron central computer system, and one input/output channel was connected to the ticket printer. Two input/output channels were spares for connecting such options as a mark-sensing optical reader. Lottery tickets are small—business card size. They are printed on a small, inexpensive dot matrix printer.

When the terminal is first turned on, a short program contained in the ROM (which is not erased when power is turned off) takes control of the microcomputer and calls for the central computer to load over the telephone line the terminal data entry and verification program into the

RAM. This program, like all start-up programs, is called a bootstrap, because the microcomputer is figuratively pulling itself up by its bootstraps. Both ROM and RAM are necessary because RAM is wiped clean every time the power is turned off. Down-line loading is slow. In the demonstration the task took several minutes. The CRT screen displayed the section of the program being loaded so that the operator could tell how the process was going. I asked Larry why he didn't put the entire data entry and verification program in ROM, thus making a down-line load unnecessary. He replied that, if a software "bug" were discovered or if Ticketron wanted to upgrade the program in any way (and one condition or the other was almost inevitable), then he would have to send service personnel to each of the several thousand terminal sites to replace ROM chips. With the down-line load, he would only have to correct the one copy of the program in the central computer, and all terminals would be automatically upgraded the first time that the power was turned on. Also, down-line loading reduced his spare terminal inventory problem. He could pull a terminal out of inventory and send it to any lottery knowing that it would be automatically upgraded to the rules of that particular lottery when it was connected to that state's central computer system. Ticketron used the same terminal, connected to a theatrical-type ticket printer, for sports and entertainment ticketing also. The keyboards for the different applications are different, but the keyboards are separate plug-in units and so are easy to change.

The data entry and verification program running in the terminal was designed to coach the ticket seller by messages on the screen. It would display blanks to be filled in for the date, choice of number, etc., and it would not allow the seller to transmit the wager to the computer until all the blanks were filled in correctly. The program also kept track of the number of tickets sold and the amount of money collected for audit reports. I was impressed with the cleverness that had gone into the design of the program.

Bidding for a state lottery's business requires a fine feel for the business and a gambler's instincts. The high capital cost to Ticketron for the computer system and for the terminals must be balanced against the uncertain revenue stream, based, as it is, on the amount of wagering done by the state's residents. Adding to the hazard is the fact that, when a state finally decides it wants a lottery, often after years of debate and a voter referendum, it wants to see the lottery in operation *right away*. Short schedules to install and get the lottery operational are the rule. Penalty clauses calling for payments to the state of thousands of dollars per day for delay in the start-up schedule are commonplace. Under these conditions

Fred Bandierini was a master at coming up with winning bids that also make money for Ticketron. He has been something of a corporate hero since the first successful lottery was implemented in Pennsylvania. Larry Littwin is equally adept at getting the hardware and software installed with a minimum of expensive delays.

After several years of using the first generation of the programmable Ticketron terminals described, Larry decided that he wanted an upgraded terminal to include an integrated wagering ticket printer, a mark-sense reader, and a more powerful 16-bit-word microprocessor. Mark-sense readers are useful for entering certain types of wager in which the customers mark their selections on cards by blackening in a space between two lines, somewhat like computer-scored questionaires or multiple-choice exams. This request for a new wagering terminal started a royal political battle. It seemed there was now a corporate strategy group that had concluded that Control Data was using too many types of microprocessor, thus duplicating software development efforts and complicating the training of programmers. Their solution: standardize on a single micro-processor model in each capability range. The corporate choice for a 16-bit microprocessor was a proprietary design of a leading minicomputer manufacturer—emphatically *not* the micoprocessor that Larry wanted to use. Larry argued that the Ticketron programs were unique and of no value to anyone else in the corporation. All his terminal programming was done in assembly language anyway, so what difference did it make to anyone but Ticketron which microprocessor his terminal used? The Terminals Division, following corporate policy, refused to budge: Take the corporate standard microprocessor or nothing. Larry's boss, the president of Tick-etron, backed Larry's position. A heated standoff followed. Finally Tick-etron pulled an end run. They awarded funding for the development of the new terminal to a Control Data division in La Jolla, the same division from which Nate Dickinson had come and where he was now the vice-president. La Jolla Division was designing the small computer system used by Ticketron, and they had some engineers available to work on Larry's new terminal. He did not get the microprocessor he wanted from La Jolla either. The project engineer there had his own ideas of the best microprocessor to use. He finally convinced Larry to accept a 16-bit Zilog microprocessor rather than the Intel model Larry had wanted. The ending is ironic. The La Jolla operation was eventually closed, and the newly designed Ticketron terminal was given to the Terminals Division in Roseville to manufacture. Although it uses a microprocessor that neither Ticketron nor the Terminals

Division wanted, the terminal worked well and was built by the thousands. A third generation of programmable Ticketron terminals is being designed now. I expect that it will be the subject of as much controversy as the first two generations of terminals.

One day I got a phone call from a friend that I had known since my Univac days. He asked if I was going to Unihogs this year. "What's a Unihog?" I asked. He explained that a growing group of ex-Univac employees had for years arranged an informal get-together once a year on Groundhog Day. The combination of Univac and groundhog suggested the name "Unihog." Unihogs form a loose nonorganization. Originally, to participate, one must have left Univac. Returning to Univac does not disqualify a member once qualified. Some attendees have left Univac three and four times! The requirements were later loosened to include anyone who had even *thought* of leaving Univac. Unihogs have no membership roll, no dues, no elections, no bylaws, no officers, no newsletter, no secret handshake, no funny hats, and no rituals—except for the singing of the "Unihog Drinking Song" at the close of every reunion. Unihogs are governed, if that is not too strong a word, by a self-perpetuating, six-member committee of volunteers. Two new members are added to the committee each year, and the two members who have served for three years are dropped. The treasury, consisting of an old envelope with a few dollars in it, is passed along from head hog to head hog. A small surcharge is added onto the cost of the dinners at the annual reunion to provide funds for mailing the meeting notices and for gag gifts. An artist among the membership drew the mascot of the Unihogs, which appears on the meeting notices and banquet tickets: a little black and white spotted pig with a single long horn growing out of its forehead.

The first meeting that I attended was held in the basement private dining room of a nightclub just down the road from the Univac headquarters. About a hundred hogs showed up for cocktails and gossip. Luckily someone had brought a supply of "Univac Visitor" name tags, which everyone wore. I had not seen many of the attendees in fifteen years. At a later reunion my old friend, Dick Karpen, now living in Herkimer, New York, managed to visit the Twin Cities on Groundhog Day. Dick brought me up to date on the whereabouts of some of the Philadelphia hogs.

Typically, after an hour or so of socializing, the hogs sit down to dinner. A short program follows dinner, always something related to the early history of computer development. One year an academic paper was presented on the founders and the original organization of Engineering Research

Associates, the predecessor of Univac St. Paul. Another year a member showed slides of the early ERA and Univac computers. At the 1983 reunion the speaker, who introduced himself, consistent with our porcine nomen-clature, as the "big boar," was none other than Willis Drake, the man at whose house I had subscribed for Control Data initial-issue stock back in 1957. Drake, chairman of Data Card, a company that makes magnetic credit card processing equipment, spoke on the need to recapture the engineer-ing creativity of the early days, a topic close to my heart. The 1984 reunion speaker was the new director of the Charles Babbage Institute for the History of Information Processing, Arthur Norberg. (Charles Babbage was a nineteenth-century British mathematician who attempted to build a mechanical "computing engine." He is considered by many to be the earliest designer of the programmable computer.) The institute, a nonprofit foundation at the University of Minnesota, was set up to document and preserve the early history of the electronic computer. The director spoke on his experiences in attempting to document the early growth of technology in Silicon Valley, where he had just completed a project.

Following the program the hogs always stand for the ritual bellowing of the "Unihog Drinking Song" (sung to the tune of "The Whiffenpoof Song"), with a final chorus:

Managers, programmers, engineers
We're all Unihogs, and we'll give three cheers
We'll program computers to recall past years
Oink, oink, oink!

The number of different companies that have been started by Unihogs is astonishing. One of the members prepared a genealogy chart listing seventy-six firms (some have merged or gone out of business), and the list is still not complete. Five generations of companies from Univac are shown, and it is only a matter of time before a sixth generation appears. I suspect that the Philadelphia branch of Univac could show as many offspring.

In due time I got a call inviting me to join the committee as an apprentice hog. When elevated by seniority to head hog, I moved the reunion, as was my prerogative, to a larger banquet facility in the midway district of St. Paul, near the original ERA plant at 1902 West Minnehaha. The meeting notice (figure 24) dates from that meeting place. A later head hog moved the reunion once again to a more luxurious private club near the new Cray Research building within sight of the Control Data headquarters tower across the Minnesota River.

Two of our most distinguished Unihogs, Bob McDonald, retired president of Univac, and Bill Norris, are invited every year, but they have not attended so far. McDonald, still held in high regard by most of the past and present Univac employees, always sends a polite reply, explaining that he would like to come but that he will be skiing in Switzerland at that time of year! Bill Norris does not reply. We continue to invite them both.

Figure 16
CRAY 1 computer system. Photograph courtesy
of Cray Research Incorporated.

Figure 17
CRAY 2 computer system. Photograph courtesy
of Cray Research Incorporated.

Figure 18
TOOS poster.

A PARABLE

In the beginning was the plan, and then the specification;

And the plan was without form, and the specification was void,

And darkness was upon the faces of the implementors thereof.

And they spoke unto their leader, saying:

"It is a crock of crap, and smells as of a sewer."

And the leader took pity upon his men, and spoke to the project leader:

"It is a crock of excretement, and none may abide the odor thereof."

And the project leader spoke unto his section head, saying:

"It is a container of excretement, and it is very strong, such that none may abide it."

The section head then hurried unto his department manager, and informed him thus:

"It is a vessel of fertilizer, and none may abide its strength."

The department manager carried these words to his General Manager, and spoke
unto him saying:

"It containeth that which aideth the growth of plants, and it is very strong."

And so it was that the General Manager rejoiced and delivered the good news
unto the Vice President:

"It promoteth growth, and it is very powerful."

Knowing that the President was normally saddened of heart, and was in need of
encouragement in the face of many obstacles, the Vice President rushed to his side
and joyously exclaimed:

"This powerful new software product will promote the growth of the company!"

And the President looked upon the product, and it was very good.

Figure 19
A parable poster.

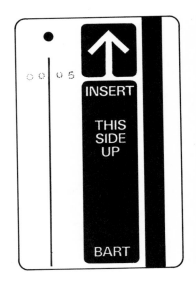

Figure 20
A BART fare card.

Figure 21
A transistor, an integrated circuit, and two microprocessors.

"We trained hard---but it seemed that every time we were beginning to form up into teams, we would be reorganized. I was to learn that later in life we tend to meet any new situation by reorganizing, and a wonderful method it can be for creating the illusion of progress while producing confusion, inefficiency, and demoralization------------

----Petronius Arbiter, 66 A.D."

Figure 22
Petronius on reorganization.

Figure 23
Ticketron wagering terminal with ticket printer. Photograph courtesy of Control Data Corporation.

UNIHOGS !   FEBRUARY 5

UNIHOGS OF THE WORLD ARISE ! REUNION TIME AGAIN !

WHEN   Friday, February 5, 1982
            5:30 PM - conviviality, cash bar opens
            7:00 PM - buffet supper - $9.00 (price is same as last year)

WHERE   Midway Twins Motor Inn (same place as last year)
            Northwest corner of University Avenue and Prior (just two blocks
            from 1902 W. Minnehaha, where it all began!) See map on back.

WHAT   Buffet supper consisting of soup, tossed salad, assorted cold meats, bread,
            potato salad, jello and beverage - $9.00 (includes tax and tip)
        Attendees not staying for supper are asked to contribute $1.00 to defer costs
            of mailings, chips and popcorn, etc.
        Short program following supper, then socializing untilthe bar closes!

WHO   All ex-Univacers, (even if repatriated) and sympathizers. Eligibility
            requirements are very loose!

HOW   You pay for dinner at the door, but we do need to know the number for dinner
            by Monday, February 1, so please contact your company representative
            or Unihog committee member below for your reservation. (Those not
            staying for dinner need not make a reservation.)

Company	Representative	Phone
CDC ARH	Bob Egemo	482-3864
CDC RVL	Dave Lundstrom	482-4314
CDC HQR	Al Brandon	853-5944
CDC NRM	Dale Strand	830-5016
CDC GSD	Jim Wright	853-5376
CDC PLY	Roger Ranzinger	553-4179
3M	Chuck Mortenson	736-0996
NCR Comten	Bill Saed	638-7513
Univac RVL	Wally Emerson	631-6125
Univac Eagan	Jim Button	456-4892
Data Card	Pat Ryan	933-1223
Cray Research	Janette Robidoux	452-6650
Honeywell	Hank Valo	870-6465
Lee Data	Jim Vellenga	932-0300
Micro-Comp.Tech.	Dick Hencley	482-5103
Check Technology	Roger McCumber	941-9400

1982 UNIHOG Committee

Historian Hog - Clete Tauer - 483-4859
Hog Emeritus - Dave Lundstrom - 482-4314
Hog Emeritus - Ross Rash - 638-7965
Head Hog - Bob Schultz - 482-4495
Head Hog - Don Sampson - 830-5569
Apprentice Hog - Jim Nickitas - 456-2182
Apprentice Hog - Bob Blixt - 854-2963

SEE YOU FEBRUARY 5 !

NOW IS THE TIME FOR ALL GOOD UNIHOGS TO COME TO THEIR ANNUAL REUNION !

Figure 24
A Unihog meeting notice.

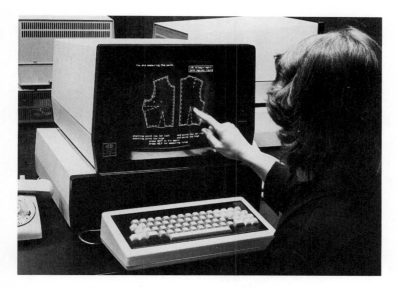

Figure 25
Control Data IST-1 Plato terminal. Photograph courtesy of Control Data
Corporation.

Figure 26
Joel E. Laurance.

Figure 27
FTP/80 prototype (promotional photo with professional model). Photograph
courtesy of Control Data Corporation.

22

Microspin and Spin and Spin

When I transferred to the Terminals Division, another application-specialized terminal that was clearly needed was the Information Systems Terminal (IST). The IST, in one of its variations, is the terminal used with the Control Data Plato computer-based education system. Plato is a totally computer-based learning system, originally developed by Donald Bitzer at the University of Illinois in the 1960s. Bill Norris became interested in Plato, so Control Data acquired rights to it and continued to refine it. Computer programs have been developed for Plato courses to teach subjects ranging from basic reading skills to robotic technology. The student works at a screen and a keyboard that are connected to a large Control Data computer.

The first ISTs, developed at the University of Illinois and manufactured by Magnavox Corporation, used plasma display panel technology rather than CRT displays. You have probably seen small plasma display panels. The displays used with supermarket checkout scanner systems that show the item description and price are usually plasma panels. They can be identified by the pattern of small orange dots that form the characters. Many automated teller machines also use plasma displays. The early Magnavox terminals used a large plasma panel, about ten inches square. On the face of the screen was a touch-sensitive surface. The student could select an answer, choose a figure, or indicate a decision just by touching a selected image on the screen. The coordinates of the point touched are calculated by the terminal and sent to the computer, which then interprets the student's choice among the images displayed on the screen.

Plasma panels have a number of advantages over CRT displays. The panels can be made thin and can be hung on the wall like pictures because they do not have a bulky CRT tube behind them. They can be made to have no flicker, which might cause eye strain. They can be made environmentally rugged to take more abuse than CRTs. And they can be used with a rear-projection slide projector, which superimposes a picture on the image formed by the plasma. Plasma panels are made by placing a layer of parallel, closely spaced fine wires over but not touching a second layer of wires that are at right angles to the first wires. Both layers of wires are enclosed within a sealed panel filled with a gas, for example, neon, that glows when subjected to a high voltage. The word "plasma" means an ionized (electrically charged) gas. A plasma panel is in essence a matrix of tiny neon bulbs.

The original Magnavox terminals were large, square, and ugly. They looked like tabletop microwave ovens with keyboards attached by two-foot cords. They had provision for the rear-projection feature, which was rarely used. They were also expensive. In order to be able to announce the Plato system as a viable product, which was done in 1976, Control Data decided to have Terminals Division build the terminals.

The first model designed by Terminals Division was so constructed that it could use either a plasma display panel or a high-quality CRT display. It was constructed in two pieces, with the display unit sitting on top of the controller unit. A keyboard on a two-foot cord plugged into the controller. Control Data tried for years to produce large plasma display panels at a cost competitive with CRT displays, but they finally gave up. Plasma panel cost, in contrast to CRT cost, is almost directly proportional to the size of the screen, or, more accurately, to the number of lighted dots. Thus, although a small panel for a supermarket checkout display may be cost effective, a panel large enough for student training was judged too expensive. A high-quality CRT display, of a resolution much better than the usual alphanumeric conversational display (though not so good as a sophisticated graphics display), was designed for the IST-1, the first product from Terminals Division. The touch-sensitive panel, a key feature used in Plato courses, was retained in the CRT display of the IST-1.

In an attempt to get more funding for terminal development and to extend Plato system sales into the oil-rich areas of the Middle East, Control Data formed yet another joint venture for technology transfer. The result was, as usual, disastrous, but for a unique reason. The partner chosen was the Shah's Government of Iran; the venture was named Computer Terminals of Iran (CTI). The managing director of this new international enterprise was my old friend and sometime boss, Jay Kershaw. One of the features of the IST was the ability to display any alphabet or symbols. Building ISTs in Iran was thus a logical choice because the terminals could easily be programmed to display in Farsi, the language of Iran, which uses characters similar to Arabic. The Shah of Iran at this time was spending his oil income prodigally on development of high technology industry for his country. Because another of his priorities was education, what was more logical than building high technology terminals for computer-based education with the Shah's money?

A number of Iranian citizens were hired and sent to the Terminals Division in Roseville, Minnesota, for training. The new model IST-2, a redesigned and cost-reduced terminal developed with funding from the joint venture, carried a little sticker on the front panel with the Computer Terminals of Iran name and logo in English and Farsi. A demonstration program for the IST was written that displayed on the screen a formal portrait of the Shah, complete with his resounding titles in English and Farsi—a good likeness, too. After the Shah's flight and the revolutionary takeover, I asked the joint venture employees if they wanted to reprogram the Plato system to display the formal portrait of the Ayatollah Khomeini! Although some of the Iranian nationals privately admitted that they favored the Ayatollah (after the takeover, that is), my suggestion met with a cool reception.

Jay Kershaw had visited Iran a number of times to negotiate for factory space, hire personnel, and meet the high Iranian officials responsible for the Shah's push into high technology. He would regale us privately with stories of the Tehran traffic jams and the corruption, both of which seemed to be equally extreme. He never got to meet the Shah, but we at Roseville were favored by a visit from a group of Iranian dignitaries, headed by, I believe, an admiral of the Iranian Navy. The visit caused quite a stir because the Iranians wanted permission to land a helicopter in the grassy area between the Roseville plant and the shopping mall next door! No one had ever landed a helicopter there. Permission was somehow obtained to fly from the Minneapolis–St. Paul International Airport direct to the Roseville plant. After the one brief visit we never saw the Iranian officials again.

Jay Kershaw had planned to move to Iran with his wife, but fortunately he was not in the country at the time of the American Embassy takeover. The swiftness of the collapse of the Shah's regime and the takeover by the Ayatollah seemed to surprise the CTI employees as much as those of us with no knowledge of the country. The Shah's portrait on the IST-2 screen and the CTI stickers on the front of the terminals quietly disappeared.

A far more significant event for the Terminals Division and for the entire computer industry was the first availability of the flexible disk. The flexible disk, or floppy disk, was introduced by IBM. It filled a need for a rugged, low-cost, mass-storage device. Together with the microprocessor, the flexible disk made practical the low-cost personal computer. The term "flexible disk" implies the existence of a "rigid disk" or "hard disk," which, of course, is a far older product. The flexible disk is conceptually closer to magnetic tape than to the rigid disk. Magnetic oxide is deposited on a disk of

Mylar just as in the coating of magnetic tape. The first flexible disks on the market were 8-inches in diameter and could be used on only one side. Later disks were offered in 5¼-inch diameter and most recently in 3½-inch diameter; they can be used, depending on the model, on one or on both sides. Flexible disks are enclosed in a cardboard sleeve much like a record jacket. The disk is sealed in the sleeve, but a slot is cut out of the sleeve to allow contact with the magnetic head of the disk drive. Floppy disks, of course, can be removed from the disk drive mechanism, as the early rigid disk packs could be removed by the operator. The key difference between the flexible and the rigid disks is that the magnetic head actually rides in contact with the surface of the flexible disk, just as magnetic tape rides in contact with the tape transport head. A lubricant is included in the formulation of the magnetic coating on a flexible disk so as to minimize wear, but in time a flexible disk will wear out. A rigid disk will not. The heads of all modern rigid disks "fly" on a thin cushion of air at heights measured in millionths of an inch. The heads are designed using aerodynamic principles to fly at these extremely close tolerances over a smooth, highly polished, and perfectly clean disk surface. As a result, a rigid disk surface and its head will never show wear unless contaminated by dirt.

A flexible disk, with its head riding in contact with a less smooth, less clean surface, is able to tolerate a modest level of contamination caused by normal handling and shipping. The price paid for this greater tolerance to dirt is a much lower storage capacity and speed of access. A single-sided 8-inch-diameter flexible disk would typically store half a million bytes (0.5 megabyte) of program or data. A single surface of an 8-inch-diameter rigid disk would store a minimum of ten times the data (5 megabytes), and versions of rigid disks storing twenty, thirty, or more megabytes per side are available.

The speed of access to data is similarly much slower for the flexible disk. Eight-inch rigid disks typically rotate at 3600 rpm, whereas flexible disks rotate at one-tenth that speed. The lower rotational speed is necessary to keep the head in contact with the disk without bouncing and to minimize wear. The speeds of the head positioners, which move the heads radially across the disk to the desired track are correspondingly slower for the flexible disk. The great advantages of the flexible disk are its low cost and the ruggedness of the disk media, which can be removed and even mailed from site to site without damage or loss of data. Rigid disks, even those intended to be removed and stored, are much more fragile and expensive.

The Magnetic Peripherals Incorporated plant in Oklahoma City, acquired from Honeywell when MPI was formed in 1975, was soon delivering flexible disk drives to Terminals Division for inclusion in some new and exciting products. One of the first attempts at Terminals Division to combine the new technologies of the microprocessor and the flexible disk was still another joint venture, this time with Hitachi, the Japanese electronics firm. The project, called JTS for Joint Terminal System, was to be funded by both companies and developed by personnel from both companies. The products would incorporate microprocessors, flexible disks, printers, and CRT displays into several models of user-programmable remote terminals. A series of management meetings were held in Japan, Minneapolis, and Hawaii. Hitachi seemed eager to send their engineers and programmers to work in Minneapolis rather than the other way around, so in due time a group of up to thirteen Hitachi employees worked at Terminals Division. The Hitachi people and their Control Data counterparts developed detailed design specifications, but no hardware resulted from three years of the program life. The joint venture was quietly abandoned by mutual agreement.

Terminals Division picked up the pieces of the JTS, simplified and redefined it into a single model, and pushed through to completion a user-programmable terminal known internally as Pegasus. Pegasus, later given the model number Control Data 760, included a popular 8-bit microprocessor, software, and a CRT display, all built by the Terminals Division, a dual 8-inch flexible disk drive and controller from MPI Oklahoma City, and a dot matrix printer from the CPI Division in Rochester, Michigan. It was good looking, massive, and solidly built, like all Control Data products. The software was limited, but the product seemed to fill the need of users of large Control Data computers for a remote, user-programmable data entry station. I worked on the pricing approval, the color brochure, and the formal announcement package to be sent to all Control Data field sales representatives. The model 760 was announced, and mention of it appeared in the trade press. Then the division vice-president (already the third vice-president to head the division since I had joined it) decided that the product had been introduced too late in the marketplace, and he withdrew it.

Those of us who had worked on Pegasus were furious. There was some truth to the argument that the product was late—competitors had had similar products on the market for several years—but Pegasus was the first product of its type to be designed by the division. The market for this type of terminal was certain to grow rapidly. Given the large and competent Control Data sales force and the expected sales to large Control Data computer users, we believed that Pegasus could have carved out a respectable market niche while the division learned from experience how to design an improved model. It is difficult to learn to swim without getting into the water! The vice-president had his own favorite project, a line of peripherals for the IBM Series/1 minicomputer, which he had heavily promoted with senior management and on which his reputation depended. The Series/1 peripherals were completed and sold in modest quantities until Control Data withdrew entirely from the plug-compatible peripherals market in 1984. The vice-president was by then long gone.

I had earlier noted with dismay that there was no single brilliant cutting-edge designer at Terminals Division. There were many able, competent engineers and programmers, but no outstanding individual with the unique ability to formulate and keep an entire development concept in his head, as had some of the "point-of-the-wedge" individuals profiled in earlier chapters. In discussions with old-timers and in reviewing the human history of the division, I concluded that the lack was due to the near total decapitation of the division management that had occurred when the original group that had founded Data Display had left to found Data 100 some years earlier. Talented designers had since been brought into the division or had grown from junior engineers to positions of cutting-edge talent, but such individuals found themselves without any executive-level support. With a new and constantly changing management that was unsure of itself and hence susceptible to political pressures, the most highly talented (and often most controversial) designers found themselves severely limited in what they were allowed to do. A weak management always chooses the safe path of following policies and procedures re-ligiously. The innovative designers become frustrated and quit the corpora-tion. The pattern tends to be self-perpetuating, and I saw it repeated over and over. With no top designers the division can still develop products as authorized by the corporation using the available competent designers, but the process takes longer and the result is never as elegant as a design spearheaded by a brilliant individual of the George Cogar type. Because the authorized product is often late to the market or mediocre in performance or both, corporate management lacks confidence in the division's ability and keeps it on a short leash. Bootlegging, the diverting of funds for unauthorized favorite projects, is almost entirely cut off. Management is afraid of criticism and will not back an unauthorized project even if everyone in the division believes in it strongly. The designers feel straitjacketed, find other jobs, and leave. The best usually have the lowest threshold of frustration and so are the first to go.

The most advanced models of terminals, of personal computers, and of personal computer software usually are developed by small specialized companies. The capital equipment requirements for these products are modest compared to, say, the capital equipment requirements for manufacturing disk files or semiconductors. The successful small firms invariably have a technical genius somewhere in the back room. I remember visiting one of the small firms building programmable terminals at a time when Control Data decided to buy synchronous conversational terminals OEM. I spent two hours or so in a conference room with the president of this company and a blackboard. I came away awed. He had that same total grasp of microcomputers that Seymour Cray has of supercomputers. There is no way that a company with merely competent designers can keep up with the speed of development of a firm with one of these cutting-edge talents if he has free rein to work flat out. This same small terminal firm also provided all their programmers with their own personal programmable terminals that they were urged to take home. The low cost of these microprocessor-and-floppy-disk-based devices makes it practical to encourage formally the Greg Mansfield types who may invent their own unique software on their own time.

Terminals Division never made a technology assessment and decided to maintain certain key technologies in-house, as Lloyd Thorndyke had done years before in the disk file business. Without any commitment to vertical integration, the division remained at the mercy of vendors who supplied such vital components as keyboards and CRT "bottles." Because they could not be a low-cost vendor of "plain vanilla" general-purpose terminals, the division was most successful in designing custom application-specialized terminals for the many Control Data application-oriented organizations.

One of the more successful designs combining microprocessors with flexible disks was the Micro-Plato development. In the original concept of the Plato system, all execution of the educational software, known as courseware, was done in a large Control Data computer at a central site. The various models of IST each contained a microprocessor and a large memory, but their function was limited to managing the visual presentation on the screen. This was complex because the IST, in order to draw realistic pictures and to show animation, had a resolution of 512 by 512, or 262,144, individually addressable spots of light. Many Plato customers objected to the cost of the telephone lines linking the terminals to the central computer, and they asked why courseware could not be executed locally in a free standing microcomputer with flexible disk storage. Terminals Division was given the assignment of designing a microcomputer–flexible disk combination that could be plugged into the IST. The same IST had to retain the capability of being connected over a telephone line to a central Plato computer. The division designed a product that combined an 8-bit microprocessor, memory, and a disk controller with an 8-inch double-sided flexible disk in one package, and an add-on second flexible disk without disk control logic in a second package. The two packages could be stacked, one on the other. Some of the courseware was rewritten to run on the microprocessor, and Micro-Plato was announced.

A screen-copy matrix printer (from Japan) had been available as an option to the IST, so now all the hardware elements for a personal computer were in place. Bob Price, now president of Control Data (Bill Norris had moved up to chairman), reportedly suggested that a popular general-purpose operating system be purchased from a software company and that the Micro-Plato hardware be offered as a personal computer. This was done, and the resultant product was named the Control Data 110, the first Control Data personal computer. It proved to be popular among employees for CDC internal use but unsuccessful in the marketplace because of its cost and relatively large size.

One day in late 1978 two visitors from Commercial Credit Company (CCC) arrived at Terminals Division. Commercial Credit is Control Data's big financial services subsidiary headquartered in Baltimore. It was acquired in 1968 at the conclusion of an unfriendly takeover attempt. To avoid the unwanted suitor, Commercial Credit allowed itself to be taken over by Control Data, in the largest and probably the wisest acquisition ever made by Control Data. Like most Control Data employees, I did not know much about Commercial Credit's operations. CCC had a small loan office in downtown Minneapolis, which I had never visited, and some executives in the headquarters tower, whom I had never met. There had been little mixing of Control Data and Commercial Credit personnel until Paul Miller was appointed chairman of CCC. Paul had moved to Baltimore shortly after I had moved to Terminals Division. He brought a number of Control Data people into the CCC organization, including the two who were now visiting us.

Jim Benson had been a vice-president in the headquarters marketing organization when I was there. He was now in the CCC Baltimore headquarters in charge of all CCC computer operations. Joel Laurance was an old friend. We had first met when I was investigating OCR back at the Peripheral Equipment Division. Joel was then a young engineer at Control Data's Palo Alto data services center. A local Ph.D. had approached the Palo Alto data services center with a scheme to use a simple optical scanner and a Control Data 1604 computer program to read printed mailing labels. Before the widespread use of computers, mailing lists were commonly kept on embossed metal plates. Adding a name to the list involved making up a new plate and manually inserting it in an alphabetized stack. The conversion of these lists to computer form was a large task and a natural business for data service centers. Joel and I looked into the suggested process and tried some experiments. We concluded that the process was economically impractical because of the amount of computer time required to recognize characters by computer analysis. Since then I had seen Joel occasionally as he moved around the company. Now he was with Commercial Credit—head of a two-man computer laboratory some twenty miles from Jim Benson in Baltimore. His assignment was researching improvements in CCC's terminals and communications networks, at which he was extremely competent. Joel is a tall, dark haired, pleasant mannered native Californian from the Palo Alto area. Like Lee Granberg at Univac who "thought like a transistor," Joel lived and breathed microprocessors and integrated circuits. As I found out later, he read semiconductor manufacturers' specification sheets for recreation! He had maintained friendships with engineers at semiconductor companies in the Silicon Valley region. He usually knew all about the latest advances in chip technology long before they were announced in the trade press.

Joel's hobby is flying. He had a private pilot's license, a hot-air balloon rating, a multiengine rating, and an instrument rating, and he was taking lessons for a helicopter rating. On one of his later visits to Terminals Division Joel told me about his adventure on the previous weekend. He and the instructor were practicing one of the required maneuvers, touching down and immediately taking off again. The instructor at the controls descended a little too rapidly; the helicopter hit the ground too hard. The main rotor blades flexed downward, striking the small stabilizing rotor in the tail and cutting it off! The now unbalanced main rotor blades then literally tore the helicopter to pieces as Joel and the instructor sat petrified in the cockpit. Both walked away unhurt, but the helicopter was a total loss! Joel had the idea of starting a helicopter rental service in the Washington, D.C., area. He arranged financing and leased a helicopter, but after a *second* somewhat similar experience, he abandoned the idea!

Jim Benson and Joel wanted the Terminals Division to document and manufacture an application-specialized terminal already designed by Joel. Commercial Credit operated a thousand or so small loan offices around the country. In each office was an old, wired-program Cyberloan terminal made by Nixdorf, a German computer firm. These terminals were connected by telephone lines to Control Data computers located in the Baltimore headquarters. They were used with magnetic ledger cards for keeping consumer loan payment records. The Cyberloan terminals were obsolescent, and it was becoming next to impossible to get spare parts for them. Joel had designed his own microcomputer based on the Zilog Z-80, an upgraded and improved version of the Intel 8080—not surprising because the founders of Zilog had come from Intel. He had "turbocharged" his processor by adding an optional dedicated arithmetic-operation chip and optional input/output chips, actually dedicated specialized microprocessors in themselves. Joel had selected a dot matrix printer for his terminal, not a Control Data standard model. He wanted the Terminals Division mechanical designers to build a single-sheet page feeder and an optical mark sensor to mount on the printer. In operation the terminal would be used like this: To record a loan payment, the operator pulls from a file cabinet the ledger card for this particular loan and drops it into a sort of funnel on top of the printer. Under control of the microcomputer the ledger card is stepped down into the printer until the optical mark sensor locates the last line that was printed in the last transaction. The operator types in the payment data on the keyboard and the printer then records the payment on the first blank line. When the transaction is complete, the printer sheet feeder reverses under microprocessor control and delivers the completed ledger card back to the operator to return to the file.

Joel wanted to combine the microprocessor, the printer with its custom-designed single-sheet feeder and optical mark sensor, and a conversational CRT with keyboard into a handsome desk work station. He would program his microprocessor to emulate the Nixdorf Cyberloan terminal. As each of the older terminals wore out, it would be replaced with a new terminal, and the communications to the central computer would be unaffected. His long-range plan was more ambitious. His microcomputer, with its turbochargers, was clearly far more powerful than was needed to replace the old, slow Nixdorf processor. Joel wanted space provided in the desk work station for a pair of 8-inch flexible disk drives. Eventually he planned to upgrade his new terminals to do the loan processing locally in the terminals and to give up the expensive dedicated (that is, permanently connected, not dialed-up) telephone lines to Baltimore. The terminals would then be programmed to automatically dial the computer center in Baltimore at night and transmit a copy of the day's transactions for auditing and backup purposes. The savings in communications cost would pay for the new terminals in a short time. Joel had plans even more ambitious than these, but I only found out about them later.

The division was nervous about the whole concept. If Joel specified the design, who would take the blame if the terminal did not work reliably? I drafted a Memorandum of Understanding that in essence stated that Commercial Credit had full design responsibility. Terminals Division would provide mechanical design assistance, drafting, and manufacturing on a time-and-materials basis. After several rewrites of this document, both organizations were satisfied, and both Jim Benson and the division vice-president signed the document. The Cyberloan Replacement terminal project was off and running.

Joel spent much of the next several months at Terminals Division. I was astonished at the energy with which he delved into every department, sitting down with the mechanical designers, the drafters, even the "tin benders" in the model shop to work out every detail of the terminal. There was a certain level of resentment among the electrical engineering staff, the Not Invented Here factor causing them to criticize his microcomputer design, but Joel's pleasant personality served to smooth over most objections. We had lunch together frequently. We both had a fondness for Mexican restaurants, which are in short supply in the area north of Washington where Joel lived. I grew more and more impressed with his abilities. I suggested that he contact Larry Littwin, then in the midst of his battle for the second-generation Ticketron terminal, to discuss microprocessor performance. That was a mistake. Their personalities were totally different, and they could not agree on *anything*. I should have remembered that the only thing worse than having no cutting-edge talent is having two such talents on the same project.

Almost six months to the day after the first visit of Jim Benson and Joel Laurance, the first prototype terminal was ready for a demonstration. The desk work station, handmade in the model shop, was handsome—solid and expensive, in the best Control Data tradition. A phone line to the Baltimore headquarters computer center was installed in the largest conference room at Terminals Division. All the new product lacked was a name. Cyberloan Replacement Terminal lacked class. Joel and I ran a contest to pick a name. The winner was FTP/80, for *Financial Transaction Processor* for the *80*s. A data sheet and a set of 35 mm slides were made up for the presentation using the FTP/80 name. The demonstration went well, and ten more terminals were ordered for pilot installation in CCC's small loan offices.

Because Joel had the cutting-edge talent that the Terminals Division lacked and because Commercial Credit had both funds for development and a staff of application programmers, why shouldn't the division ride on Commercial Credit's coattails and exploit the product? With the addition of the dual flexible disks and substituting a general-purpose printer for the Cyberloan ledger card printer (the printer interface was industry standard), the terminal would be a much more powerful version of the deceased Pegasus. Commercial Credit planned to buy some software and develop additional software with their own programming staff. Division management had changed once again. I wrote a memo urging active cooperation rather than passive response to Commercial Credit and gave my opinion that Joel was a near genius. The memo rose to heights of exhortation:

[In] 20 years no really good product has ever been developed at Control Data that was not driven by a single, very strong individual. Maybe IBM can design by committee, but CDC demonstrably cannot.

I received no reply.

Several months later I got a phone call from Joel in Baltimore. He was chuckling. "Jim and I have a job that we think you would be good at," he said. Jim Benson wanted to announce formally and demonstrate the FTP/80 to Commercial Credit management and the field sales force at the Commercial Credit President's Forum the following January. The President's Forum was the Commercial Credit equivalent of the Control Data 100 Percent Club. It had been started by Paul Miller. The January 1980 President's Forum was to be held at the Boca Raton Hotel and Club on the Atlantic coast of Florida. Jim wanted a fancy trade-show-type booth, with data sheets and photographs for CCC visitors to take home to their local offices. I had a number of old friends in the sales promotion and trade show groups at corporate headquarters, a fact known to Joel. If I would coordinate getting the booth prepared and handouts made up and shipped, I would be rewarded with a trip to the President's Forum at Commercial Credit expense.

A trip to Baltimore was now necessary to discuss exactly how the demonstrations would be conducted and what features of the FTP/80 should be featured on the lighted backdrops of the booth. Joel met me at my motel and we drove to Baltimore. I got my first look ever at Commercial Credit headquarters. It is a sixteen-story building in the heart of the business district, unimpressive except for the top floor executive offices. Paul Miller had redecorated in a modern, white-and-chrome style, far more elegant than Control Data's fourteenth-floor executive headquarters. I was disappointed that Paul was out of town, as I did not get a chance to say hello.

The President's Forum proved to be another four-day party much like the 100 Percent Club. On the flight from Minneapolis I met two senior vice-presidents and their wives who were invited to the club as guests of Paul Miller. When we arrived at the Miami airport, there was a black chauffeur-driven limousine waiting to take them to Boca Raton. Because I knew both vice-presidents, they courteously invited me to share the limousine, and I arrived in style at the Boca Raton Hotel and Club. This is a rambling 1920s building built in an ornate Spanish style, with the intercoastal waterway in the front and a golf course in the back. It was a delightful old place, and I enjoyed it thoroughly. Before checking into my room I checked on the FTP/80, which had been assembled in its booth in a central lobby area where the visitors could not miss it. The booth was well done, with the Commercial Credit logo and the features of the FTP/80 on illuminated backpanels. The woman responsible for the training of the terminal operators had come to Boca Raton to run demonstrations for the visitors. Joel and his assistant in the lab, fearing that they might need spare parts and test equipment, had rented a motor home into which they loaded virtually their entire laboratory and had driven down from Baltimore!

Jim Benson and his group of managers adopted me as one of their own. We ate together, went to meetings together, and went deep-sea fishing and sailing together. At an awards ceremony a special surprise award for technical achievement was given to Joel by Paul Miller. His prizes included a video recorder and camera—not your usual pen and pencil set! The forum was an interesting opportunity to meet a number of the Commercial Credit people and to find out just what they did. For the Commercial Credit attendees it was also an opportunity to find out what the rest of CCC did. The story was told that Commercial Credit had been run as a number of small companies, with so little contact between groups that there were presidents of operating companies (the CCC term for subsidiaries) that had never met one another until the President's Forums were started!

Joel had confided in me earlier that he had decided that a more powerful 16-bit microprocessor was going to be necessary to run the Cyberloan application locally in the terminal. He had selected a new microprocessor chip just available from Motorola, purchased a sample, built up a micro-computer system on a printed circuit board, and interfaced it to a dual flexible disk drive. At the President's Forum he had the new micro-computer, hidden behind the booth, programmed to run an electronic message center for the attendees. His choice of chips was the same model judged highest in performance of all available 16-bit microprocessors in an independent study done at Terminals Division and the chip later used by the Apple MacIntosh. What Joel had *not* done was cover the company politics at headquarters adequately. When his proposed switch to the 16-bit microprocessor became known, he ran into the same group that had opposed Larry Littwin's choice of microprocessor. At first Joel's arguments seemed to be accepted. He was given corporate permission to continue with the understanding that his work be strictly limited to the one Cyberloan replacement application. However, in the absence of any political supporters at Control Data headquarters, his detractors had time to prepare a case against allowing him to continue. In a later showdown meeting he was directed to discontinue his work on the 16-bit micro-processor terminal.

Joel had run his own small electronics assembly business on the side for several years. He remained in his CCC laboratory for some time after his political defeat, but in early 1983 he resigned to work full time at Laurance Digital Systems. Joel bought from Commercial Credit much of his labora-tory equipment, including some unfinished FTP/80's. His assistant at the lab resigned to work with him. I expect to hear more about Laurance Digital Systems in the future.

23

East Wind, Rain*

Joel Laurance was the last of the brilliant technical project leaders to cross my path during my long career in the computer business, so my reminiscence of heroes, villains, and computer projects ends with him. Even before Joel's political defeat, a new threat, perhaps even more menacing than the highly political vice-president, had begun to appear on the computer scene. Like most Americans I had watched the Japanese inroads into one industry after another with concern but without any emotional involvement. The problems of the American auto industry I thought to be largely of their own making. After all, had not American automakers ignored the small economy car for twenty years with the clear example of Volkswagen in front of their eyes? When the gasoline crunch came, they were caught with uneconomical designs, clearly a failure in their corporate product planning. I had always bought General Motors cars, working my way up from Oldsmobile to Buick to, finally, Cadillac. In 1979 I bought my first foreign car ever, a 1980 Dodge Colt, built by Mitsubishi in Japan. Waxing my new little Japanese bug alongside my 1978 Cadillac, I learned something.

I had expected to find the "fit and finish" of the Japanese car superior; everybody said it was. Everybody was right. The paint job was fantastic, absolutely flawless, with no pits, no overspray, and no running in the corners of the door posts, all flaws that I could see on my Cadillac. What I did not expect to find was better engineering design. The remote hood release worked far more easily, the remote trunk release was far more clever, the dashboard instruments were much better positioned for visibility, and all the controls were easier to locate in the dark. Every detail of operation had been painstakingly thought out, the very hallmark of good engineering. Could it be possible that Japanese automotive engineers were better than ours? That belief would be hard for me to accept. I am a registered

---

* In November 1941, just before Pearl Harbor, Japanese diplomats around the world were informed by Tokyo that the plain language weather broadcast message "East wind, rain," would have the meaning "Japanese-United States relations in danger."

professional engineer myself; most of my friends are engineers. I could accept that Japanese assembly line workers are more conscientious than ours, but Japanese engineers more competent? There must be another explanation.

Two years later I bought my first video cassette recorder. While researching available models and formats beforehand, as engineers tend to do, I found that all VCRs on the market, including those with RCA and GE nameplates, were made in Japan. I vividly remembered an engineering conference field trip held more than twenty years earlier when we visited the factory of the Ampex Corporation in Redwood City, California, in what was not as yet known as Silicon Valley. We were shown the early video magnetic tape recorders that Ampex had developed. They utilized a 2-inch-wide reel-to-reel tape and were being sold to commercial TV broadcast stations. They employed an unusual recording technique: helical scan. In helical scanning the tape is moved diagonally past a rapidly rotating set of magnetic heads. This is the exact same principle used in home VCRs today. Why had no American company developed a consumer version of this American invention? Had the product planners at RCA, the firm that virtually invented home television, all been asleep? Had the development engineers at RCA been unable to design an inexpensive foolproof mechanism suitable for the home market? Or was there a third explanation?

The first intrusion of a Japanese product into my own area of computer terminals was innocuous enough. The mechanism selected by Larry Littwin for printing wagering tickets was made by a firm called C. Itoh in Japan. This was an inexpensive, small dot matrix print mechanism that could be held in the palm of the hand. Designed for the printing of calculator tapes and such, it seemed to be reliable. The larger sports and entertainment ticket printers had been custom designed and built for Ticketron years before by the Control Data Printer Division in Rochester, Michigan, later part of the CPI joint venture. The Rochester division showed no interest in designing an inexpensive matrix printer that was out of the mainstream of their business. No one thought too much about the selection; after all, everyone knew the Japanese were leaders in calculators.

Next, a printer from Okidata, another Japanese firm, was selected for the printing of exact copies of the screen images on the IST series of Plato terminals. This printer was neither small nor inexpensive, but it was the only one on the market that could print an accurate copy of the screen in a reasonably short time.

A third printer was to be selected and sold as a part of the Control Data conversational terminal standard product line. This was to be a "letter-quality" or "correspondence-quality" printer; that is, its output was to look as perfect as electric typewriter copy. All the leading vendors of letter-quality printers were contacted and asked to provide pricing and sample printers for evaluation. Most letter-quality printers use the so-called daisy wheel print mechanism. This mechanism was invented some years ago by Diablo, a California firm later acquired by Xerox. A group of engineers split off from Diablo to form another company, Qume, later acquired by ITT. These two American firms, Diablo and Qume, had the daisy wheel printer market to themselves for years. A daisy wheel printer works much like an electric typewriter mechanism except that the characters, instead of being on the ends of type bars or on a ball, are on the ends of petals or spokes radiating out from a central hub. The printing element thus looks somewhat like a plastic daisy. To print, the daisy spins on the hub until the next letter to be printed is at the top. A hammer behind the daisy pushes the petal forward—it flexes easily—until the letter at the end of the petal is pressed against the ribbon and the paper, leaving an impression. The type style can be changed by changing daisies. The mechanism is simple and fast compared to an electric typewriter but slow compared to most other types of computer printers. The winner of our open competition, which included the two industry pioneers, was a daisy wheel printer submitted by C. Itoh of Japan.

Tom Kamp, then president of Control Data's Peripheral Products Company, was the first high Control Data executive to warn his employees of the Japanese threat to their successful disk file business. In 1982 he sent to two thousand management and senior technical employees of Peripheral Products Company a reprint of an article comparing an automobile factory in Japan with one in the United States. He asked for comments on the article's relevance to the disk business. Tom stirred up quite a controversy when he announced that those employees who had *not* replied to his request for comments would have their salary reviews delayed by one month. Corporate pressure forced him to back down on his threat, but I believe that Tom was quite right in his insistence that *everyone* think seriously about the Japanese challenge. At my invitation, Tom spoke to the Terminals Division management group on the same subject in 1983.

The vice-president of a small custom disk-controller company was invited to Terminals Division to submit a proposal for a special disk controller. His company's specialty is the custom design of controllers to adapt any disk file to any computer as selected by the customer. As a result, he works with disks from nearly every vendor. Over lunch this man remarked that both Control Data and Fujitsu of Japan make good disks but that Fujitsu is more consistent. The waveforms of the electrical signals coming from the Fujitsu disks are the same as those coming from the Control Data disks (they even copied the imperfections), but the signals from the Fujitsu disks are absolutely consistent, like photographic copies, from disk to disk.

In 1983 Tom Kamp was replaced as head of Peripheral Products Company and was given a high corporate staff position. In 1984 he retired from Control Data. In late 1984 Control Data announced that it was withdrawing from further marketing of the large, high-performance IBM-compatible disk files, which had a history of technical problems and had reached the market late. Control Data's withdrawal left only four vendors of the high technology disk files apart from IBM: Memorex Division of Burroughs Corporation (now Unisys Corporation), Storage Technology Corporation (struggling in Chapter 11 bankruptcy proceedings), Fujitsu, and Hitachi.

The Institute of Electrical and Electronics Engineers, reportedly the largest technical society in the world, has run a series of articles in their publications stressing the need of the United States to retain leadership in the design of supercomputers. Frankly, I had not paid much attention to stories that NEC (Nippon Electric Company), Fujitsu, and Hitachi had gained a lead in supercomputer performance until I saw the name of Sidney Fernbach in the article. Dr. Fernbach, the reader will recall, was director of the computer lab at Livermore when the Univac LARC was being designed. He is without a doubt one of the leading authorities on the use of supercomputers in the world, and he is reportedly one of the few users to whom Seymour Cray listens. If Sidney Fernbach says to worry about the Japanese lead, I worry!

A supercomputer is hard to define precisely because performance standards are increasing continually. Yesterdays's supercomputer could be today's ho-hum, average-fast computer. Also, it is much easier to design a one-of-a-kind, never-leaves-the-laboratory prototype that is maintained and serviced by computer science professors and their graduate students than it is to design a commercial supercomputer that can be shipped across the country and installed and maintained by ordinary customer engineers. Early supercomputer attempts by Univac (LARC) and IBM (STRETCH) have been mentioned in this story. Some years later Burroughs Corporation and Texas Instruments both attempted supercomputers that were later withdrawn from the market. A small Colorado supercomputer firm, Denelcor, recently went out of business. There are far more losers than winners in supercomputer design. The only commercially available machines built in the United States today that considered to be supercomputers are the Control Data Cyber 205, a direct descendant of the STAR 100 computer designed for Livermore Laboratory by Jim Thornton and a group of engineers from the Control Data Arden Hills plant, and the CRAY 1, the CRAY 2, and derivative machines designed by Seymour Cray and a small group of mostly former Control Data engineers. Nearly all the successful designers of supercomputers in the United States today know each other and could meet in a medium-sized conference room. On such a narrow base does US supremacy in supercomputer design rest!

Another recent story from the computer trade press is rich in irony. It recalls the fable of the Arab who allowed his camel to put the tip of his nose in the tent during a sandstorm. Before long the camel was entirely inside the tent and the Arab was entirely out in the sandstorm! It was reported that Honeywell had signed an agreement with NEC to buy NEC's large-scale computers on an OEM basis and to resell them as part of the Honeywell computer line, replacing Honeywell's own large computers. Seventeen years earlier, the article reported, Honeywell had licensed NEC to use the Honeywell architecture to get started in the computer business in Japan. Now the pupil was selling computers to his teacher.

Sometimes the aggressive, rapidly industrializing countries of the Far East, particularly South Korea and Taiwan, outdo even Japan in the speed with which they produce low-cost imitations of high technology products developed in the United States. The trade papers have carried a number of articles about the perfect counterfeits of the Apple computers made in Taiwan and sold for a small fraction of the price. In 1982 I served on a task force at Terminals Division that examined in detail the manufacturing cost of our lowest-priced conversational CRT terminal. The task force concluded that with considerable engineering redesign the cost could be reduced by 20 percent.

The next year a group from the division visited Taiwan at the invitation of a large Taiwanese electronics firm. They visited a large, messy factory where CRT terminals were being built by the thousands. It is interesting that color monitors for the IBM personal computers were being built in this factory, complete to packaging them in boxes with the IBM name. The CDC visitors, all veterans of the terminal industry, were absolutely astounded at the vertical integration and the level of automation in this plant. The Taiwanese were designing and blowing their own CRT "bottles," almost unheard of for a terminal manufacturer. The visitors suspected but did not actually see that the factory was making its own glass from silica sand! The Taiwanese firm asked to bid on supplying, on an OEM basis, a CRT terminal that was the functional but not the physical equivalent of the terminal whose costs I had studied. I saw the Taiwanese terminal later with the cover removed. I have examined the insides of a lot of CRT terminals over the past ten years, and I saw no radical departures from the usual construction. The terminal was small, neat, and well packaged, and it worked well. The OEM price to Control Data: just under half the manufacturing cost of the US terminal!

"But, of course," says the reader, "labor costs in Taiwan are a fraction of labor costs in the United States." "True," I reply, "but components account for typically 80 percent of a CRT terminal's cost; labor is only 20 percent!" The dramatically lower cost of the Taiwanese terminal must result more from good design and a high level of vertical integration than from the use of sweatshop labor. The Taiwanese firm, with a minuscule domestic market for CRT terminals, had invested millions of dollars in capital equipment on the wager that they could export almost all of their CRTs in competition with the US and European manufacturers. The decision to design and blow their own CRT tubes reminded me of the decision made at Peripheral Equipment Division years before that critical elements of disk technology could not be trusted to outside suppliers. Control Data now buys its low-cost CRT terminals from this Taiwanese firm.

In 1985, after trying offshore subcontracting, Control Data announced that it was abandoning the flexible disk business altogether. The business had gotten so competitive, so the announcement said, and the market prices so low that it was impossible to produce flexible disks profitably. A few holdouts still do some assembly in the United States, but the flexible disk is now largely a Far East product, as consumer electronics is.

Could it be that the Japanese and Taiwanese have engineers more competent than the likes of George Cogar, Seymour Cray, Lloyd Thorndyke, Bob Oslin, Joel Laurance, and the others profiled in this story? Try as I will, I cannot believe that. Could the astonishing successes of these Far Eastern companies be due in large part to their greater willingness to take risks, to research the market and the technology thoroughly and then bet their companies on their ability to design and build competitive products? Time will tell.

24

E Unum Pluribus?

What remains to be told? One more good Dave Cahlander story, two interesting quotations from industry leaders Bill Norris and Seymour Cray, an attempt to summarize and to make sense of all I have witnessed, and a suggestion for the future.

The technical advances that I have watched have been astonishing, nearly unbelievable. When I pick up a $1000 home computer and realize that it has the computational speed of the million-dollar Univac I, I can hardly believe what I see, despite having watched the evolution step by step. Joel Laurance's turbocharged 16-bit microcomputer would have outperformed Control Data's first computer, the model 1604, a much more advanced machine than Univac I or II. Rigid disk storage systems small enough to fit in a shoe box are now available in capacities greater than the gigantic SPIN file, which filled a small room and weighed two tons. And yet the basic principles remain surprisingly the same. The logic diagrams of the Univac I, if implemented on silicon, would still create a useful computer not too different from the newest models today.

In contributing to this technical progress, quite a number of ordinary engineers and programmers that I knew, among whom are scattered a handful of genius or near-genius types, have founded a dozen or more multimillion-dollar corporations and have become in the process millionaires themselves. Starting with a good idea, the right timing, and a willingness to leave a safe job and take a risk, these entrepreneurs are a textbook example of the capitalist system.

Perhaps even more surprising to some readers is that I have not seen any evidence of systematic dishonesty. Apart from some rumors of payoffs to sales agents in some of the flakier Third World countries and one unsubstantiated story of a kickback scheme perpetrated for a short time in an overseas operation, all of the computer business in which I have participated or been aware of has been squeaky clean. Once or twice a sales representative has been perhaps a little overenthusiastic about a product or a little forgetful about the problems encountered, but payoffs or kickbacks or dirty tricks played on the competitors—never!

And yet this story has told of at least as many failures and frustrated projects as successes, and the proportion of failures has increased in recent years. I have maintained contact with hundreds of engineers and programmers through holding office in the Unihogs and in various company-sponsored management groups, through membership in technical societies, and through highly valued personal friendships. The overwhelming majority feel a similar frustration: Why does every project take so long today? Why is timidity creeping into the company like a fungus? Why can't anyone make a decision? Why does all the innovation come from small start-up companies? And why have so many of the brilliant designers identified in this story left the companies where they made a reputation?

A quick look at some of the "heroes" of this narrative is revealing:

Stayed at Univac/CDC	*Left Univac/CDC*
Lloyd Thorndyke[a]	George Cogar
Dave Cahlander	Hi Osofsky[b]
Larry Littwin[c]	Jack Rabinow
	Seymour Cray
	Greg Mansfield
	Vic Benda
	Bob Oslin
	Jack Keilsohn
	Joel Laurance

[a] Spun off as president of ETA Systems
[b] Left Univac, later returned
[c] Remained with Ticketron subsidiary

Bill Norris, in his book *New Frontiers for Business Leadership* (Dorn Books, 1983), makes a somewhat similar point, although his statement is confined to top technical talent from acquired companies:

A recent study of all acquisitions made by Control Data over a 22-year period showed that fewer than 15 percent of those employees who had been identified at the time of acquisition as members of the innovative team in each organization were still with us. (p. 174)

I have a theory based on long observation that there is a deep underlying hostility between a certain level of corporate vice-president and the most brilliant of the technical innovators. I have sensed but never heard verbalized a feeling of positive relief at the resignations of some of the most talented individuals profiled in this book. This hostility can never be expressed openly, at least not by a vice-president. For an executive of a firm that is dependent on technical innovation to say openly, "Whew, am I glad that troublesome S.O.B. is gone," would be shocking, heretical, as if a United States Marine would say, "You know, 'From the Halls of Montezuma' is really a dumb song!" The vice-president cannot openly express his true feelings, but he can work behind the scenes to discredit and even force the resignation of an innovator who has somehow bruised his ego.

Another Dave Cahlander story illustrates the essential clash of personalities. This one is not rumor; I heard it from Dave himself. It seems that a certain vice-president hired from outside Control Data was given responsibility for forming a group to develop new software. He conceived of a scheme for a radically new operating system that would enable a number of the medium-size Control Data 3000 series computers to work together with the power of a supercomputer, an attractive prospect and one that he sold to corporate management. He assembled a programming staff and spent R&D funding for several years on this project. Dave thought that the whole concept was unsound and badly oversold, and he would tell anyone who asked him his exact opinion on the topic. Word got back to this vice-president, who summoned Dave to his office. "Dave, I understand you have been referring to me as a phony," said the vice-president. "No sir, that is not correct," replied Dave. "The word that I used was charlatan!"

Fortunately for Dave, the facts as they emerged clearly supported Dave's opinion. The software project was quietly abandoned, having resulted in no useful product; the vice-president disappeared from the organization charts.

Along with a fine analytical mind often comes a gift for the devastating verbal riposte, as some of the "Seymour stories" demonstrated. For a vice-president with a large and easily bruised ego, these brilliant guys can be painful to have around.

The best designers of hardware or software invariably know that they are good and that they will have no trouble getting another, quite possibly higher-paying job. With no fear of unemployment they can be virtually unmanageable on fundamental technical issues. Most, for the sake of friendship and to avoid painful confrontation, will compromise on minor issues (the vice-president can choose the color of the cabinet), but they are absolutely adamant on fundamental design issues when they feel that their technical integrity is at stake. The executive who finds himself with a brilliant maverick, nominally reporting to him but actually doing just as he pleases technically, really has only two choices: He can get on the bandwagon and support his designer in the political infighting (as the president of Ticketron supported Larry Littwin in the microprocessor wars), or he can arrange to get rid of the troublemaker and replace him with more pliant (and almost certainly less competent) designers. In my experience far too many executives have chosen the second alternative. In their heart of hearts they much prefer to direct a group of mediocre designers who will do exactly as they are told rather than face the frustrations of dealing with a brilliant individual whom *they* have to accommodate. The mediocre group will require more development funding and a longer schedule and they will produce a less elegant product, but it will be much easier on the ego of the executive in charge.

Consider once again the archetypical protagonists of my tale. Brilliant engineers and programmers almost never have a desire to hold high administrative positions. Budgets, personnel problems, and public relations bore them. They have a great deal of self-confidence based on their knowledge of the technical state of the art, and they are intensely driven to produce and to show the world that their latest designs are absolutely the fastest, the smallest, the least expensive, and the most capable gizmos of their kind ever conceived. The middle or upper executives are also very bright, and they also have a lot of self-confidence, but there the resemblance ends. The executives seldom have *current* technical expertise; they have been away from the technical side too long, if a technical field is where they started. They feel uncomfortable when discussions of technical alternatives get too detailed, but they feel the need to have a technical position to defend in discussions. They search for a consensus among their peers; if there is a committee or task force studying the issue of concern, they get appointed to it. Once a company position or "party line" emerges from the political interplay, they adopt it with all the enthusiasm of new converts to a cult. The company position is now *their* position, and their vocal support of the company position will not hurt them when it comes to promotion time either. Then along comes this maverick designer who tells the executive: "That position may have made sense six or eight months ago, but new chips have come out that will outperform it like a Ferrari outperforms a wheelbarrow !" What is the executive going to do? Go back to his colleagues and say: "Guys, things have changed since we made that decision on technology?" or proceed in the agreed-on direction even though the resultant product may be obsolete by the time it reaches the market?

Notice that this depressing scenario applies most convincingly to middle-level executives. The top executive in a large corporation or in a truly autonomous subdivision of a large corporation has a different motivation; he is much more likely to want the best possible product even if he has to reverse his previously expressed opinion to get it. Thus in a small, independent, or quasi-independent organization, the driving motivations of the technical leader and the administrative leader are much more likely to align. I personally hold with the classic definition of a leader as someone whose job is making it easier for his subordinates to get their work done.

Why are we engineers so much less effective in developing new products than we were in the past? My unofficial and wholly unscientific poll indicates that the computer engineers of my acquaintance believe that the productivity per person of their organizations is less than half, perhaps only one-third of what it was in the early days at Control Data!

In the twenty-odd years since the completion of the NTDS development project, I have never again participated in a project so well managed. NTDS utilized all the management techniques recommended today: involvement teams, great emphasis on quality, computer-assisted project-monitoring tools such as PERT, intense day-to-day informal communications among the workers, and high-level management involvement at every stage of the project. (PERT, for Program Evaluation and Review Technique, is a sort of diagrammatic representation of all the tasks to be performed and their interrelationships. It looks much like a diagram of computer logic circuitry, with which it has much in common.) Never have I participated in or even heard stories of a formal review or a postmortem at the conclusion of a major project, either successful or unsuccessful. Why is management reluctant to learn from the past?

The morale and team spirit at Control Data in the early years are unforgettable. Everyone from the receptionist to the vice-president was intensely proud of the company. We believed Control Data to be the most competent computer company in the world, with the best engineering—the Mercedes-Benz of computer companies. Everyone was eager to show this image of pride and competence to the world. Phone messages *never* went unanswered for days, letters *never* went out with typing errors, and calls or visits from customers caused even such senior technical managers as Lloyd Thorndyke to put aside whatever they were doing and rush to welcome the visitors. This atmosphere was not entirely the result of the organization's being small and the personnel's being largely from a common (Univac) background. Employee compensation had a lot to do with attitude. Reportedly the top salary at Control Data when I started there in 1963 was $40,000 per year, and that was reserved for Bill Norris. Everyone else got correspondingly less. Clearly no one planned to get rich by being promoted within the existing organization. Nearly everyone held Control Data stock, whether obtained by stock option or by open-market purchase, and everyone expected to get rich through the appreciation of their stock. A better motivator than a low salary structure combined with a lot of stock options is hard to imagine. No one can realize his financial dreams unless the corporation prospers, and the contribution of every employee is important to this goal. Of course, this motivational tool's effectiveness is reduced as the corporation gets larger and, especially, as it diversifies into unrelated businesses whose contribution is not obvious.

IBM apparently decided that a radically different organization structure was needed to design and to bring to market quickly their highly successful personal computer. The group established in Boca Raton, Florida (a long way geographically from New York headquarters), was reportedly allowed unprecedented freedom to make decisions and to deviate from long-standing IBM policies. IBM had traditionally designed and manufactured all the computer equipment that it sells (with one or two low-volume exceptions), but the IBM Personal Computer when introduced used a color monitor from a Taiwanese firm, a printer from a Japanese firm, and disk drives from several competitors, including, at one time, Control Data. Earlier chapters in this narrative derided IBM's engineering innovativeness, but in recent years, most certainly in the last five years, IBM has demonstrated engineering leadership much more often than its smaller US rivals. I believe that this is more the result of IBM's maintaining the same pace of innovation while that of the smaller US computer firms has drastically declined, but the result is the same: a continual improvement in IBM's relative position. IBM appears to be the one sure survivor among American computer companies as the Japanese firms move in on a wider and wider product front.

Control Data has started one hopeful experimental venture. A partially owned subsidiary called ETA Systems was set up in 1983 to develop the next generation of supercomputers. Staffed mostly by former Control Data engineers and programmers who worked on the STAR 100 and Cyber 205 supercomputers, the new company is headed by Lloyd Thorndyke. ETA Systems will be partially owned by Control Data, partially owned by the employees, and partially owned by outside investors. Such a venture would seem to combine at least potentially the small-firm advantages of unified team spirit and high financial incentives together with the large-firm advantages of a stable support structure and an established marketing force. I could visualize a whole complex of partially owned subsidiaries or operating companies within the overall structure of a large firm, much like an economic version of the US state-federal system. The subsidiaries (states), which could compete with one another, would have complete control over internal policies, personnel, and budgets while ceding control of foreign relations (marketing) to the parent firm (federal government). The tricky part, of course, would be the establishment of the formula for dividing the profit made on a product designed and built by a subsidiary and sold by the parent company. This would require the wisdom of a Solomon; nevertheless, this organizational structure would seem to have more promise than most other structures that allow decisions to be made by executives who are far removed from the realities of the product.

Incidently, I was quizzing Lloyd Thorndyke some time ago about the meaning of ETA. "Is it true," I asked, "that the 'T' in 'ETA Systems' stands for 'Thorndyke'?" Lloyd claims that the letters officially stand for nothing except the three letters themselves. All the words even vaguely appropriate to the new firm's mission were already in use. Unofficially, the employees think of "ETA" as "Engineering Technology Associates," a nostalgic throwback to Engineering Research Associates in whose plant this story began.

Testimony has been given before the US House of Representatives about the necessity of government funding for supercomputer development to maintain the US position in the forefront of a number of critical technologies that require great computing power. It is interesting to read the comments of the foremost designer of supercomputers in the world on government-funded and government-coordinated development efforts. Seymour Cray, in an interview in the University of Minnesota newsletter *Update*, said:

I have really strong feelings about that. I feel that the bigger the group that works on the project, the lower the chances for success. I'm appalled at our trying to make a country-wide coordinated effort. I just can't imagine it ever being successful. I believe that you want a lot of independent people thinking their own thoughts and trying their own things. We're not going to participate in any national effort and I don't want any money from the government. We've got competition within the company. I've got a group here five miles away who I know are trying to outdo me. (*Update*, Spring 1983, vol. 10, no. 2, pp. 10,15)

I wholeheartedly agree with Seymour. Government funding for laboratories and other *users* of supercomputers may be a good way to stimulate more and faster designs, but government funding and "coordination" of design and development would be a disaster. Such a program would inevitably be taken over by professionals in federal grant funding whose behind-the-scenes political machinations would make Lucrezia Borgia look like Mother Teresa! All of the heavy funding would go to the least controversial and most skillfully promoted projects. The few good designers with novel ideas and abrasive personalities would get no funding, and their time would be wasted in endless meetings attempting to reach compromises.

The best hope for the United States to retain its technological edge lies in the encouragement of individual cutting-edge designers, each motivated to demonstrate that his own vision is the best. In high technology it is still true that *the individual makes all the difference* between mediocrity and excellence.

Epilogue

In early 1985 I was still working at the Terminals Division in the suburb of Roseville. Yet another financial crunch hit Control Data. The corporation had been trying for some months to sell the entire Commercial Credit subsidiary to raise cash. When no takers were found after seven months, Commercial Credit was taken off the market. As a part of the overall cost-cutting drive, an announcement was made that the Terminals Division would be disbanded. I was once again "between assignments." I looked into a number of Control Data organizations to find another job. Most other groups were also contracting, and there were no expanding and challenging projects anywhere that I could see. Many of the senior executives that I had known, Tom Kamp and Paul Miller among them, had retired. I was 56 years old and had worked over twenty-two years at Control Data; I was eligible for early retirement. I was offered a lump sum severance payment, a small monthly pension, continued medical and dental benefits, and a gold watch. I grabbed them, and September 30, 1985, was my last day at Control Data.

The financial condition of Control Data continued to deteriorate, and for the whole of 1985 the company reported a loss of over half a billion dollars! Control Data was in technical default on its bank lending agreements. In early 1986, a few months short of his seventy-fifth birthday, Bill Norris retired as chairman of the board. Bob Price, already president and Norris's hand-picked successor, replaced Norris as chairman.

Personnel cutbacks continued. The company put the Ticketron subsidiary up for sale. A buyer was found, but the negotiations were so unsatisfactory that the sale was canceled. The headquarters complex of buildings was sold and leased back to Control Data. Eighty percent of Commercial Credit was then sold in a public stock offering. The former Terminals Division plant in Roseville was sold. A Farewell to Roseville party, which I attended, was held. I still meet regularly with my former co-workers for lunch. I am enjoying my retirement immensely.

Sperry Rand, later known simply as Sperry Corporation, has also been much in the news lately. In 1983 Sperry officially dropped the Univac name from their line of computers. They were to be sold as Sperry computers, a decision that struck us old-timers as peculiar, giving up a proud name in computer history to honor Elmer Sperry, the inventor of the gyroscope. In 1986 Sperry Corporation was taken over in a not-quite-hostile bid by Burroughs Corporation, another computer manufacturer of nearly equal size but stronger financial condition. An employee suggestion contest was held to choose a new name for the merged companies. The winning name: Unisys. At least they have half of the old Univac name back!

The effect of the acquisition has been traumatic on those of my friends who have remained at Sperry. Layoffs have been widespread and seemingly capricious. It is hard to judge whether the Control Data or the Unisys employees are suffering more from organizational chaos. A third computer company having facilities in Minneapolis is also in turmoil. Honeywell recently announced the sale of a majority of its computer business to Machines Bull, a French computer company, and NEC of Japan. It is hard to conceive of a French-Japanese-American computer company, but I guess that the world is soon going to see one!

When I reread this manuscript I became convinced that many readers will complain that I have been terribly unfair in my criticism of management, both at Univac and later at Control Data. I do not disagree. I made no particular attempt to understand some of the constraints that forced management into making unpopular decisions. I have been knowingly partisan and passionate in presenting the viewpoint of those who have spent their lives working at the project level with engineers, programmers, sales reps, and customers. From where we were, senior management seemed overly political, frequently wishy-washy, and occasionally downright dumb, working against their and our own self-interests. Set against this basically critical position, I have described only a few senior executives who I genuinely admired: Bob McDonald at Univac, and Frank Mullaney, Tom Kamp, and Paul Miller at Control Data. In all honesty I should say that there were many more at lower levels who were competent, open, and accessible, but they seemed to be replaced over time by others who were much more politically oriented, who seemed to look first at the effect of a decision on their own careers and, only later, if at all, at the effect on the company.

In defense of management I should clearly emphasize that the computer business is a difficult business to manage. For the reader unfamiliar with the overall history of the computer business, I should say that three of the largest, most technically oriented companies in the United States— General Electric, RCA, and Xerox—all entered the computer business, lost hundreds of millions of dollars apiece, and withdrew, having failed to establish viable businesses. In this, the first quarter of 1987, many computer companies are reporting poor earnings. Even IBM's performance is disappointing. Two US mainframe manufacturers are doing great financially—Digital Equipment Corporation (DEC) and Cray Research.

So let this reminiscence remain a biased personal view, reflecting my deep admiration for the technical innovators with whom I worked. I can only hope that I have captured a bit of the passion that these designers feel for their projects, a passion that is the *best* assurance of outstanding products.

Chronology of Significant Events

1946   Engineering Research Associates (ERA) formed; occupies building at 1902 West Minnehaha in St. Paul, Minnesota
1950   Eckert-Mauchly Computer Corporation sold to Remington Rand
1952   ERA sold to Remington Rand
1955   Remington Rand merges with Sperry; I join Sperry Rand Corporation
1957   I am appointed to head Univac II test in St. Paul; Control Data Corporation formed in Minneapolis, Minnesota
1958   Control Data announces Model 1604 transistorized computer
1959   I join Naval Tactical Data System (NTDS) project
1960   First Control Data Model 1604 delivered
1961   First NTDS computers delivered to Navy
1963   I resign from Univac, join Control Data Peripheral Equipment Division; Control Data announces Model 6600
1964   IBM announces System/360; First Control Data 6600 delivered to Livermore Laboratory
1965   I transfer to Computer Systems Division
1968   Control Data announces Model 7600; TWA proposal effort begins; Control Data sues IBM, charging unfair marketing practices
1969   TWA sends Control Data a letter of intent
1970   TWA withdraws letter of intent
1972   Seymour Cray resigns and forms Cray Research; Northwest Airlines agrees to test IATA tickets; Computer Peripherals Incorporated (CPI) formed with NCR
1973   CDC lawsuit against IBM settled out of court; Northwest Airlines orders twenty magnetic ticket printers
1975   I transfer to Terminals Division; Computer Terminals of Iran (CTI) formed; Magnetic Peripherals Incorporated (MPI) formed with Honeywell; Northwest Airlines cancels order for ticket printers
1976   Cray Research delivers first CRAY 1 supercomputer; Control Data announces Plato system
1978   FTP/80 Development is started
1979   Trial of Control Data versus Northwest Airlines
1983   Control Data forms ETA Systems to build supercomputers; Sperry Corporation drops Univac name for computers; George Cogar killed in plane crash
1985   Cray Research delivers first CRAY 2 supercomputer; I take early retirement from Control Data
1986   Bill Norris retires as CDC chairman; plaque is unveiled at 1902 West Minnehaha commemorating the fortieth anniversary of the founding of ERA; Sperry Corporation is acquired by Burroughs and the newly formed company is named Unisys

The MIT Press, with Peter Denning, general consulting editor, and Brian Randell, European consulting editor, publishes computer science books in the following series:

ACM Doctoral Dissertation Award and Distinguished Dissertation Series

Artificial Intelligence, Patrick Winston and Michael Brady, editors

Charles Babbage Institute Reprint Series for the History of Computing, Martin Campbell-Kelly, editor

Computer Systems, Herb Schwetman, editor

Explorations in Logo, E. Paul Goldenberg, editor

Foundations of Computing, Michael Garey, editor

History of Computing, I. Bernard Cohen and William Aspray, editors

Information Systems, Michael Lesk, editor

Logic Programming, Ehud Shapiro, editor; Fernando Pereira, Koichi Furukawa, and D. H. D. Warren, associate editors

The MIT Electrical Engineering and Computer Science Series

Scientific Computation, Dennis Gannon, editor